Meeting the Professor

*Growing Up in the
William Blackburn Family*

Meeting the Professor

Growing Up in the
William Blackburn Family

By Alexander Blackburn

John F. Blair, Publisher
WINSTON-SALEM, NORTH CAROLINA

*The paper in this book meets the guidelines
for permanence and durability of the Committee on
Production Guidelines for Book Longevity
of the Council on Library Resources*

*Design by Debra Long Hampton
Cover photograph by Elizabeth Blackburn*

Library of Congress Cataloging-in-Publication Data
Blackburn, Alexander.
Meeting the professor : growing up in the William Blackburn family /
by Alexander Blackburn.
p.   cm.
Includes bibliographical references and index.
ISBN 0-89587-294-3
1. Blackburn, William, 1899- . 2. English teachers—United
States—Biography. 3. English philology—Study and teaching—North
Carolina—Durham. 4. Blackburn,
William, 1899- —Family relationships. 5. Fathers and
sons—North Carolina—Durham. 6. Blackburn, Alexander—Childhood and
youth. 7. Duke University—Faculty—Biography. 8. Durham (N.C.)—
Biography. I. Title.
PE64.B59B58 2004
820.9—dc22
[B]

2004014677

To the Memory
of

William Maxwell Blackburn
and
Elizabeth Cheney Bayne Blackburn

Table of Contents

Foreword

Meeting the Professor is, as its subtitle indicates, a double portrait. Alexander Blackburn the son, in composing a partial autobiography, intermingles a memoir of William Blackburn the father. The whole offers a study in contrasts as well as in similarities. We see in Alex the same useful respect, the same protective ardency, for the classics of our literature that we see in the elder professor. But we also see in the son an ambition to add his own pages to that treasury of thought and expression, an ambition almost wholly lacking in his father.

Many of his students wondered why William Blackburn, this great teacher of creative writing, never attempted the art of fiction. He had such innate feeling for it, such judicious taste, such undisguised love, and such heartfelt reverence, that a few of us conjectured he wrote secretly, his suitcases and closet jammed with the pages of novels and short stories. We fancied that upon his passing these would be discovered, published to enormous acclaim, and immediately enshrined in the canon along with the works of Marlowe, Milton, Joyce, and Conrad.

But it was his reverence, along with his dark self-distrust, that prevented the effort. The man who at the end of his life declared that he was at last beginning to grasp the English sentence could never have set down any obligatory first phrasing of a story that would have satisfied him. The first sentence of Reynolds Price's *A Long and Happy Life* could satisfy him, and of William Styron's *Lie Down in Darkness*, and of Mac Hyman's *No Time for Sergeants;* he could see in these beginnings their necessities and their excellences and he admired the authors who produced them. But if he had penned them himself, in that unsteady, spidery lettering in blackest ink, he would undoubtedly have pronounced them unusable.

His modesty, though it may have sprung from an unhealthy source, was one of his great assets as a reader and as a teacher. He stood before such works as, say, Thomas Browne's *Religio Medici* as a trembling penitent might stand before a phalanx of effulgent saints. And he showed an almost identical degree of respect for the works he truly admired by any of his students. Once, when I remarked upon a felicitous phrase in Mac Hyman's *No Time for Sergeants*, the ever-solicitous Dr. B., quickly rejoined, "Oh, Mac is a true *artiste.*" This was a judgment the hardworking writer would have rejected out of hand, but his friend and mentor meant what he said.

For, though he was a demanding critic as a teacher, as a friend and champion of the published work, he was fervently loyal. When Styron's second, cautiously experimental novel, *Set This House on Fire*, received some mixed comment, Dr. Blackburn was as incensed as if his own personal honor had been called into question. "It's not inferior to *Lie Down in Darkness,*" he snapped. "It's *different.* These birds need to understand that." In defense of achievements he admired, especially those of his friends, he could become eloquent, even voluble.

But taciturnity was his more familiar mode. Once, after she had become a friend of the good doctor, my wife Susan visited him upon impulse. She was strolling by his apartment, saw the desk lamp glowing beside the window, made her way up the quiet stairs past the impassive portrait of some gent resembling Chester A. Arthur, and knocked timorously upon his door. He invited her in, pressed upon her a glass of supermarket sherry, and placed a recording of Schubert's Trout Quintet on the turntable. There they sat for forty minutes, complete and companionable, without speaking. When the music ended, Susan rose, shook hands, and departed. Greeting and farewell were the only words that passed between them.

If, in the pages that follow, there are many descriptions of Dr. Blackburn's "body language," it is because his habitual silence underscored this manner of communication. Long silences were punctuated with profound sighs. William Styron has described him as one of the great "sigh-ers." His intimates learned to wrest meaning from these lengthy exhalations, but in my case I shall not dare to say that my interpretations were correct. He was a person from whom one sometimes had to wrench comment, especially analytical remarks, almost by force.

His reluctance to criticize a new work or one in progress in detail was another characteristic of his modesty. He intuited the nearly preternatural esteem in which his favorites held him and feared to utter a mistaken judgment that might imperil the project underway. I speak now of the stories and novels undertaken by his friends in their early professional stages. Toward their undergraduate themes and essays he was pitiless. Of the old-fashioned school, he held to the view that undergraduate composition courses comprised a sort of intellectual boot camp where the necessary first step was to knock the nonsense out of the tenderfoot. He fretted endlessly about the justice of the grades he awarded papers, but he was liberal with Cs and Ds and would deliver the fatal F when he thought it particularly well deserved. When I described his grading procedure to one of my contemporary colleagues at the University of North Carolina Greensboro, she observed, "These days he would probably be sued." I have tried and failed to imagine the student who might bring legal proceedings against Dr. Blackburn.

He had such a manner about him, such an aura, that impudence like smart-ass retorts, frustrated rejoinders, and even lawsuits simply would not wash. *Gravitas* has become a trendy term of late, but it might have been coined to describe the powerful totality of impression he made. His figure was tall but slumped forward; his suit seemed to have acquired its impressive rumple about 1926 and to have retained it with steadfast determination. The bow tie he often affected added no hint of jauntiness and served instead to emphasize the resigned nobility of his features. But if he was grave in aspect, he was not ponderous and there was a sort of uncanny grace in his movements.

He was never humorless, but even his most cheerful conversation flickered with uneasy shadow. He was patient and generally stoic, but there was also a power of bitterness in him that was never long in abeyance. He felt that Duke had treated him unjustly in the past and was continuing to do so. In practiced aggrievement, he would repeatedly announce, "I am the lowest paid professor in this university." Then he would nod sagely, as if he had affirmed some law of nature like the inverse square of gravitation. He considered that he had accrued enemies in the English department, colleagues who were out to do him dirt. "They'll get you right *here*," he would say, plunging an imaginary dagger into an invisible torso before him and twisting it viciously. Once I suggested that if there really were a conspiracy against him, it couldn't be as sinister as he made out. His face first registered bafflement ("Has Chappell lost his wits?"), then a flash of suspicion ("Fred hasn't gone over to *them*, has he?"), then weary comprehension ("My friend is too young to comprehend the depths of villainy that some men descend to.").

His fears were not completely unjustified. Jealousy is as much a hallmark of the second-rate academic as is the ostentatious footnote. Some of his colleagues openly referred to him as "that old fraud." When the anticipatory gossip about the national television appearance on "Meet the Professor" was round the halls, one of my graduate instructors halted me on the way to the classroom. "Just what do you fellows propose to talk about?" he demanded. "How Blackburn made you the great men you are?"

Still, even though there was a continual low-temperature friction between Dr. B. and many of the rest of the English professors and a more heated relationship with the University administration, he was ever the faithful partisan. He believed that Duke possessed the possibility of becoming a truly great university and he would look upon the pretensions of Ivy League institutions with a sardonic smile. It was his tacit vision of what Duke might be that so irritated him when he considered it in its contemporaneous state.

And yet it was probably a pretty good place to teach and to learn. My buddies and I enjoyed and greatly profited from the lectures and class discussions of Drs. Ferguson, Williams, Sanders, Nygard, Heninger, and others. The only class that ever disappointed me was a course offered by the religion department on the ancient epics. It was all unctuous moralistic pabulum, a queasy pail-full of what Mark Twain called "soul butter." Otherwise, the classes I attended were sturdy, well planned, informative, often challenging, and if some of them were sometimes a little dull, they were not meretricious.

For all his nervous skepticism, for all his melancholy outlook, Dr. Blackburn was an idealist and thus doomed to disillusionments. His colleagues simply did not measure up to the status of educators like Francis Bacon, Baldassare Castiglione, and Thomas More. The inevitability of his disappointment may be illumined by the fact that a certain few of them would be surprised to hear that they were not ranked with these titans. I believe that he did try to think the best of them and I know he did try to develop friendships among the younger faculty. These overtures often fizzled. "Do you know what he told me?" he began after one of his attempts at a meeting of minds. "He actually said that at least fifty percent of scholarship in English studies remains to be done." He wagged his head slowly, sadly, leaving me to conjecture if he thought much more scholarship than fifty percent needed to be written or if the existing heap were already too ample.

He was not averse to scholarship. His discovery of the Conrad-Blackwood correspondence is landmark and his editing of it solid without being coldly punctilious. The acclaim he received was less than he expected, partly because the book was released during a newspaper strike so that admiring reviews were written but not distributed. This disappointment seemed, however, but one more instance in a long series; he was of such melancholy disposition already that misfortune had lost much of its power to depress.

He distrusted much of the scholarship he read because it was based upon what were to him dubious premises. Marxism and psychoanalytic criticism he deplored, along with anthropological theorizing and reflexive politicizing. When the University brought in a crew of pundits for a seminar program it titled "Post-Christian Man," Dr. B. fumed like a Cub Scout campfire. "Post-Christian," he railed. "The *insolence . . .*"

"Maybe Non-Christian would be better," I proposed. "Or Pre-Christian."

"*Un*-Christian would be more accurate," he replied and sulked for the rest of the evening.

Christian humanism was the philosophy he favored, though he would chafe under any programmatic description of it. A print of the Holbein portrait of Erasmus hung in his living room-cum-study and I have seen him look up from the papers on his desk to study the lineaments of the great humanist as if seeking advice or succor. Perhaps one more student had averred in an examination paper that Sir Philip Sidney wrote poetry because he was conceited or that a sonnet consisted of an octet and a sextet. He made the usually successful effort not to regard an undergraduate howler as a personal affront, but there were some blunders for which Erasmus could offer no palliative.

I note that Alex Blackburn and I, along with others, fall into the habit of speaking in negatives. "He was not this, he was not that— *but . . .*" This is the desperate ploy one resorts to when the task of description has become almost impossible. So many of the salient details and revealing anecdotes are anomalous that to report them is misleading. Perhaps he did once chuck a chair at a student, but that is not an example of typical behavior. Maybe he did resort to sarcasm when his patience ran thin, but mostly with students he was kind and generous and humorously disposed.

He rarely engaged with students on a personal level. That privilege was reserved for a few in whom he thought he saw grains of possibility. To many he seemed aloof, though I believe he did not desire to present that appearance. His distance was not so much a distance of attitude as of time. In this double memoir we can observe the son engaged with the currents and movements of the years he lived through while the father stands apart, unchanging, so absorbed by the great literature he taught that he was almost absorbed into it, something of a stranger to the decades he inhabited.

This distance was both an advantage and a drawback. The main allegiances of a teacher are two and they are in conflict. The teacher must respect the integrity of the materials, not debasing these for ideological purposes or "dumbing them down" to curry favor with students. The second duty is to make them interesting, relevant, and urgent to be known and, if possible, loved. Dr. Blackburn succeeded beautifully in the second duty, but his more ardent allegiance was always to the first. James Applewhite's poem, "William Blackburn, Riding Westward," glimpses the dedicated teacher preparing for the morrow's presentation: "you were suffering for us the thornier passages,/ Transfixed by Lear, or staring ahead to the heart/ Of Conrad's Africa."

Suffering is the immensely accurate word. Dr. Blackburn went at texts with a desire to comprehend that was almost savage intensity. But his efforts could not satisfy him. It was common for him to discard all the notes on a work that he had made previously. "I was wrong, all wrong, about number 45," he would say of a Shakespeare sonnet, the timbre of his voice close to anguish.

When he felt he did understand to some degree, that he had something of value to impart about Henry Vaughan or Sir Walter Raleigh, he would present it with the vigor of St. George dispatching the dragon. When he thought he saw classical humanism disappearing from the world ("Post-Christian Man—the *insolence* . . ."), western literature took on the lineaments of the maiden in distress that he must defend.

Noble resolves, those—but quickly superseded by feelings of inadequacy and impotence. The gloom came down again.

Alexander has ventured the idea that his father was all the more valuable as a figure because he allowed his vulnerabilities to show, that he did not always attempt to stand as a heroic personage, unsullied and impervious. I believe this to be a true statement, though I would add that he also allowed, perhaps even desired, for his *contradictions* to show. In order to form a picture of him, one must add all the contraries together. What emerges then is a profound but not easily defined harmony.

The quality about this man I shall longest remember is the rueful resignation that had been wrung from hurt and self-hurt. His favorite saying was that of King Lear: "Thou see'st [deep sigh] how this world goes."

Now that I am old and full of days and have seen much hurt and given much and felt much, I can reply, as does Gloucester in the play: "I see it feelingly."

Fred Chappell

Acknowledgments

Special thanks to:

Inés, for encouraging me to make a book of memories.

Pia Hoffman, Sunshine Literary Agency, Mims, Florida, for providing a cheerful professionalism that gives sunshine a special meaning.

Ruth Wild, for preparing manuscript with her usual wizardry.

Carolyn Sakowski, President, John F. Blair, for putting her faith in this project.

Grateful acknowledgment for excerpts from:

Absalom, Absalom! by William Faulkner, Random House, Inc.

Anti-intellectualism in American Life, by Richard Hofstadter, Random House, Inc.

My Ántonia, by Willa Cather, Houghton Mifflin, 1995.

An Open Life, by Joseph Campbell, Larson Publications.

The Art of Teaching, by Gilbert Highet, copyright © 1950, Alfred A. Knopf, 1969.

Neurosis and Human Growth: The Struggle Toward Self-Realization, by Karen Horney. Copyright 1950 by W. W. Norton & Company, Inc., renewed

Already in thirteenth-century Europe, when the prestige of an enforced Levantine religion-for-all was at its height, there had dawned the realization that every individual is unique, and every life adventure equally unique. In the Old French prose version of the Grail adventure known as the *Queste del Saint Graal*, for example, there is a line that makes this point with the greatest clarity. The Holy Grail, hovering in air but covered with samite cloth, had appeared before the assembled knights in the dining hall of King Arthur and then, again, disappeared. Whereupon Arthur's nephew, Gawain, arose and proposed to all a vow, namely, to depart next day on a general quest, to behold the Grail unveiled. And indeed, next morning they departed. But here, then, comes the line. "They thought it would be a disgrace," we read, "to ride forth in a group. But each entered the forest at one point or another, there where he saw it to be thickest and there was no way or path." For where you are following a way or path, you are following the way or destiny of another. Your own, which is as yet unknown, is in seed (as it were) within you, as your intelligible character, pressing to become manifest in the unique earned character of an individual life.

Joseph Campbell
The Mythic Dimension

ONE

Legacy

They say the apple never falls far from the tree. According to this theory, which apparently has a background in patriarchal social systems, a son never deviates far from what he learns at the knees of his parents. Perhaps, then, if I try to remember my years of growing up in the William Blackburn family, up, say, to the age of twenty-one, I can learn something about trees and knees. Having no more raving urge to write primarily about myself than to make a public appearance in the emperor's new clothes, I shrink before the very idea of autobiography. If, however, in writing about myself I can evoke the presence and influence of the unique and noble figures of my parents, I may hope to erect a lodge in a cucumber patch.

I believed by the age of twenty-one that I had loosened bonds to parents and gained sufficient power over myself to live responsibly and to take my own path. Paradoxically, as I now perceive, the path of divergence leads to convergence. Apple theory resolves the apparent contradiction: my life had in fact never ceased to be part of my family's life. I was no island, I was part of the main. Try as I might to deny an

William Blackburn with Mary April and Alex, Brookgreen Gardens near Myrtle Beach, South Carolina, 1939 (Photograph by Elizabeth Blackburn)

inherited sense of wholeness, I cannot. The simple reason is that my consciousness had bequeathed to it a family environment of freethinking. It is true, my parents' inability *faire bon ménage*—to live happily together—could have bequeathed me a world in bits and pieces. Instead they gave me the wonderful liberty to be myself—the gift of love. When it came my time to nurture them in turn, I discovered that the only genuine assurance of love is loving, itself. I do and shall remember love with love, and shall explore as best I can the mystical union of love and freedom.

Among circumstances of life about which children exercise no control but learn in maturity to accept as a sign of great fortune, there is the imperfection of parents as human beings. What charming and delightful companions, what courteous and urbane friends most parents could be were they not so egregiously and piously perfect! But imperfect parents may earn their children's devotion with every misadventure, every pratfall, every delusion. The child who worships a parent as a god is sooner or later bound to be disappointed, whereas the wise parent is also a fool, albeit a fool at a later stage of development than that of his or her ridiculous offspring. My parents were successful failures. By virtue of this paradox they inscribed themselves in the book of humanity.

As a critical spectator of family, I was part of its world, engaged, not detached, not an outsider. I opposed the dogmatic values and pretensions of the older generation, that of my grandparents; but, then, so did my parents. They dared to seek new values. In passing these along to me, they took care that I should fall under their judgmental gaze, which was superior to mine not simply because as a child I lacked power and influence but because, their troubles and imperfections notwithstanding, they were gifted with intelligence and with the courage to uphold the honor of living. I moved on from them, as I said, took my own path. Because it was sometimes the way of error, independence sometimes warranted their displeasure. My freedom to choose my own path was nevertheless exactly what they wanted. Again paradoxically, and to repeat, the further I wandered from their world the nearer I came to it; the more I rejected it, the more I accepted it.

Father's parents followed a tradition rendered in a scripture dated 2,000 or more years ago. Confined to dogmatism, which is the fear of freedom, my grandparents lacked the imagination to set an example of living for their son as much as he might receive from following a light of his own. At cost to his nerves and equilibrium, without rancor or remonstrance, he seized upon the possibility of change: he became a teacher of literature. Father thereby could claim, in reach if not in grasp, the entire range of human experience—written, thought, or felt—as his province.

Mother's parents were bound to the tribal, bound to social, economic, and military rivalries. They were confined to the cult of individualism, the denial of community. Their America was one in which Earth was considered as merely inanimate nature, as opportunity for exploitation. It was also one in which "mind" was considered synonymous with "reason." They regarded intuitive and emotional life, especially that of women, as inferior. She, too, found possibility. She also rebelled. She gathered in herself an open life.

Father and Mother, both of them, grew into cultured and world-related beings. Although distinctions of nation, class, race, religion, and sex would not be altogether discarded as superficial, or the ego-fog altogether dispelled, they were precursors of a new world. With the creative will to leap into new contexts of living, with compassion to perceive the world as others see it, and with a wisdom not all sprung from learning but rather from an almost mystical participation in an Otherness beyond in-groups, they had the consciousness of poets.

This consciousness left a legacy, most evident in the lives of Father's students. I, for my part, benefited from both a mother's and a father's faith. Long before I sensed something like personal destiny, they perceived and encouraged in me a vital design. Mother, for instance, wrote to me when I was twenty, still in college, still inchoate, as follows:

> As a "poet," your mother has nothing to express but feeling. I do not know, but suspect, that you have ideas to express. I believe you can and will; for you have the best of your Dad in you; I have always known him to be a true poet, though he has never written a line of poetry.[1]

I would say that Mother was here perceiving—both parents perceived it since my early childhood—the individual element, one much akin to her own. She understood my concerns, emotional needs, and personality traits as those which push themselves forward and form, perchance, the compulsion of the poet. As to the relation between poetry and "ideas," she could not have guessed any more than I did at the time that the fundamental themes were already bred in the bone, already in the American grain, already manifested in her life and in Father's, transmitted to me as if on a rising tide.

One need not align oneself with catch-all trends such as New Age and Aquarian Conspiracy to perceive the emergence of a world culture. Whereas only a century ago peoples of the Earth were not commonly aware of themselves as citizens, let alone stewards, of a planet that is a speck of blue dust in the cosmos, they are now. A hundred years ago the separation of mind and matter was considered, except by mystics, as infallible scientific truth, but no longer. As humanity surges higher in the evolutionary journey toward enlightenment, we discover the interconnection of all life from the spurt of the subatomic particle/wave to the stone, the flower, and the tree, from the individual to society, from society to the planet. It is all one. Further, as we situate ourselves in space and time to the point of recognizing our responsibility in and to the terrestrial future, perhaps even in a cosmic plan, the arrogance of solipsism yields through a free and imaginative outpouring of the spirit over the surface of the globe to a humble and generous compassion. Our primal ancestors separated into small groups and spread themselves thinly over the planet; these groups increased to tribes and nations, to dynasties, to empires, to today's multinational standardizations and enslavements. We have seen the destruction of vast areas of the Earth, the fear of annihilation, the growth of a human population into a thronging weight, one not felt during the last 20,000 years, but felt now. Nevertheless, slowly, but inexorably, it seems to me, an in-the-same-boat spirit is moving in us and through us to create a stage of consciousness where the future matters more than the present. With a collective imperative for preventing destruction and for bringing up children to identify themselves not with in-groups but with humanity, itself, we could all pass along to generations as yet unborn—as my parents passed along to me—the legacy that unites freedom and love.

If one thinks of an infinite, numinous power welling up from an underlying creative source, and then considers this movement as evolution, one begins to grasp the idea that evolution proceeds on psychic as well as on physical levels. When awakened, we may find ourselves in a new age coming as an old age reaches its climax. In America the ideal of that old age was to withdraw from industrial civilization and to begin a new life in a fresh, green landscape. This ideal crumbles before the onslaught of history, leaving those of us who still have access to rural felicity and the liberating beauty of nature to fear that time for the civilization we inherited may be swiftly running out. But there is a version of the future of Man—emergence—that does not concern itself with beleaguered ideals, with escape, with withdrawal, with retreat. Sentimental pastoralism[2] still has a hold over the native imagination. So does Puritanism with its concept of the "elect." Put those two cultural impulses together and we have the contemporary urge to abandon our Mother Earth altogether and to send a few righteous, enraptured, and sexually potent pilgrims into space to find a virginal planet amongst the trillions of stars. We mortified earthlings, of course, as the pilgrims blast off, will be left as if on a sinking ship to ponder the words of a Pilgrim Father, one Robert Cushman who lamented in 1622, "Our dwelling is but a wandering; and our abiding, but as a fleeting; and, in a word, our home is nowhere but in the heavens."[3] There is notwithstanding such melancholic and misanthropic visions the likelihood of a new world of the mind. The fresh landscape into which our minds are emerging is already here and now. It is Earth, our home, our place of unity between freedom and love, nature and society, heart and spirit. Our emergence is then in an evolutionary perspective and in true devotion the greatest voyage of discovery that humanity has yet undertaken.

That voyage began for me in the North Carolina city of Durham. Angels surprised me there. The angel of place rooted me in wonder and mystery. The angel of time gave me a family with reverence for the full and open life. Then Mom and Dad, whom I formally call Mother and Father, left me the ineluctable legacy of a sense of plenitude.

It is a curious cultural fact that the relationship of a son to his father is presumed to be the decisive one. Mother, herself, glorified Father and set him up as the model to emulate. Willy-nilly, although I stubbornly resisted until my mid-twenties the very idea of becoming another teacher of literature, I became one. It is now clear that what I had feared was not the paternal vocation itself but the shadow of nepotism. I desired no patronage bestowed upon me in consideration of relationship to a widely and justly celebrated professor. Little by little, I accepted the father-part of myself. Then I realized I had been meeting The Professor all along.

TWO

Sketches of Father

William Maxwell Blackburn was born in Urumiah, Iran, on April 20, 1899; he died in Durham on December 9, 1972. His parents, Charles Stanley Blackburn of Midwestern background and Amy Malvina Waring Blackburn of Columbia, South Carolina, were Presbyterian missionaries in Iran. His paternal grandfather was a church historian and college president. His maternal grandmother was a writer. From her, Father could claim descent from John Howland, a Mayflower colonist, as well as from Joseph Ball, grandfather of George Washington.[4]

When he was five, Father came with his parents and a younger brother, George, to live in the upcountry of South Carolina. A sister, Malvina, and another brother, Clark, were born there.[5] The family of six moved from small town to small town, living off the meager rewards of the father's ministerial vocation. Father's early education proved a hit-or-miss affair, but Malvina Sarah Black Gist Waring, his highly cultured grandmother, encouraged his independence and

Malvina Sarah Black, ca. 1860. William Blackburn's maternal grandmother more than anyone else recognized young William's strength of character and intellectual promise and sent him through college at Furman University. (From Elizabeth Waring McMaster, *The Girls of the Sixties,* Columbia, 1937.)

intellectual growth and in 1917 sent him to Furman College (now University) in Greenville, where he was graduated in 1921 with A.B. in English. There followed a year of graduate study at Yale and a year of teaching in Pittsburgh at the Carnegie Institute of Technology. Then came recognition of his learning and strength of character:

William Blackburn, Instructor of English, Duke University,
1927

he was awarded a Rhodes Scholarship. The years at Hertford College, Oxford University, 1923-26, led to B.A. and M.A. degrees in
English literature and, of greater importance, confirmed his sense of
mission as a humanist educator.

In 1926 Father was drawn to Duke University. There he was to
teach English for most of his career, with the exception of an assign-
ment with University Training Command, Florence, Italy, in 1945 and
an honorarium position at the University of North Carolina, Chapel
Hill, following his retirement from Duke.

After Duke University Press published *The Architecture of Duke University* in 1939, he edited three successive volumes of narrative and

*William Blackburn (second from left) at Oxford University in
1924 with fellow Rhodes Scholars*

verse by Duke students and faculty—*One and Twenty, Under Twenty-five,
A Duke Miscellany.*[6] His edition of Matthew Arnold's *Literature and Dogma,*
for which Yale awarded him a Ph.D. in 1943, was partially published
in journals and later recognized by scholars in the field as a pioneering achievement and model of painstaking research.[7] In 1958 his inge-
nious discovery and penetration of materials published as *Joseph Conrad:
Letters to William Blackwood and David S. Meldrum* earned international critical acclaim not least because, as perhaps only the personally tormented
editor could reveal, of the heroism of Conrad's early struggles to win
success and recognition.[8] In 1969 there appeared *Love, Boy,* an edition
of letters by Mac Hyman, one of my father's former students and the
best-selling author of *No Time for Sergeants.*[9]

With imaginative power and a gift for sympathetic insight, Father
was able to grasp the essential design of a literary work as it begins to

surface from the creative process. This almost uncanny perception of design, this expression of an archetypal apperception, was crucial to his success as a teacher of writers. In spite of his modest claim that he helped writers to become good readers, it was clear to the writers themselves that his discovery and encouragement of their talents were really the decisive events. His unifying qualities of courage, humor, and moral integrity inspired an entire generation of Southern writers, including winners of the Pulitzer Prize, the National Book Award, the National Book Critics Circle Award, the T.S. Eliot Award, the Bollingen Prize for Poetry, and many more.

‡ ‡ ‡

The contrast between Ernest Pontifex and his father Theobald in Samuel Butler's *The Way of All Flesh* (1903) and between Edmund and his father Philip in Sir Edmund Gosse's *Father and Son* (1907) has a parallel in the relationship between my father and his parents. In these instances Puritan theology is revealed as an unwholesome influence on human life.

As described by Larzer Ziff, Puritanism, taking its rise in the days of the Armada, never relinquished its overwhelming insistence on the centrality of the Word—the Holy Spirit that enters the soul via interpretation of the Bible.[10] The band of true believers who transmitted this Word were, for Puritans, Christianity's core, "purified" because they considered themselves elected to redemption through receipt of the gift of belief in Jesus. Charged with conveying the Word through his own words, the Puritan minister had an awesome responsibility as he faced his fellow men in the vocabulary of callings and duties and tried to put conscience, God's vicar, to the work of saving the unenlightened. This missionary impulse to be the vehicle for lofty and unchanging truths—truths separated from the details of daily reality and from the scholarly evidence that distinguishes myth from history in Christianity's origins—sparked the endeavors of the family Blackburn until Father came along and together with his brothers took, to paraphrase Gosse, the human being's privilege to fashion inner life for themselves.[11] A modified strain of small-*p* puritanism lingered on in the family, converted to "service," Father and Uncle George becoming teachers, Aunt Mallie a nurse, Uncle Clark a social worker who would eventually be executive director of hundreds of family counseling agencies. Father, in particular, believed not in the Word but in words, in language as almost holy.

‡ ‡ ‡

My great-grandfather William Maxwell B. (1828-98) was born in Carlisle, Indiana, and trained at Princeton Theological Seminary for a career as Presbyterian minister and educator. He served churches in Illinois, Ohio, and Pennsylvania; he wrote a *History of the Christian Church from its Origin to the Present Time*, now superseded. In 1884 he accepted a call to become founding president of the Territorial University of North Dakota and in 1885 to become founding president of Pierre College, now Huron University, in South Dakota. His opinions of Custer's Last Stand and of Wounded Knee have not come down to us, but it is probable that he wished to save Native Americans, not annihilate them. According to the *Dictionary of American Biography*, he presented a redoubtable figure. He taught "mental, moral, and political science" and was, we are told, "dignified and even courtly, producing the impression of one who was a forceful thinker but was indisposed to impose his thoughts upon others."[12] When he discovered fossils in the Badlands, according to a story told me by Uncle George, he had the intellectual curiosity to read Darwin's *Origin of Species*. It is unlikely that he synthesized science and religion. In my imagination he is perpetually stooped over a fragment of dinosaur, his feverish brain pondering how to fit the monster into mental, moral, and political science.

His son, my grandfather Charles Stanley B. (1870-1946), was trained in evangelical institutes in Chicago and in Princeton. He hated with a lifelong passion "the modernists," as he called them—presumably Darwinists and European textual critics of the Bible—and believed, to quote him, that "the Lord will provide." According to Uncle Clark, Grandpa Charley refused to practice birth control or to borrow money with the idea of paying it back. Even though the Lord failed to provide his children with food and shoes, Grandpa Charley was content to have them live in hillbilly parsonages without heat, running water, or indoor plumbing. His concept of economy was to purchase a cow, said animal to be milked by little Clark, to spend savings on dry oil wells in Wyoming, and to stock his own bookstore with Christian books that nobody bought. As I remember Grandpa Charley, he was a handsome, short, sad, sweet man who called his wife "Mother" and showed symptoms of dementia praecox.

"He was paranoid." So Uncle Clark said, aged ninety-four in 2002.[13] Clark escaped home—and milking the cow—to attend Mercersburg Academy and Yale. When I asked him what he meant by "paranoid," he spread his arms wide to illustrate a chasm. "On the one side was reality," he explained, "and on the other side there was the Reverend Blackburn. And there was something else." Clark lowered his eyes in remembered fear, anger, and humiliation.

"What was that, Clark?"

"He tried to do himself harm."

"What do you mean?"

"He. . . ." There was a pause before Clark went on in low voice: "He slashed his wrists."

Clearly, Grandpa Charley's children didn't have a father they could respect, a masculine father they could depend on, be proud of. Worse: they had a legacy of insanity to worry about. They forgave their father but credited their endurance to their grandmother and mother.

My great-grandmother Malvina Sarah Black (1842-1930) married in 1863 William Gist, son of "States Rights" Gist, governor of South Carolina. After William Gist's death in a skirmish the night before the Battle of Chickamauga in the Civil War, she served in Richmond, Virginia, as a treasurer for the Confederacy from February to April 1865. She married Clark Waring (1827-1913), a widower with two boys, in 1867. He had been a member of the Columbia City Council when in 1865 he, two other councilmen, and the mayor rode with a white flag

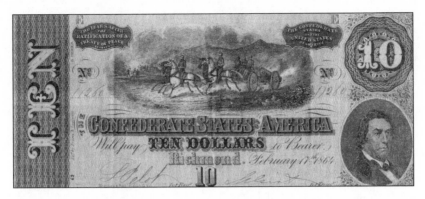

A rare $10 Confederate bill signed "M. Gist" (Mrs. Malvina Gist) in Richmond, February 17, 1864.

in a carriage toward the river and surrendered the city to General William Tecumseh Sherman. "They had to go out and shake hands with General Sherman," Uncle George recollected once. "I don't know if they said, 'glad to meet you' or not." In 1869 the Warings moved to 1428 Laurel Street in Columbia where their five children were born, including Elizabeth (22 June 1869–27 March 1971), my Great-Aunt Bessie, and Amy Malvina (31 January 1872–2 April 1971), my Grandma Amy.[14] When Bessie died at the age of one hundred and one, Amy aimed to whip her record for longevity but followed her into the grave at the age of ninety-nine. Each sister had a program for long life. Amy's was to marry—she married Charley on July 29, 1896—and to walk a mile a day. Bessie's was to marry—she married Fitz Hugh McMaster, Lieutenant Governor of South Carolina—and to eat three hot, cholesterol-frantic meals a day.

I well remember the meals Father and I were served during visits to 1428 Laurel Street. In from the kitchen would come long-suffering Ella, Bessie's octogenarian African-American cook, bearing trays with platters of hominy grits, hot biscuits, bacon, pancakes, scrambled eggs, fried chicken, hush puppies, yams, lima beans, and deep-dish peach cobbler smothered with whipped cream. Bessie ordered Ella about, as if to dismiss the Emancipation Proclamation as a historical discourtesy. It bothered me but not Bessie that poor Ella had fallen arches and toes that poked from holes in her flattened moccasins. Before we could eat, Grandma Amy bowed her head and delivered an interminable prayer to Jesus, blessing the food in His name while I wondered, in childish gluttony and ignorance, why He would want the food to get cold. Anyway, we "et," and Bessie, a tiny creature with the looks of a desert tortoise and with the spitfire personality of Scarlett O'Hara, apparently never gained an ounce of weight.

One hot, humid afternoon Bessie showed me around the living room. High ceilings and Irish-linen draperies provided relief from heat. On top of great-grandmother's piano rested a signed photograph of General Robert E. Lee. Over the mantelpiece there was hung, gleaming, a wicked-looking saber. It had a dark spot on the blade.

"What is that spot, Aunt Bessie?" I asked. I pronounced "Aunt" as "Ant" in order to allay suspicion concerning my recent schooling Up North. She drew herself up stiffly. Her eyes blazed. "Yankee blood!" she rasped in her hen-cackle voice. She added that the saber had belonged to a Confederate officer, a "Major"; I didn't catch the name. I

Malvina and Clark Waring's home at 1428 Laurel Street, Columbia, South Carolina. Now torn down, this was the birthplace of William Blackburn's mother, Amy (Mrs. Charles Blackburn). Father would remember this house as a place to get candy and new shoes once a year.

guess she meant Major Gist, my ancestor by family association who died for states rights. Another time I asked Aunt Bessie about "The Mayflower Society" to which she and Grandma Amy belonged, as could, I believe, many an American who hires a genealogist.

"Well, Elleck, I'll tell yuh.....Yo ancestuh was John Howland, Gent. of Plymouth. He had a misfortunate love affair-yuh and went down yonder to the h'yarbor to commit suicide. Seein' him, the Mayflower folks, they declared, 'If you-all wont to die, why not come with us?' Come he did. And he was the on'y gentleman on the bo-at!"

Grandma Amy was a tall, big-boned woman with a primal bicameral mind: one room for a Southern belle, the other room for a god. To a boy looking at her eyes enlarged by bifocals, she focused on very distant horizons. Leaning forward as she walked, she seemed to be in a hurry to get to them. She exercised her thoughts with expectation not just of the sudden appearance of the Lord but of her right to be forgiven by Him ahead of us other rascals. Often she approached strangers and asked them if they were Saved in the Precious Blood of the Lamb. When, as they invariably did out of an embarrassment I could fully comprehend, they tried to excuse themselves, she would thrust into their hands, like a bailiff serving summons, one of Billy Graham's latest announcements about the End of the World.

She took me, then about ten, to an old-time gospel revival. This was held in a brightly lit and unventilated tent on the outskirts of Durham. Outside the tent everything smelled of gas exhaust, cigars, and horse manure; everything inside smelled of ladies. Because Grandma was partly deaf—she had neglected for decades to clean the wax out of her ears—she had us sit in folding chairs on the first row in front of the preacher with his microphone. He was a balding, red-faced true believer who wore a white shirt with sin-soaked armpits. When he preached, I could, as the saying goes, have located Hell on an atlas. And when he suddenly paused, pointed an extended arm right at me, and shouted, "YOU are going to HELL!" I resolved to abandon my diabolic habit of eating Colgate toothpaste when nobody was looking.

She was fond of saying prayers in an effort to discover in what manner she had sinned. For instance, there was the time when she fell down a flight of marble stairs at the National Art Gallery in Washington. Crumpled in a heap, moaning from justified pain—she had broken her hip bone—she cried out, "Lord, what have I done to offend thee?"

When she was a very old lady and living in the King's Daughters Home in Durham, I called on her and took her out for a walk. While we were resting on the lawn of Duke's East Campus, she spoke of losing a first-born infant after her arrival in Iran. "I was so naive," she said with winning self-mockery, "I couldn't make the milk stop. The Muslim ladies brought me their babies for nursing, but I couldn't make the milk stop. The Muslim ladies brought me puppy dogs and goats for nursing, but I couldn't make the milk stop." Leaving her story unfinished, she threw back her head and whooped with laughter.

‡ ‡ ‡

Because Father never spoke to me about his early childhood in Iran, for a description of Urumiah I draw upon reminiscences of an English traveler who visited it in 1903.

Urumiah lies in the alluvial plain of the "Paradise of Iran." A river flows past the city on its Southern side, and streams formed by the snow melting on the Kurdish hills to the west assure a plentiful water supply and irrigation source during the heat of the summer. The country, for miles around, is covered in summer with gardens, orchards and vineyards. The Blackburns and other missionaries could always rely upon an abundance of fruits and vegetables and cereals. Moreover, the city itself afforded them considerable security. It was girded by a wall some three or four miles in compass, pierced by seven gateways, and strengthened by a moat at the more vulnerable points. The value of this double defense had something of a test during a Kurdish raid upon Urumiah in 1880, when the city was besieged and threatened with destruction; the Kurds had plundered the surrounding villages,

Urumiah, Iran, birthplace of William Blackburn in 1899. (From a 1903 photo published in A.V. Williams Jackson's, *Persia Past and Present.*)

burned, ravaged, and murdered throughout the region, and were checked only after much bloodshed.

But Urumiah at the time of Father's birth was not in all respects a paradise. Streets were paved with large round stones from the river-bed. There was no system of drainage, save the water channels from the moat and the river, and these served alike to receive refuse and furnish a washing place for the women to launder their clothes. During the winter when snow was shoveled off the roofs into the streets, thoroughfares were at times impassable. And since burying grounds were unrestricted, the main street into the city actually led directly across a cemetery. One can imagine the surprise my grandparents must have experienced when horses' hooves beat hollow over excavations beneath the sod. Indeed, the air of the city must often have reeked of sewage and decomposing corpses, especially when the temperature suddenly soared to a brutal 116 degrees Fahrenheit.[15]

Urumiah has no public edifice of any importance, but it has a church of great antiquity associated with the biblical story of the Magi and indirectly with Zoroaster. This is the old Nestorian church of Mart

Mariam, the Blessed Virgin. Popular tradition says that at least one of the Magi who came to worship the infant Christ at Bethlehem lies buried in its crypt. A legend regarding these Wise Men is found in the apocryphal New Testament Gospel of the Infancy, recounting how the Wise Men received from Mary the swaddling clothes of the infant Christ as a gift. On returning to their country, they made a fire with which to worship and consume the clothes according to their religion, but the blessed garments remained unseared in the flames and became a sacred relic. A church was built in commemoration of the miracle, and it is this edifice that serves as the burial place of the Magi. The story, now transparent to mythologists, illustrates the attempt to suppress Zoroasterism in favor of Christianity.

This was enchanted country for my grandparents. Once, while I was dining in Cambridge, England, with a Kurdish prince familiar with the modern city of Urumiah and with the work of missionaries there, he told me, "They built a school and a hospital, for which the people remain most grateful, but they never made any converts." I didn't tell him the story of infidel Grandma's breast-feeding of Muslim infants.

‡ ‡ ‡

Married less than two months, my grandparents arrived in Urumiah on September 23, 1896, with nineteen pieces of luggage, Amy and Charley having traveled four hundred miles from Batumi on the Black Sea. They had taken a Russian train to Tiflis and Akstafa, then gone by horse-drawn post-carriage over the formidable Sevan Pass (elev. 8,000 feet) and down to blue, briny Lake Urmia (elev. 4,000 feet). Amy would never forget the sight of snow-capped Mount Ararat (elev. 17,000 feet) or the sacred shrine at Nakhchivan, popularly believed to be Noah's grave. She noted in one of her letters home that "the plough used here is the same Nebuchadnezzar used, or at least one just like it."[16]

They were welcomed at the gates of Urumiah by fellow missionaries who presented them with a samovar, as it would be necessary for

"Billy," ca. 1902 (left front facing camera), at a party in Urumiah for the missionaries' children. Amy (center) holds George.

them to serve native guests with tea. Then they were escorted to their new home, a mud house inside the mission compound. The mud floors were covered with Persian carpets. Father—"Billy"—would be born in this house two and a half years later. He would remember during an interview at Duke the mud walls and the carpets. The samovar would be used when he served tea to his students at Duke.

The beautiful sincerity of Amy's faith shines through passages of her letters:

> When I realized that we were almost at our destination—our field of labor henceforth—I could not suppress a few tears, it seemed so very solemn and sweet, and yet so very unreal. I asked the Lord to bring to mind some of His precious promises, and there came "Ye shall go out with joy and be led forth with peace," the promise I had chosen in connection with my coming, and "Lo, I am with you alway."

She observed native customs with the detachment of an accomplished journalist:

> Housekeeping in Persia is quite different from what it is in America. I was thinking of how Ralph used to wheel to the bakery in a few minutes for the bread. Here, as fall comes on, our manservant must be on the lookout for good wheat. After some days, when he finds it, it is brought on donkey's back to the house. After half a dozen women have separated the good grains from the bad, the manservant must be on the lookout for a good mill. When he finds one, he takes the wheat to it early in the morning and stays all day, or goes early in the evening and stays all night. Then a sieve of regular bolting cloth must be made—i.e., if one has been told before leaving America to bring regular bolting cloth; otherwise, organdie does nicely. A sheet is spread upon the floor, and for two or three days a woman sifts the flour. It is well to be around occasionally to see that she does not put her feet on top of the sheet and into the flour. Finally, the flour is sealed up in large earthen jars and taken out when needed, to make bread.

For all her belief in biblical certainties, Amy was driven by an insatiable curiosity about life.

Benjamin Labaree, son of the president of Middlebury College in Vermont, had come to the mission in 1860 to translate the Gospels into Azerbaijan Turkish. Grandpa Charley assisted him in routine duties. On March 9, 1904, something happened that had Charley and Amy worried about the safety of their sons, Billy, almost five, and George, aged two and a half: Labaree's son Benjamin was kidnapped by Kurds, carried away to a mountain ravine, and stabbed to death with daggers and swords, his body stripped and left in the snow. "I still remember," Father told a reporter in 1949, "the horror I felt as a child in being told of how one of the medical missionaries had been waylaid and murdered and his body left on the snow by some fierce nomadic tribesmen named Kurds."[17] He would retain a horror of death for the rest of his life.

The Blackburns left Urumiah late in 1904. This time they traveled in a caravan accompanied by well-mounted armed guards. The

"Paradise of Iran" sank slowly out of sight: the roofs of mud houses, the palm trees, the ash mounds of Zoroastrian fire-shrines, the ultra-marines of Lake Urmia. They were in an ox-cart, not a post-carriage, for many of the hundreds of miles of barren desert and snow-drifted mountain trails. Every dawn the tough, weather-beaten caravan leader with Mongoloid features, a scarf wrapped around his face to protect it from bitter winds, awoke the motley assembly of pilgrims, merchants, and animals after pauses at caravansaries for the night. The dull *dong dong* coming from the huge copper bells attached to the dromedaries and mules staggering under crushing loads must have lulled the little boys to sleep in their cart. When after many weeks the family reached the shores of the Black Sea, little Billy asked, "Is this America?"

‡ ‡ ‡

Excerpts from Ben Robertson, *Red Hills and Cotton: An Upcountry Memory* (1942)[18]:

> We are farmers, all Democrats and Baptists—a strange people, complicated and simple and proud and religious and family-loving, a divorceless, Bible-reading murdersome lot of folks, all of us rich in ancestry and steeped in tradition and emotionally quick on the trigger.

> Like almost all Southerners, white and black, we were born with manners—with the genuine grace that floods outward from the heart.

> It is from our ancestors that we have faith. They have taught us our responsibility, and obligation and duty. We must amount to something, we must be somebody, we must put something by for our old age, we must spend less than we take in. We must stand for complete freedom of conscience, for absolute liberty of the soul. We alone must be responsible to God for our salvation, and the Holy Scriptures form the only absolute standard of faith; and we deny the controlling authority of catechisms, and reject all union between the church and the state. No magistrate has any power over us in faith.

The Reverand Charles Blackburn and family, ca. 1916. Front, left to right: *Clark, Charles, Amy;* back, left to right: *Mallie, William, George*

We must stand alone. . . . What our ancestors have taught us is this: we are ourselves, we are to be ourselves, and except to ourselves we owe no obligation to anyone or anything except the Almighty, the government, and our fellow man.

We laugh a great deal—perhaps because deep within we are melancholy and brooding and touched with the mystic.

There is something lost in all of us—lost in us as a type, I think. It is that something that sometimes strikes us with a pang when we see, high and free in the sky, a wedge of wild ducks flying—that something that disturbs us when we listen to the lonesome rumbling of a train. It is that quality within us, I think, that always has sought perfection and that never gives up searching. It is all or nothing for so many of our kinfolks, and that perhaps is why we are so restless— why flight, why motion disturbs us. We feel that somewhere there exists the complete unity we long for, we feel that if we keep on looking for it, surely somewhere we will find it. It is at the base of our strength and of our weakness—this desperate craving we have for the absolute in existence.

‡ ‡ ‡

Father made one attempt as a memorialist, revealed in the following excerpts from "Sketches for a Memoir."[19] Although the date is uncertain, internal evidence suggests that it was written about 1948, a time of "midlife crisis" in which he found at least some partial sense of identity in Robertson's book about the Upcountry—behind which looms the "lost" motif of Thomas Wolfe's novels.

One of the books I wish I had written is Ben Robertson's *Red Hills and Cotton*, a loving evocation of life in Piedmont, South Carolina. I spent my boyhood in Seneca, a small town on the main line of the Southern Railway, between Greenville and Atlanta. Seneca is at the foothills of the Blue Ridge. I went back there about ten years ago. When I saw the contour of the hills, I realized I had returned home.

On that visit I was astonished at how things and events and people, long since, apparently, forgotten, flooded my memory.

— The family of Charlestonians up the street who taught me that all South Carolina is divided into two parts:

(1) Charleston and (2) the unfortunate remainder of it.

— The first automobile I ever saw, a Maxwell ("Get Out and Get Under"), owned and operated, much to the astonishment of the population, by the enterprising dentist, who lived just down the street from us.

— My first fight in the woods behind the schoolhouse and making up afterwards with my erstwhile enemy by giving him a pocket-knife—just to make everything square.

— My visit with other boys to the town calaboose, where the local prisoner, furious at our intruding on his privacy, dashed water at us through the iron bars above the door.

— The Sunday afternoon reader sessions in the family, when Mother read the Bible to us and the *Youth's Companion* or, sometimes, Bunyan's *Pilgrim's Progress*. This last book, a sure means of conjuring up visions of Old Nick himself, as soon as it got dark.

— Hayrides on summer nights to the deserted railway tunnel above Walhalla, singing all the way.

— Feeling noble the night John Cary and I brought Julian Holloway, who had been bitten by a snake while we were on a camping trip, to a doctor in John's donkey cart.

— Hearing my father taking the tenor part in "Lead, Kindly Light" at Gus Tribble's funeral and wondering about death and of how Gus had met it, driving his taxi on a lonely road.

— Fabulous tales of Train No. 97, the crack mail train, Atlanta to New York, and sometimes hearing it at midnight blow for the crossing. "She was going down grade, making ninety miles an hour."

— The summer visits of Grandmother Malvina Waring, from Columbia. The climax of the visit, an annual pilgrimage in a hack, to Clemson College, nine miles away. Our admiration for Fort Hill, the old home of John C. Calhoun, and Mother's constant reminder: "Now, Billy, you must always remember that your great-great grandmother was the sister of John C. Calhoun's mother." I never got the family connection, but I think I know what she meant.

The grand event of the year was the family trek at Christmas to Columbia—a distance of 120 miles, covered in about seven hours in a train as picturesque as it was slow. There in the big house on Laurel Street the clan would foregather: Grandfather Waring, a great hulking figure of a man, with a white beard and a twinkle in his blue eyes and a genius for guessing when exactly children wanted stick candy; Aunt Bessie, who ran the house with quiet efficiency and great good humor; her husband, Uncle Fitz, with his laughter and sarcastic wit; Uncle George Waring, boisterous and great-hearted, who used to take us four children to the shoe store and have us shod for the year— as a gesture of good will toward a poorly paid profession; and, of course, there was Grandmother, who, though going blind, had an infectious cheerfulness and an amazing knowledge of the heart, particularly of the young heart. Up to the time when she went completely blind from cataracts, she would play on the piano daily and sing the old songs. She wrote poems and novels. Her last novel, a story of Reconstruction, was published when she was well over eighty. To me, she was the personification of courage, and I owe to her precept and example more than I can say.

She would tell us stories of the Civil War, of Sherman's March to the Sea and of the burning of Columbia; of her marriage to Major William Gist, son of the "States-Rights" Governor of South Carolina;

and of how, one day while she was taking a walk on the Gist plantation, a little Negro girl ran up to tell her that her husband had fallen
at Chickamauga: "Miss Mallie, Mistah William—he done dead, done
dead."

Then she would tell how, after her loss of the major, she went to
Richmond and there signed banknotes in the Confederate Treasury.
Among my most priceless sentimental possessions are some notes
signed in a clear, bold hand, "M. Gist."

Grandmother had a way of encouraging her grandchildren to
try their mettle, and my brother George and I began early the game
of making a shining penny when we could. We used to meet Train
No. 38, the Crescent Limited, at Seneca, and sell baskets of figs to
the, presumably, rich Yankees on their way south. We sold newspapers. And one summer we went to Akron, Ohio, to work in the
Goodyear Tire factory. I never quite learned the art of making cord
tires, and I have often wondered how many blow-outs I have been
the unwitting cause of.

I came along before the Fuller Brush Man entered into his present
fame, but in my time I have sold brooms in a house-to-house canvas.
And once, the year before I went to college, I dispensed "The Knowledge Book" wherever I could find innocent takers in Orange County,
Virginia. There's nothing quite like a house-to-house canvas to learn
both the hardheartedness—and the kindness—of the world. Or to
learn that one is not cut out to be a salesman.

It was Grandmother who sent me to College. I attended Furman
University, Greenville, S. C., during the years 1917-1921.

Soon after the beginning of my sophomore year, the Student
Army Training Corps was organized. I found myself corporal of the
first squad, working under the critical eyes of some of my friends
who had been to Plattsburg and had there learned the art and tough-
ness of being sergeants. The fact that our commanding officer was a
composer and had written the then popular marching song—"It's Not
the Pack That You Carry on Your Back. . . It's the Last Long Mile" —
did not make soldiering any the more palatable for me. When I was
just about to be sent to an artillery O.T.C., the war obligingly came
to an end one November night.

I was definitely not a soldier; nor was I an athlete. I did, however, contribute my enthusiasm and lungs to the cheering section on
Saturday afternoons. What with this contribution of wild frenzy and
what with smoking black cigars, which somehow seemed appropriate

to the occasion, I remember thinking that football, even for spectators, is strenuous fun.

In those days the college literary society was a powerful organization on the campus, particularly in the South. I had begun my oratorical career back in Seneca, winning a medal for reciting, with grandiose gestures, "The Georgia Volunteer." I carried on these adventures in spell-binding in high school and college. Medals shown upon request. With the general decline of Southern oratory (over which decline I have no regrets), I seem to have lost faith in the business of emoting in public. I have few regrets, but I could wish that I had belonged to some dramatic group in college. . . . But there was no dramatic group in the Furman of my day. On the other hand, we did have an excellent glee club, of which I was a member for four years.

I wrote for the college newspaper and for the literary magazine.

My teachers at Furman I remember with affection, even those who despaired of my abilities in chemistry and mathematics. I have space, however, to mention but one of them—Robert Norman Daniel. It was he who awakened my interest in English literature. He awakened it by reading poetry as if it has life in it.

My parents had hoped that I should follow the family tradition and become a minister. . . . But English poetry and perhaps the more worldly wisdom of my grandmother—together with my distaste for the role of being a preacher's son—turned me toward a more secular career.

I drifted into teaching. I was lucky enough to win a University Scholarship in the Graduate School at Yale and, after that year, I got a job as an instructor of freshman English at the Carnegie Institute of Technology, Pittsburgh. That settled it.

The year I was at Carnegie Tech, I had the good fortune to win a Rhodes Scholarship from South Carolina. . . . I look back upon my three years at Oxford as being the happiest college years possible. It is a city of infinite charm: the college quadrangles and gardens, the walks on the banks of the rivers, the bookshops and the innumerable bells ringing on Sunday morning. . . What I am most grateful to Oxford for is the opportunity I had there to read. When I wrote the comprehensive examination in English language and literature, I won a Second Class Honours. Only three Americans in the history of the Rhodes Scholarships have won "Firsts" in English—a fact which has consoled me over my "Second," as it has many others.

One of the South Carolina towns I lived in (after Seneca) was Greer. There I had known William Preston Few II, a nephew and namesake of President Few of Duke University. Remembering that name (and sharing with President Few, although the fact was not known to him, a hometown), I wrote to ask whether he had a job for me. He did.

When I arrived at Duke in the late summer of 1926 and called on President Few, he took me out to the plateau where the West Campus now is: "Let me show you where we're going to build the Oxford of the South."

Dr. Samuel Johnson complained of his experience as a teacher that it was dull and unvaried—"One day contains the whole of my life." I must confess I haven't found it so. English literature is so rich in connotation that, even in handling the old assignments, I see something new and, to me, wonderful every year. Nor are the students all alike but, on the contrary, as varied as human nature itself. The ones I admire most are those who come to college badly prepared but are willing to put up a fight to get an education. This is not, of course, a plea for poor preparation.

THREE

Tris

Elizabeth Cheney Bayne Blackburn was nicknamed "Tris" in childhood because of an association, affectionate but obscure, with a brand of biscuits. She was born October 16, 1898, in South Manchester, Connecticut. In spite of a long and distressing history of illness, she lived to the age of ninety-six and died on December 23, 1994, in Colorado Springs, Colorado.

When she was still in her teens, a dental infection led to the removal of one of her kidneys. Three times she survived pneumonia, a second time in the 1930s when doctors at Duke Hospital had little hope for her recovery. In her sixties, she had a mastectomy for cancer; it did not spread. At the age of seventy-nine, after lonely years spent in apartments in Santa Barbara, California, she moved to a retirement home in Colorado Springs and was soon showing off her skills as a ballroom dancer. At the age of eighty-three she suffered a blood clot and the amputation of a leg, a trauma which she was not expected to survive. Survive she did, and soon she was living with me and my wife, Inés, in our home. She received round-the-clock nursing care for nine years until at the age of ninety-two she requested to be moved to a nursing home. There either Inés or I visited her almost daily for the next four years. Just before Christmas of 1994 she passed away in an instant—as she was joyfully reaching for a cookie being offered her by a nurse.

I say "joyfully" because a dream of her lifetime had just been realized through me: she believed that the publication of my second novel, *Suddenly a Mortal Splendor*, had established solid artistic credentials. She had invested in me, ever since I was a child, her own literary ambitions.

If I were to characterize Mother in a nutshell, I would say she was a Connecticut Yankee with a Katharine Hepburn-style cocky awareness mixed with reckless gusto and stiffened by pride.

‡ ‡ ‡

The rather tall, slender young woman wearing a cloche hat and ankle-length organdy dress had booked passage on the steamship *George Washington* for $80, student third class. It was scheduled to sail from Cherbourg on July 22, 1926, and to arrive in New York on the first of August. Her face bore a solemn, deceptively sad expression enlivened by bright brown eyes and set off by strikingly attractive auburn hair.

She was completing a journey around the world, sometimes accompanied by a Spanish girlfriend, "Chuchi," but, for once, not tethered to her mother or other family chaperon. There had been a lengthy stay in Manila and Baguio in the Philippines—a cousin, General Halstead Dorey, was aide to Governor Wood there—and she had stopped over in Singapore, Johor, Cairo, Naples, Genoa, Monte Carlo, and Marseilles. She had just spent two months in France, staying most of the time near Paris where her father lived in contrived Rabelaisian style on a small estate with his second wife.

The journey had been a reward for successful completion of nurses' training at Presbyterian Hospital in New York. It was also a chance to recover from an unrequited love affair. Midway through training (1921-22), she had suffered a nervous breakdown precipitated by a

"Tris" in Russell Cheney's studio, ca. 1914

writer named Donald Ogden Stewart as well as by exhausting work in the hospital.[20] Through sheer stubbornness she graduated with a Nightingale Pin. Now tan and healthy, she did not lack for beaux. There was that officer in Manila who had escorted her to full-dress military balls and taken her by boat for midnight swimming in the middle of the bay. Had he asked her to marry him, she might have accepted. As she traveled on, he became a distant memory and, upon reflection, dull. She still wanted a husband who was intelligent and gifted, preferably someone with whom she could share her love of literature—someone, in fact, like Don Stewart.

When news reached her at Genoa of Don's first marriage, she imagined that he would be honeymooning in Paris where his close friends, the Hemingways, lived. Dreading an encounter with him there, she almost changed her plans but pressed on to Paris. No such encounter took place. She dined at the Ritz and danced there with Pavlova's ex-partner. At Brunoy, her father's estate, she was introduced to some of Don's chums from Skull & Bones, the Yale secret society, when they showed up, inebriated, for tennis, swimming, and more cocktails. Some of them might have posed for the character of Tom Buchanan in *The Great Gatsby*, the rich boy who gleaned "scientific stuff" from a book called *The Rise of the Colored Empires*. Brunoy offered gaiety, of course, that forced cheerfulness for which her father was celebrated, but Tris had no stomach for faking spontaneous feeling. Upon her return to New York, she planned to resume her nursing career in an asylum for lunatics. That had been part of her triumph, nursing in an asylum. It had brought out in her a deeply compassionate nature.

One day out of Cherbourg and Southampton, aboard the *George Washington*, she was sunning herself on deck, her legs wrapped in a steamer rug. Nearby stood some American men grouped about a person who made tall, dark, and handsome into a fresh cliché. Although he wore the requisite white shirt with bow tie, white flannel trousers, and white shoes, he didn't seem to be a character in a Fitzgerald novel—like one of Don's friends. This man's conversation, of which she caught snatches out of the breeze—he held forth on William James but who or what were "Balliol noetics"?—made him seem an unabashed highbrow. Still, he was a charming highbrow. He listened to admiring companions with an air of friendly, if detached, amusement.

She went to the ship's library and borrowed William James's book, *The Varieties of Religious Experience*.[21] The next morning she went on deck with the book and seated herself in the same chair she had occupied the previous day. She let the breeze ruffle her hair. After a while the interesting gentleman appeared, alone and smoking a cigarette. He glanced her way, then approached and peered at her through round-rimmed spectacles.

"That's a good book," he pointed. "May I join you?" He drew up a chair and introduced himself in a throaty Southern voice sharpened at the edges by British inflection. After conversation and cigarettes together, this fellow named Bill invited her—Tris—for the captain's gala that evening. She discovered that he did not dance as gracefully as Pavlova's ex-partner but well enough to make her feel that a year of intimacy had passed between them in a matter of hours. He was grave and mature, not self-centered, not like Don. Before the *George Washington* docked in New York, Tris and Bill became engaged to be married.

It would be rash to deny the ordination of civility that leads lovers into marriage.

‡　‡　‡

Mother kept a "baby book" for me in which she wrote a "history of Alex's mother" at some time in the 1930s. Laconic and self-effacing, it is the portrait of an insecure girl who rebelled against her conventional upbringing in a family that considered itself "aristocratic."

My father was a lawyer from New Orleans. My mother was a daughter of a wealthy silk manufacturer of Connecticut. She was deaf, so she studied in an art school in Boston instead of coming out in society with her sisters. He graduated from Yale in 1892. They were married in South Manchester, Conn., in 1895 and went to live in New Orleans. After the birth of my sister, Helen, father moved his practice to New York City, where the climate was better for my mother's health. I was born October 16, 1898. Soon afterward, my mother went to Colorado Springs with "threatened" tuberculosis, leaving me in Manchester with my grandparents.

From birth I was under the care of Dr. Alexander Lambert, my "Uncle Alex," who was the husband of my oldest aunt and whose sister, Ruth, was the wife of my oldest uncle, Dexter.

For many years we moved from house to house and town to town, seeking relief for my mother's asthma. There was a rented house on Lawrence Park, Bronxville, a winter in Spokane, Wash. with the William H. Cowles family, summers with Grandma Cheney at York Harbor, Maine, a winter in New Orleans, a yellow house among the dogwood trees of Bronxville, a trip to England when I took pneumonia on the ship and lay two months in a hospital in Southampton; there was one year at the Charleton School for rich young snobs in New York, and another year at Brantwood Hall in Bronxville; but most of my education was in the hands of an endless series of governesses. I studied what I liked: English literature and composition, and left the rest alone. I read a great deal of everything from the age of eleven on; but the infectious stupidity of my teachers prejudiced me for life against other subjects, with the possible exception of music, which I worked upon fitfully.

At thirteen, while we were living in Grey Arches, a large house in Bronxville, the uncongeniality of my parents began to wear on my nerves. Helen was away at boarding school. My father brought a stream of gay friends to the house; there were dances, theatres, house parties, tennis parties; my mother protested with neurasthenic invalidism. I lived in loneliness on weekdays and frenzied excitement on weekends. They sent me off to boarding school, Miss Bennett's in Millbrook, N. Y.

There I spent the four happiest years of my life. I made many life-long friends, was president of my class, citizenship leader, editor of the school magazine, class song writer, leading man or leading lady in many plays, and member of the advanced dancing class. I wrote plays, songs, poetry, a novel, a masque, and many stories. I rode horseback, played field hockey, took ten-mile walks, did high and broad jumping, played a little baseball and basketball. My consuming interests were drama, aesthetic dancing, and pageantry (including especially costuming). I let the routine studies go, as usual. My vacations were crowded with dances and theatres and parties of all sorts. We always spent Xmas and Thanksgiving at Grandma's.

The year I left school, my father sailed to France as Judge Advocate on General Pershing's staff in the World War. We went out to spend the winter in Colorado Springs and then to visit the Cowles in California. I had decided now, since my mother would not allow me to study dancing for the stage, to prepare for college. I went to girls' schools in Colorado and in Santa Barbara, but I did not study because I was becoming mildly popular with boys my own age, for the first time, in spite of my prettier sister Helen and beautiful cousin, Harriet Cowles.[22]

It was this year that my parents were divorced. My father soon married Emily Ward in Paris, a young, intelligent, and charming widow with two children. They had one son, Hugh. After the War, my father bought a place near Paris and settled there to live.

In two summers and two winters I managed to make up enough gaps in my education to graduate at the Manchester Public High School. They were hard years, because of my undisciplined mind, because I was four years older than my classmates, and because of the antagonism of the town people to anyone related to the rich Cheneys. The last year, however, I made some friends, became editor of the magazine, and started a dramatic club[23] and a girl's basketball team. I was not permitted to play on the tennis team because it was unmaidenly.

Instead of going to Smith College, I became interested in nursing during the great influenza epidemic in the War, and entered the Presbyterian Hospital Nursing School in New York. It was uncongenial, exhausting work, but I stuck it out until I graduated (in five years) from sheer stubbornness. In my second year, owing to night duty and falling in love, my health broke down completely. For two years I was in bed or having operations most of the time. But I was finally able to go back and finish training, nursing three months in an insane asylum.

As already noted, the insecurity of Mother's home life is a ready inference: those moves from town to town and from school to school; the sick, querulous, domineering mother; the seemingly solicitous, party-loving, gregarious father who in reality was a recidivistic social climber "cheated" of a male heir by his first marriage; the stupid governesses and unencouraging teachers; the Victorian strictures against artistic expression and "unmaidenly" exposure on the tennis court; the constant reminder that she was an ugly duckling as compared with her sister. The fact that Hugh A. Bayne, her father, is not mentioned by name, whereas Dr. Alexander Lambert is, is significant because she was financially dependent upon Bayne but emotionally dependent upon Uncle Alex for the paternal model. Such security as she had she found in the related clans of the Cheneys of South Manchester and the

"Tris" in nurse's uniform, class of 1923, Presbyterian Hospital, New York. After the influenza epidemic struck South Manchester in 1918, "Tris" decided against college and in favor of nursing school.

Cowleses of Spokane and Santa Barbara. It is true to say, the Cheneys were as remarkably kind and benevolent as they were rich; the Cowles cousins, descended from newspaper publishing tycoons of Chicago and the West, were similar godsends. That said, Mother struggled within her world and within herself in order to get a purchase on a worthwhile, independent life.

She got it by pluck and "stubbornness." She got it by following the dictates of her heart: "Instead of going to Smith College, I became

interested in nursing during the great influenza epidemic in the War"....
she tells us in understated fashion, omitting the details of a turning
point in her life.

She was an eighteen-year-old girl raised for what might be called
an aristocratic career in czarist Russia instead of in South Manchester,
a provincial town virtually owned by her family, when the epidemic
hit. At great risk to her life she volunteered to give assistance to her
sick and dying fellow citizens. Cheney Hall, a cultural center dedicated in 1867 by Horace Greeley, had been converted into a tempo-
rary hospital. She became "interested," there, in nursing.

I have fictionalized the scene and offer it here by way of drama-
tizing events as they might well have been:

> Heartwell Hall was usually a large single room with a stage at
> one end, an organ loft at the other, tiers of seats in-between. Now
> the seats had been removed, replaced by tiers of bunk beds, and the
> blackness of walnut-paneled walls was broken only by pale squares
> of open windows. In the daytime, shafts of sunlight slanted across
> unshaven, haggard faces with glazed eyes. In the dark, electric torches
> or lanterns would pick out a bed, turn upon a face flushed or deadly
> white—or, worst of all, a dull bluish color—upon delirious lips and
> blank eyes, gaze inward. Death was an actual presence in the room,
> a stirring in the troubled air of majesty and terror.
>
> When Trinc first entered this hospital, its foul odors repelled
> her until she heard the caterwaul of dying men, the gasping, the
> coughing. She was met by a doctor who called her "Miss Derryman"
> and seemed to believe that anyone acquainted with the famous
> Dr. Knight already knew how to give hypodermic injections, take
> pulses, collect sputum cups, change sheets, and wrap up corpses to
> look like mummies. For he put her to work at once. But she had
> done these things, soon moving as if in a trance as the first day be-
> came a landslide of the nights and days that followed. Relief came at
> odd intervals; sleeping at home was like touching shore when you
> had begun to wonder if you could swim any further.
>
> There was a youngster of eighteen who called, "Rosy, Rosy, I
> need you." When Trinc went to him, he seized her hand and began
> to kiss it all over, crying, "Ma, take Sis away, she bothers me." He sat
> straight up in bed, whimpered, trailed off into feeble curses, asked

for a glass of beer and died. There was a fine-looking boy who was not delirious and who seemed only humbly concerned not to be a bother. He said to her, "Don't feel badly," and died. There was a tough-looking Swede who said in dim light, "Hello, girl. I like you. I like you better than any girl I've seen. I'd like to go to town with a god-damned girl like you and have a hell of a time!" Trinc poured out some bitter medicine in a big iron spoon and gave it to him; he seized the spoon, tried to hit her with it. The doctor came and she helped him to tie the Swede's hands and feet to the ends of the bed, to fasten a sheet tight over his body, to tie the sheet under the bed. The doctor put a gag in the Swede's mouth. Trinc asked him not to do it. The doctor said, "Miss Derryman, a man who cannot move or curse becomes more tranquil." The muffled curses became fainter and fainter. Then the Swede died.[24]

The family opposed Mother's decision to undertake nurses' training in New York rather than attend Smith College. A nurse's career, after all, involved disciplined care for patients with, to them, "unacceptable" social, economic, or racial backgrounds. Only Uncle Alex encouraged her.

Mother was, as she writes, "related to the rich Cheneys," thus assumed to be rich, herself. She was not. Yet the assumption would be made by people wherever she went whether in New York or Manila or Paris, or in Durham! My grandmother Helen Bayne, one of the twelve children of Knight Dexter Cheney, though "looked after," had little money. After her divorce, she lived in South Manchester not in the grand mansions of her brothers but in what had once been "the coachman's cottage." At her death in 1937 she left Mother $15,000, just enough for her to build a house in Durham. (I at the age of eight was left the complete works of Ralph Waldo Emerson, Henry David Thoreau, and Robert Louis Stevenson!) When Mother married Father, her entire capital amounted to $44,000. She spent much of this capital to meet Father's expenses as a graduate student and to educate her children.

In those days an educated woman was not highly prized. For this reason, perhaps, Mother puts emphasis in her "history" on a disinterest in learning even though, it is clear, she had been an outstanding student at Miss Bennett's. Her course work at Presbyterian Hospital, moreover, had not been easy. Anatomy, for instance, might have floored her contemporaries who went to liberal-arts colleges. All the same, the morbid depiction of herself as a nonintellectual made her vulnerable to Father's *Pygmalion* lapses into scorn. He writes, as follows, in a letter to her dated 29 February 1928:

> I long ago concluded that you were almost entirely uninterested in my work, and from that particular point of view our marriage was perhaps a failure. You are, it is true, interested in your husband's getting ahead in his profession—like all other women, supplying ambition to husbands who apparently are lacking in it. But for the materials I have to work with, you'll have to admit, my dear, you have little sympathy. This may be due to the fact (1) that you left off schooling with prep. school & (2) that you are convinced—as I am secretly too—that scholarship is a dull business—that is, scholarship as practiced by most of its devotees. You are interested in being amused: you have been amused all your life, & apparently count me a dud because I cannot furnish you with the particular kind of gaiety you must enjoy. This may be another way of saying that Dullness has already overtaken me—if I were not, to begin with, dull. In either case, it is a pretty bad outlook for the future.[25]

Although Father's attitude—the "superior" male demands female compliance—may have been one to which his young wife subscribed, it was ambivalent. When she wrote a novel based upon her experiences in nurses' training, he condemned it so harshly that she never sought its publication. She sold a short story to *Tomorrow Magazine*, but he expressed no interest in the fact.[26] She published book reviews, but when she risked the word "genius" in praising Thornton Wilder for *The Bridge of San Luis Rey* (1927), Father gave her a scolding she would never forget. And yet he relied heavily upon her literary judgment, making her the first reader of manuscripts turned in by his students. He used her cogent remarks as the basis for his own remarks, the ones he returned to students—including discoveries of potential genius. His students never knew that "Tris" had been involved in evaluation of talent.

The Cheney Homestead was probably built in 1785. Timothy Cheney (1731-95), a clockmaker, left a record in his account book dated 1784, saying, "Paid this day for lumber for my new house."[27] It was situated on the side of a hill in what was then East Hartford Woods, or Orford Parish. The little brook running before it and a high hill rising beyond it created a picturesque valley. In this house lived George, Timothy's son; George's eight sons, the first generation of Cheney brothers, were all born there.

Today the Homestead is maintained as a museum by the Manchester Historical Society. Many of the great elms and oaks that once surrounded the house have been lost to disease or to the hurricane of 1938. Interstate 384 now commands the valley. Commuters speeding on their way to the great insurance empire of Hartford, about nine miles away, see only an exposed remnant of a bygone era.[28]

George's sons John (1801-85) and Seth (1810-56) were successful engravers and portraitists whose financial support helped the budding silk industry founded by their brothers. After extensive study in Europe, John and Seth became intimate with and made portraits of some prominent persons of their day, Transcendentalists, Daniel Webster, Longfellow, Emerson, Dorothea Dix, James Russell Lowell. According to a family historian the portraits were exhibited at the Boston Museum of Fine Arts and are still in demand today. In 1853 Seth married Ednah Dow Littlehale (1824-1904), a prolific writer involved in the antislavery movement and an ardent feminist who in 1897 gave a two-hour address to the Mechanics Institute of Boston on "The Reign of Womanhood." Here are strands woven into the fabric of Mother's heritage: artistic pursuits, civil rights activism. Although Cheneys were not churchgoers, they held fast to a tradition of conscience. Mother would do the same.

It was about the year 1835 that the brothers, with the exception of George Wells who had died, and John and Seth, established in South Manchester a nursery for the propagation of mulberry trees essential to supply food for silk worms. With establishment of the Mount Nebo

A 1957 photo of the Cheney Homestead, built ca. 1785. Preserved by the Manchester Historical Society (South Manchester, Connecticut), the Homestead was the birthplace of the eight Cheney brothers, two of whom became celebrated artists, five others founders of Cheney Brothers Silk Manufacturing Company. (Photograph courtesy of the Manchester Historical Society.)

Silk Company the manufacture of sewing silk was begun in 1838. Even though the mulberry-tree bubble burst, by 1855 the Cheneys had made a practical success of spinning waste silk. Prior to that time all the raw silk used in American factories was that which had been reeled by an expensive hand process from perfect, that is, unpierced cocoons. The attempts which had been made, both in America and in Europe, to utilize the large quantities of pierced cocoons and also masses of silk fiber which had become too tangled to be reeled, had proven unsuccessful. By the adaptation of machinery from cotton and woolen mills, and by the use of special machines invented by them or imported from Europe, the Cheneys were able economically to card and spin into

Cheney Brothers Mills in 1923. Knight Dexter Cheney served as president during its heyday from 1894 until his death in 1907. Elizabeth Blackburn, his granddaughter, was born in his home in 1898. (From Spiess and Bidwell, History of Manchester, Connecticut.)

yarn the silk waste. Incorporated as Cheney Brothers Silk Manufacturing Company, the firm expanded at an exceptional rate. By the end of the nineteenth century Cheney Brothers, producing every variety of silk thread and fabric and conducting every process of manufacture from raw silk to finished product, had become the leading business of its kind in the world.

Knight Dexter Cheney (1837-1907), Mother's grandfather, served as president of the firm from 1894 to 1907. Ednah Dow Smith Cheney (1841-1915), a niece of the formidable Ednah Dow Littlehale and Mother's grandmother, presided over a four-story, forty-five-room mansion, Mother's birthplace. Its dining room easily accommodated over a hundred guests at Thanksgiving and Christmas gatherings. When the Persian carpets were rolled up in the Big Room, guests would dance there, provided that they were at least twenty-five years old. Anyone younger than that was defined as a child!

Four generations of Cheneys managed the company; most of them settled with their families in South Manchester. By the late 1920s fifteen families, all Cheneys, were living in houses near one another in a park-like area of wide lawns and big trees. Here, in short, was a green kingdom in the middle of Connecticut. It is likely that nothing resembling this "feudal aristocracy," as family members affectionately called it, existed anywhere else in America. The passionate though unspoken love and concern of the Cheneys for the Family created a sort of fairytale community. It was against this community, so comfortable and so caring, that Mother had to rebel if she were to become mistress of her own destiny.

Various forces brought about the decline of Cheney Brothers: the growing popularity of synthetics, the price of raw silk, unionization, single-family management, little diversification of product. The company was gone by 1954. Today, the red-brick shells of the factories that once covered twenty acres now bear a resemblance to Roman ruins. Executives from the insurance companies in Hartford now occupy some of the mansions that Cheneys could no longer afford to heat or pay taxes on. The lawns are occasionally used by golfers practicing tee-shots. It was once the custom of Knight Dexter Cheney at Christmas to take his horse-drawn sleigh into the village to distribute presents to his workers. No sleigh bells ring now.

‡　‡　‡

My grandmother Helen Cheney Bayne (1868-1937) reminds me of Isabel Archer in Henry James's *Portrait of a Lady*. Like that romantic character, she aspired to a marriage with a man of noble and artistic sensibility, found in Hugh Bayne the semblance of such a person, but in fact married a conventional egotist. Helen, like Isabel, renounced personal happiness. Deaf she was and domineering she may have seemed to Mother, but Grandma Bayne was a gifted painter in a family of painters. One of her oils, painted when she was an art student in Boston, has in my opinion the quality of Vermeer's great *Girl with a Pearl Earring*. Although she quit painting, her brother, Russell Cheney (1881-1945), Mother's Uncle Russell, gained a reputation as "an American Cézanne."[29] He studied at the Art Students League in New York and then for three years at the Academie Julien in Paris, under Jean-Paul Laurens. After assimilating the Impressionists, he discovered his own style by going beyond the outward appearance of a chosen subject to its inward reality. Whether he was painting a still life in Venice or a poor Mexican in Santa Fe or a landscape in California or Maine,

Russell Cheney, the "American Cézanne," in his South Manchester studio, ca. 1916. The two large canvases flanking him, right and left, depict New England and California and demonstrate his assimilation of French impressionists. (From F.O. Matthiessen, Russell Cheney, 1881-1945, A Record of His Work, The Andover Press, 1946.)

he showed a powerful will to express life in a philosophic manner. He could not divorce life from art, a fact that influenced his companion, F.O. Matthiessen, in a synthesis of literature and culture. Harvard Professor Matthiessen's *American Renaissance* (1940) was written in Uncle Russell's house at Kittery, Maine.

My grandfather Hugh Aiken Bayne (1870-1954) had the intelligence, charm, and generosity to earn an admiring portrait.[30] His exhibitionism and racism ruin it. He was descended from John Gayle, Governor of Alabama, 1831-35, whose daughter, Anna Maria Gayle, married Thomas L. Bayne of New Orleans, a lawyer and colonel in the Confederate Army. Grandpa quarterbacked the 1891 Yale football team and immortalized himself, I think, by inventing the use of numerals in signal-calling. A photograph of the team shows Grandpa in a jaunty pose, his bushy mustache looking as if it has been glued on as, indeed, his personality had been. His enormous popularity at Yale rested upon footballing but also upon his singing of slightly risqué French songs. When he was tapped for the Skull & Bones society, a freemasonry of the future power elite, doors opened for him, including an introduction to the Cheney clan. When he became engaged to Grandma, the clan dressed up in Prince Alberts and tuxedos and Parisian dressing gowns, gathered in Cheney Hall, and listened to a speech combining persiflage with witty insolence:

Peaceful as may have seemed the mission which has so often brought me from the far South to share your Northern hospitality, I have come in a spirit of retribution for the invasion which my country suffered at your Yankee hands thirty years ago. I have come hoping to square the account by a complete reversal of the events of the War. Then, in 1864, the North invaded the South and captured many of her best people. Now, in 1894, the South, personified by me, is for the Union, and Helen Cheney, personifying the North, has, after a futile resistance, accepted the union I have campaigned to impose upon her. And so my toast shall be "To the United States—the State

Lt. Colonel Hugh Aiken Bayne, Elizabeth Blackburn's father. Judge Advocate on General Pershing's staff in World War I, he returned to civilian life, but was fond of posing in military uniform.

of Maidenhood and the State of Bachelorhood—where North and South shall be one forevermore."

At the beginning of American involvement in the First World War, one of Grandpa's Yale cronies, "Corny" Vanderbilt, remembered the French songs and recommended the now-wealthy Wall Street lawyer, on the basis of fluency in French, for appointment as Judge Advocate on General Pershing's staff. For his service in France, which included impersonating Pershing at a ceremony honoring French aviators, Grandpa was awarded the Distinguished Service Cross. After cultivating acquaintance with Marshal Foch, commander-in-chief of Allied forces, Grandpa was awarded the Croix de Guerre. Years later, Yale men were guided to his estate at Brunoy by means of a blue "Y," the size of an IMAX screen, he had painted on the side of the house.

Left a widower when his second wife Emily died of TB and retiring from the practice of law at the age of fifty-five, he devoted himself to painting rigid portraits in oil, to playing paddy-cake tennis and aggressive backgammon, to drinking heavily, and to circulating petitions in New Haven designed to deny admission of African Americans to Skull & Bones.

We pots should hesitate before calling kettles black. Grandpa Bayne, when I knew him in his late seventies, was broken-hearted over the debauchery of his only son, upon whom he doted. Hugh Gayle Bayne (1921-56), Tris's half-brother Uncle Hughie, though kicked out of numerous schools and colleges, had been an Air Transport pilot during the war and a legitimately decorated hero for courage during the Normandy landings. His appetite for drinking and gambling overwhelmed him, as did five marriages, the last to Hollywood pin-up Chili Williams. Uncle Hughie's debts, perhaps totaling a million dollars, were always paid by Grandpa, who nevertheless attached lawyerly strings to Hughie's inheritance so that when Hughie died, aged thirty-five, in Majorca, in mysterious circumstances, he may have been murdered for failure to pay gambling debts.

Grandpa's Bones connection yielded brilliant friends for Helen, my "Aunt Hen," and for Mother. One was the Hartford lawyer, Farwell

Knapp, who married Aunt Hen in 1923; they had two daughters, Emily (1928-64), the inspiration for my first novel, and Betsy.[31]

Before that marriage, Hen and Tris found a protective big brother in the poet, H. Phelps Putnam (1894-1948). Good-looking, amusing, and endowed with a gift for mockery, this romantic personality seemed almost comparable in his day, in the opinion of critic, novelist, and historian Edmund Wilson, to Scott Fitzgerald, Ernest Hemingway, and Edna Millay. The career that might have been of that quality was destroyed by asthma and by the alcohol that "Phelpie" drank in an attempt to relax its hold. Descended from a family that included two Revolutionary heroes, Putnam often sounded, with characteristic eloquence, notes that remain surprisingly contemporary, as in these lines from "Putnam Battle Cry":

> Think of the rascals
> Thrown out of England on their ears
> Because a Putnam cuckholded a king.
> The Putnams were farmers, rifle-boys,
> They were preachers, scholars; they
> Were atheists, free-thinkers, bums;
> They were always revolutionists.

> ────────

> They won't be home until they find
> Who loosed the terrible swift sword—
> They won't be home until they meet
> The enemy, until their feet
> Are muddy on the dispossessing floors.

Like Robinson Jeffers, Putnam was one of our first poets to denounce the exploitation of nature. His Earth acts vengefully toward descendants of her ravishers and boasts that she has

> molded fools in the images of men,
> Making them lovelorn in all other lands,
> Making them desirous with a secret homesickness,
> Uneasy in her arms or in other arms.[32]

Mother introduced me to Putnam's poetry when I was twelve. I loved his rebellion against stuffiness. I loved his explicit sexuality. I loved his voice—derisive or solemn, bitter or erotic, ringing with the "iron clangour" of forthrightness. This almost forgotten poet has influenced me more than I can say—more, at any rate, than T.S. Eliot.

Putnam's friend at Phillips Exeter Academy, at Yale, and at Skull & Bones was Donald Ogden Stewart (1894-1980). In 1920, when Stewart was living off the charity of Grandma Bayne and Aunt Hen in their apartment on Park Avenue, he met "Tris." Within a year, on the recommendation of F. Scott Fitzgerald, he showed a literary parody to Edmund Wilson, then assistant editor at *Vanity Fair*. His career was launched. With the help of Ernest Hemingway in Paris in 1924, Stewart wrote and published a humorous novel, *Mr and Mrs Haddock Abroad*, which endures as a little classic of facetious drollery. When he was in Hollywood in later years he wrote the screenplay for *The Philadelphia Story*, starring Katharine Hepburn, and for *A Woman's Face*, starring Joan Crawford. His marriage to Ella Winter, widow of Lincoln Steffens, nudged him toward the Communist Party. Senator Joseph McCarthy's purge of Hollywood "liberals" sent both of them into permanent exile in London.

Like Mother's father, Stewart was a charmer. Both, she believed, were narcissistic persons in the original descriptive sense of being in love with their idealized image of themselves.[33] This basic attitude gave them buoyancy, resiliency, and an air of perennial youthfulness. It was the source of their charm for others. Incessantly, Stewart spoke to Tris of his wonderful gifts and qualities, expecting admiration and unconditional "love" in return for his scintillating display of feeling. He wished to appear irresistible to a girl difficult to attain, but as soon as he consummated his conquest in her emotional surrender, his interest in her receded.

Putnam wrote to Hen on November 8, 1921, deploring Tris's infatuation with Stewart:

> I will say that the situation between Stewie and Tris won't improve. It will get worse. I know this. First you knew Don & then Tris

knew him—and all the while I knew him a damn sight better. And I've always known him & liked him for exactly what I knew him to be—so this doesn't affect me that way at all. You can't really damn Don's actions because, as far as I know, he's never lied to Tris about his feelings (except to be as dramatic as he always is). You can only disagree with his personality. It has always been a surprise to me how anyone with any Cheney blood in their veins ever did anything else but disagree with that personality.[34]

‡ ‡ ‡

As a boy I was often taken by Mother for visits with Cheneys in South Manchester. They were immensely kind to me, and I remember with delight and nostalgia, though never with envy, the ways of these people in their green kingdom. Some of them were eccentric. For instance, when Tris and Hen were little girls, they were never allowed to wash their own hair or even to wipe their own bottoms. Servants were assigned to perform these tasks.[35]

The eccentricity of "The Wee-Wee's" is part of Cheney folklore.[36] Rush Cheney (1815-82) married an English woman and had four children who never married. Harry and Robert drove Rolls Royces and hung dead deer in a stone-floored room of the Homestead. Ann (1849-1944) and Louise also owned Rolls Royces but seldom drove them out of the carriage house. They kept a separate ice box for the servants' food and had a tunnel built to connect their "Italian" palace—a Stanford White monstrosity—with the clothes-drying yard located so that they need not observe the washer-women from their windows. These sisters always spoke of themselves as one: "our stomach has flatulence" or "our bowels are not in working order." They wore identical white kid gloves and carried silk parasols to tea. Mother remembered that Rudyard Kipling called them "Annie-and-Louise" in one of his stories. To the Family, they were known as "The Annies" or "The Wee-Wee's." Because there were no marriages and no children, these brothers and sisters became the richest of all the Cheneys and were called "The Royals" by townsfolk.

Their butler hated children. On May Day, various children

including Tris would sneak up to the palace, hang a basket on the door, and, when the butler answered the bell, kiss him and run for their lives. It was daring enough to kiss the butler. No one, absolutely no one, had ever dared to kiss a Wee-Wee. That would have been tantamount to bringing a curse upon one's head, perhaps sterilizing one's ability to breed—or drive a Rolls Royce. Of course a portrait shows Louise to have been, once upon a time, as stunning a beauty as Alexandra, Queen Victoria's daughter-in-law. Perhaps Louise had been kissed once or twice; Cousin Annie never. Everyone dreaded the Curse of the Wee-Wee's.

On Tuesday, December 28, 1926, Mother and Father were married in the "keeping room" of the Homestead. Does a keeping room mean a place of confinement or a place that has to be defended like a goal or, likely, a place of welcome? It was certainly kept cold. That day, outside, there was snow, and since snow was a hazard to the bride's Cheney silk velvet gown, one of her uncles tossed her over his shoulder, veil and train wound around her, and delivered her to the Homestead like a sack of flour. There she was stowed in the freezing stone-floored room that reeked of Harry and Robert's rotting deer. Finally the wedding march was played by Tris's piano teacher and by a violinist, his boyfriend. The wedding took place in the aforesaid keeping room under a clock case which had a painting inside instead of a dial. Weddings are supposed to be timeless.

There were 150 guests, mostly Cheneys with a sprinkling of Blackburns, Grandpa Charley doubtless sunk in his Slough of Despond, Grandma Amy doubtless peering around for sinners in need of salvation. When everyone joined the reception line, their teeth chattering, in order to congratulate bride and groom, Father believed it was his duty to kiss all comers. He had not been warned about the Wee-Wee's. Presently, seventy-eight-year-old Cousin Annie held out her gloved hand. Father leaned in and pecked her on the cheek.

There was a sudden freeze-frame silence in the Homestead before Annie moved on and a festive atmosphere returned. Mother whispered to Father. He felt appalled by that forbidden kiss. The incident, in fact, depressed him for many years to come.

Bridal portrait of Elizabeth Cheney Bayne. She and William Blackburn married on Tuesday, December 28, 1926, in a Protestant Episcopal service at the Cheney Homestead. Her love for "Bill"—a womanly, purely human experience of love, involving the courage to suffer for it—lasted her entire lifetime.

Had this paragon of Southern courtesy and honor inadvertently brought down upon the House of Blackburn the Curse of the Wee-Wee's?

FOUR

Crying Hither

When the newlyweds arrived in Durham early in 1927, the city had, like the human race, low repute. It was generally regarded as dirty, its population as uncultivated, and its leading citizens as worshippers of Mammon. It was a "tobacco town" famed for little else but the manufacture of cigarettes, cigarillos, snuff, and plug tobacco. Even Duke University, less than two years old, was regarded derisively as the riotous offspring of Methodism and the Tobacco Trust.[37]

Neighboring towns saw Durham as upstart and distinctly second class. Historic, "aristocratic" Hillsborough, about twelve miles away, and Chapel Hill, also about a dozen miles away, felt superior. After all, Chapel Hill was the seat of the University of North Carolina, founded in 1795, the first state university in the nation to open its doors to students. To Tar Heels such as the novelist Thomas Wolfe, Durham was chiefly useful for its railroad station. Twenty-five miles to the east the city of Raleigh, the state capital, which prided itself on culture and politics, doubted what Durham had to offer. Poor Durham doubted itself: a bride came to the city, a native of an older but smaller place, and the comment of the local newspaper was, "She might have had a brilliant social career but she came to live in Durham."

Once it was fashionable to regard all places with disdain except for Manhattan Island, and it seems to believe the U.S.A. a desert between Manhattan and Hollywood. Even tourist attractions in Europe can arouse the scorn of New Yorkers. Edmund Wilson, for instance, considered Delphi a shabby little town; he ignored Parnassus above his head. With so much condescension to be distributed, it's a wonder that Durham, boasting neither an oracle nor a home of gods, got noticed at all. The tourists who visited it in the nineteenth century wanted spittoons in public places, not hallucinating soothsayers. "We make millions of cigarettes in Durham," wrote the late Helen Bevington in her journal. "Back in the 1880s, the Bull Durham tobacco factory was the largest in the world. People came from miles around to admire the snorting bull painted on the factory and listen to the steam whistle imitating its bellow."[38] Whatever—Durham will always be to some people "Tobacco Road" even though Erskine Caldwell's novel of that name was set in Georgia; it will always be associated with warnings from the Surgeon General that smoking is injurious to your health.

Nowadays the image of Durham as thoracically incorrect has been largely replaced by another image, that of a dynamic educational center in the "research triangle" comprising Duke in Durham, University of North Carolina in Chapel Hill, and North Carolina State University in Raleigh. Yet good-natured ridicule persists. In a novel by Doris Betts of Chapel Hill and Pittsboro, Durham is populated by drug addicts who think Beethoven's Fifth is a bottle of bourbon.[39] Durhamites themselves continue to put the city down as "Durms." Few realize that this name is fairly accurate: in 1854 Dr. Bartlett Durham helped to establish a station for the North Carolina Railroad Company, first called Durhamville station, and later Durham's, the colloquial pronunciation of which would have been Durms.

The founding of Durham coincided with the rise of industrialism in the previously agrarian and slavery-bound South. This origin accounts for the disdain felt for the city by its older neighbors, but it also points to what has made the city enviable. "Durham was a new town," William Kenneth Boyd wrote in *The Story of Durham: City of the New South*, "brought into existence by industrial enterprises rather than by the needs of an agricultural community or by the necessity for a center of governmental and political action in pioneer days." The prosperity of the new town "was first established after the Civil War by the enduring toil and the indomitable spirit of plain men who possessed little capital and had not belonged to the large slave-owning class."[40] Perhaps Professor Boyd, whose book was published almost eighty years ago, could be accused of the kind of boosterism that has its source in a feeling of injured merit. The statement, however, rings true. The creation of a New South at the moment of its defeat, humiliation, and impoverishment was indeed an accomplishment of considerable magnitude by "plain" men of considerable fortitude. Durham, itself, a hamlet of about 200 people in 1869, grew into a city of about 75,000 a century later, its growth owed to the in-migration of workers, white and black, seeking jobs in the tobacco factories and in the cotton and hosiery mills. Altogether this in-migration brought a cosmopolitanism that was itself somewhat new in the South. Durham could genuinely boast of an atmosphere of toleration and of an unwritten creed of support for education.

The story of Duke University's rise from tobacco ashes has a direct bearing not only upon Father's career but also upon my imagination as a native son.[41]

It all began on April 26, 1865. At Bennett House, four miles from Durham, fifteen days after Lee's surrender to Grant at Appomattox, General Joseph E. Johnston surrendered to General Sherman the last Confederate army east of the Mississippi. Whereupon federal soldiers ransacked J.R. Green's little tobacco factory in Durham, found his "bright leaf" to their liking, spread favorable reports about it, and stimulated a smoking craze in the cities of the North. Whereupon Green went to visit one John Y. Whitted of Hillsborough to discuss plans for marketing his product nationwide. Over a morning dish of fried oysters, Whitted, pointing to a jar of Coleman's Mustard, advised Green: "There is a condiment that is manufactured in Durham, England, and its label bears the sign of a Durham bull's neck. Why not name your product Bull Durham Smoking Tobacco and adopt a whole bull as a trademark?" Whereupon Green's "Bull Durham" product became famous—still so famous today that a cowboy who "rolls his own" in a film is preparing to smoke "Bull Durham," so famous that a local minor league baseball franchise named for it would eventually inspire a Kevin Costner film called *Bull Durham*.

Washington Duke, another local tobacco grower, also had his supplies raided by federal soldiers. He peddled what was left of them as "Pro Bono Publico"—no worries then about public health—and set himself and his sons, Buck and Ben, up as W. Duke Sons and Company, manufacturers. Not until 1882 could this company compete with "Bull Durham." Then, Buck decided to make machine-rolled cigarettes, a "Duke of Durham" product that captured the market. Rival companies joined W. Duke Sons in 1890 to form the American Tobacco Company; by 1898 "Bull Durham" had come under its control. Using efficient, if ruthless, business methods, Buck expanded his "Tobacco Trust" to a gigantic $274 million industry in 1904. Whereupon philanthropy came and made a favorable adjustment to his relation with the Almighty.

A small college in Durham called Trinity had won for itself the friendship of the Dukes, father and sons. Shortly before his death Washington Duke gave the college $500,000. Buck and Ben, by 1919, had given it more than $1.25 million. Five years later Buck created the Duke Endowment of $40 million for aid to educational institutions, hospitals, orphanages, and superannuated Methodist preachers. At Buck's death in 1925, this endowment was more than doubled, and a large portion of the more than $80 million was assigned to Trinity College, which changed its name to Duke University. Whereupon construction began at once of two campuses, one of Georgian brick known as East Campus, the other of stone, in "collegiate Gothic" style, known as West Campus.

Although necessity drives professors, like their starving cousins and fellow vagrants, the troubadours, players, and artists, into all sorts of lowly paid jobs in all sorts of remote and risible colonies, Father was made for Duke and Durham. From his perch in Piedmont North Carolina he could keep an eye on his morose, suicidal father, now in Greenville, South Carolina, and on his scattered siblings who might need, and occasionally did need, the elder brother's assistance.[42] Impelled by inheritance of pioneering and missionary impulses, he was attracted to Duke as a new institution which would afford him the opportunity to assist in its growth, in particular through instigating an awareness of the arts.[43] In spite of his aversion to the "Teutonic" style in higher education—the Ph.D. mania, the swatting up of historical trivia, the emphasis given research over teaching—he correctly anticipated Duke's capacity for centering professional schools around a core of liberal-arts disciplines, as in the old English universities. At Duke he would be able to nurture in his students, against the pull of specializations, the Baconian ideal of achieving fullness and exactness through reading and writing.

He did not realize how uncomfortable and isolated his bride might feel in the South. A liberal-minded Yankee in the South could be about as welcome as Darwin's monkey. Fortunately, Duke faculty and families befriended Mother, and the city of the New South accommodated strangers. She grew fond of Duke and Durham.

I am fond of them myself. I am rooted in sense of place and have written extensively about a region where industry and academia form a special civilization. Fictionalizing Durham as a stage called "Poe's Hill," I have in a number of novels been a dyed-in-the-wool regionalist and discovered in this imaginary realm the enrichment of universal themes.[44] Durham is no provincial backwater, no Yonville-l'Abbaye. It was already, when I was born there, an actor on a world stage in business and educational operations. It has shared, too, the burden of Southern history, hence the suggestion of the grotesque in a Hill named after Edgar Poe. Its allegiance to the American dream of success has distanced it from agrarianism and from some, not all, of the bigotry of the Old South. It has flourished as a place of boundless opportunity. It has bred all-American Titans who atone for their capitalistic sins with philanthropic bonanzas. It was multicultural before that word became today's national "ism." Emma Bovary, I surmise, would have gone to college there and obtained a divorce instead of a vial of poison.

New South/Old South: I reflect the change in a novel which is a partial portrait of the Durham that the angel of place has conjured up for me from fifty years ago. In the following samples the point of view is that of Mary, a light-skinned woman raised to believe she is African American.

> Penitential madwoman in a white robe
> crosses the tracks glinting in blue glitter from
> the tobacco factories of Mill Mile.
> Piercing millwhistles
> announce the shift.
> Crowds of workers are in the night streets.
> There is comfortable raillery among them. Young old
> men women black white work together and are
> not alone.

She takes the bus downtown, alights across the street from the Bright Leaf Hotel, and enters Mrs. Zabriski's air-conditioned diner. Some boys in T-shirts are gazing into the glittering globe of a jukebox. Their faces have blanked-out expressions. The music throbs

> love me love me
> 0 0 0 bay bee. . .

"Cuppa coffee, dear, or what?" Plump, peroxided, rabbiteyed Mrs. Zabriski fingers the crucifix on her starched white blouse.

"The usual," replies Mary with a studied pause. There is something historically amusing about the way she neglects to say please. Mrs. Zabriski thinks so anyway and chuckles, pouring coffee from a pyrex globe. Mary's white cup has rings in it like a ghetto's bathtub.

> did you come
> did you fee eel

"They grow up fast." Mrs. Zabriski leans over the counter in a confiding manner. "Mr. Zabriski is teaching me to shoot a pistol. So what's new, dear?" When Mary tells her that Manny has decided to go to college, Mrs. Zabriski blinks her weak watery eyes and says, "It's a free country, dear. . . Jeez, I might have known," she suddenly exclaims.

And they are both glancing toward the glare of the street, both seeing the policeman rest one hand on the butt of his pistol and raise the other, the cars stopping and, coming across the street from the hotel, walking with pigeon-like bob, the grayhaired old lady in a white robe.

"Old Mother Pentecost," says Mrs. Zabriski. "They ought to lock her up. She found out I'm Catholic, see. She'll come in here, see. I said, 'Look, lady. Come here again and you gotta eat something in the joint, or what.' Know what she did? She orders a cuppa hot water. I think it's a gag, see. So I bring the hot water in a cup. So she takes out this used teabag—used, I am telling you—drops it in the cup, helps herself to my cream and sugar, has a cuppa tea and don't pay me a nickel. She even squeezed the teabag and took it with her. So what am I in business for—communism?"

The rock music has stopped, the T-shirted boys are leaving. Mary watches them in the big mirror behind Mrs. Zabriski. She is reaching up to adjust her hair when one of the boys holds the door open for Mrs. Pentecost. Bending over her coffee cup, Mary can hear the pneumatic door closing like a long suck of breath.

"So what's yours?" Mrs. Zabriski demands in a rude voice. "Cuppa hot water, or what?" She begins to wipe the counter, her crucifix dangling and jiggling about, her eyes not even flicked up but burrowed inside themselves.

So that Mrs. Pentecost stands alone and still makes a strange moaning sound in her throat.

Two small black boys shade their eyes and peer incuriously through the plate glass. The sun has drained their faces of color.

"The Lord will provide," Mrs. Pentecost says, quite softly.

"Well," says Mrs. Zabriski, "He's not providing today. So tell me it's unfair," she concludes with a dumb satisfied look that sweeps the diner's ceiling from end to end.

Then Mary turns, lifts her gaze.

"Hullo," she says as if out of breath. How ill and decrepit looks this old woman who was almost certainly her mother. The blue-veined hands seem to make an involuntary motion, inwardly like a pair of loose claws. At this moment Mary is not aware that she has learned to make herself akin to people, with love toward them and sympathy. She would not have dwelled upon the idea that her rising and her stepping forward to grip Mrs. Pentecost lightly by the shoulders would express a quality of affiliation. Her thought at the time is of practical remedies, of food and friendship proffered for ten minutes. She has ten minutes. "Don't you know your Mary?"

Mrs. Pentecost studies her with charmed eyes; then she is smiling and exclaiming with a sort of girlish giggle, "Mary, I declare! Goody goody. . . I was going to pay you a call but I've had no peace in my heart."

"So they know each other. So I'm an idiot," Mrs. Zabriski is muttering.

"How about something to eat?" Mary guides Mrs. Pentecost to a counter stool. "How about ham and eggs and french fries and a glass of yoghurt? Sit down."

Mrs. Pentecost sits, still smiling. Her eyes are blue and intense, and she sits upright but bulgy, like a badly stuffed bird. "Are you cooking here now, Mary?"

"If you don't mind," interrupts Mrs. Zabriski. "I hate to mention."

"I'm paying," says Mary. She picks up the menu and suggests, after a pause, "Why not Number Three, two eggs sunny side, two rashers of bacon, and a side stack of buckwheat pancakes?"

Mrs. Zabriski licks her pencil. "You trying to kill the old dame, or what?"

"Number Three and a side order of french fries and a glass of strawberry yoghurt."

"Oh," says Mrs. Pentecost, "goody goody."

"Number Three and a side french and yoghurt. Old dear must be starving, huh?"

"Mary," Mrs. Pentecost is saying with a wistful smile, "I would have invited you to visit at the Home but the ladies there, I never dreamed they'd be so old. . ."

Mary feels inspired. She sees, in her mind's eye, Mrs. Pentecost, Pap. . . "Tell you what," she is suddenly saying. "Come on down have supper with us tonight. We'll have special deluxe fried chicken just like always. You know my house on Watauga?"

Mrs. Pentecost nods. "It didn't seem fitting to pay my respects."

"Well," says Mary, "don't worry about it. Take a taxi. After six."

A hand comes to rest on the back of Mary's hand. It is like a cold kitten.

"I'd be delighted to come. Dear Mary."

With eggs and bacon sizzling on the griddle, Mrs. Zabriski says in loud voice, "Nothing personal, Mother Pentecost, but why do you walk around in a white robe and tell people they're going to hell? Are you nutty as a fruitcake, or what?"

Claw-like, Mrs. Pentecost's hand squeezes down on Mary's. Her eyes, blue and intense, are smiling.

Sharkfinned cars glide by schooled for home at five o'clock. Pyramid shadow of the statue of the Confederate Soldier lengthens across a stone bench and the whiterobed old woman slumps there asleep like Time without an hourglass and scythe.

Overhead, helicopters went pocka pocka pocka.

It's an outrage, thought Judge Debnam Babbage, observing the police helicopters from his chambers in the Court House. His bow-string tie adjusted, his Panama straw hat in place, he was preparing to go home when he thought he knew that old woman, Pentecost's widow. He shook his head.

But ah—let them out in the glorious sunshine. Bit of old America. Made them out of whalebone and vinegar then. Tough as wheat. Then, nobody pushed them around, breathed down their necks. Faith, sir, to move mountains.

Judge Debnam Babbage paused at the foot of the Court House steps, adjusted his wing collar and bow-string tie, tugged the brim of his panama, and decided to run for governor.[45]

‡   ‡   ‡

Wary of Durham doctors, Mother went to New York for the delivery of her first child. Uncle Alex, there, would see to it she received first-class care. Father met his classes, wrote frantic love letters to his bride every night, brooded. Summoned by Mother at last, he caught the train from Durham depot to Penn Station, rushed to the hospital, and sweated out the long hours of her labor.[46]

A baby daughter finally arrived on November 15, 1927. They gave her a lovely name: Mary April.

Back in Durham, the family moved into a white clapboard house, 303 Swift Avenue, midway between East and West campuses and near to friends who lived on Pettigrew Street, Lewis Patton of the English Department and his brilliant young wife, Frances Gray Patton.[47] It was good for Mother that she was making friends and becoming accepted in a party-loving circle of Duke faculty.[48] The neighborhood at unpaved Swift Avenue was a bit scruffy, visited daytimes by the whistles of Erwin Cotton Mills in West Durham and nighttimes by mournful hoots from the Southern Railroad engines. Mother was used to chaos. She had already worked in an insane asylum.

"It was during a Christmas vacation at my mother's house in Manchester that we decided to have another baby, whether we could afford it or not," she noted in my baby book.[49] I am grateful to my parents for their supererogation. Had Father foreseen the coming of the Crash and the Great Depression, I think it would have been thumbs and tools down for a child he could ill afford. As it was, the decision for Grandma Bayne's coachman's cottage was propitious: she was deaf, the house cold.

I was born at 1:15 A.M. on September 6, 1929, at Watts Hospital, Durham, under the supervision of Dr. Robert A. Ross and Miss Arrington, nurse. I weighed eight pounds, four ounces. My swollen head appeared wrinkled with grotesque grimaces. The skin of my face and hands was purple spotted with yellow.

Mother recorded this dramatic event in the baby book.

> After supper the contractions increased and came every five minutes, but there was no pain, so Bill assured me I was letting my imagination run away with me. He sat in his study reading and pretending not to be worried. At last I called the doctor, just to make sure he was in town. He was at the movies and I asked not to have him disturbed and would not even leave my name. So I went to bed to nurse my pains, feeling thoroughly ashamed of my imagination and frowned-on by Bill. When I could stand it no more, I timed my contractions again: every two minutes they came, regularly. I got up and

walked up and down the room. At 11:30 I had the first hard pain. I staggered into Bill's room and roused him. He called Dr. Ross on the telephone and said sarcastically, "My wife thinks she's in labor." By the time he got upstairs again I was in real agony—but oh so happy to have labor come on early and save me those last two weeks of waiting, so happy to know that the baby that had been kicking inside me so long would actually be in my arms, and so happy to be having "good" pains: pains so hard that you knew they must be getting you somewhere, pushing the baby out fast. I was elated and Bill was frightened and we both were excited and hurried.

Dr. Ross came in four minutes. He put his hand on my abdomen and said immediately, "Get her to hospital." As he left the room and I jumped up to dress, the "bag of waters" burst, and blood and water poured on the floor. There was no time to rest. I flung a dress over my night gown and a coat over that, a pair of stockings and pumps. . . and I was being led downstairs before I knew it.

Dr. Ross jumped in his car and sped away, beating a freight train at the crossing. We stopped to wake the cook up to take charge of Mary April while we were gone, got in the car (which had been out of order but fixed that very day) and away to hospital. I bit my lip and did not let Bill see when the pains came or how hard they were. The freight train was blocking the crossing, and we had to go around by West Durham on a rough road.

Arrived at Watts Hospital I was still too proud to let even the doctor see how bad the pains were, only asked to have a wheelchair halted until one was passed. I had a promise from him not to give me any morphine. . . The nurse shaved me in bed. Bill waited outside, steeling his nerves for another all-night torture such as he had with the first baby. Dr. Ross examined me, said it might be a short labor, and implored me to take morphine. I refused. The nurse said I must call him in as soon as I felt I was ready for the delivery room.

Dr. Ross joined Bill outside. He paced up and down, running his hands through his hair. At last he exclaimed: "I never saw such a stoical woman in my life! She won't cry out and she won't take morphine! She says she can stand it, so I suppose she can, but if it's a long labor, I can't!" They hadn't long to wait. With every pain I could feel the baby moving down the birth canal. It seemed incredibly fast; I told the nurse to run for Dr. Ross. He dashed in and said, "Get the stretcher!" They bundled me into it and started for the delivery room. I still felt happy: happy with myself now to think what I was enduring without making a cry or groan. Bill bent over the stretcher and said, "Brave girl!" I kissed him and said, "Goodbye." The next minute we were at the door of the delivery room. Along came a pain that would have pushed the baby right out, only the nurse pushed it back, and they all cried, "Don't bear down! Hold back!" I will never forget that pain if I live to be 100.

The next thing I knew Dr. Ross was saying, "No time for ether! Give me that chloroform quickly!" I took deep grateful breaths and went under. There was ether later, for I remember things while I was coming out of it: a baby's squawk, a bright light, Dr. Ross saying, "Put her under again." The next consciousness was drunkenness and pain, terrible pain. I said, "Is it over?" and a voice said, "Yes," so I said, "No, it isn't. Here comes another pain." "It's all over." "It isn't over. It must be twins." "No, it isn't twins. Just one fine boy." "Nonsense, it is twins. Just look and see." "It's all over." "It isn't." Someone gave me some paregoric for the pain. I was soon conscious enough to be interested in the baby. I wanted to ask to see it but felt too weak to shape the words. I remembered that cry I heard before they gave me more ether but thought it might all be a nightmare, every bit of it, or perhaps the baby was dead and they were fooling me; there was no baby, no crying now, only a hard narrow operating table and a bright light and white walls. Someone carried the baby in, and I tried to raise my head to see it but was too weak, so I got a fleeting glimpse only of a fat purple little creature in blankets, with swollen eye lids and masses of black hair.

Mother's narrative needs clarification.

For instance, this business about Dr. Ross coming in four minutes: there's a period piece! Was Durham so medically backward in those days that an obstetrician came to a patient's house? In four minutes? Although North Carolinians are according to the usual custom conscious of time, it is not always of this world. In Moore County, I've heard, folks live in perpetual puzzlement, "studying up them Ten Commandments what taken the Lord forty days when he done done the world in only seven."[50] Be that as it may, I'm going to trust Mother on this one. She was a trained nurse with a wristwatch, and dear Dr. Ross seems to have been infected by kindness. As for the old-fashioned word "stoical," was Mother giving herself a compliment? Yes, she was.

Her Cheney mother and grandmother seldom went to bed at night without reading *The Meditations of Marcus Aurelius*.[51]

When I was in college, I took a course called "Classical Civilization," taught by an inexperienced Greek scholar who was so nervous upon first sight of us barbarians that he lost his voice for ten minutes. What a voice when he found it! Explaining Homer's *Odyssey* through decipherment of key names in the text, he showed us that Calypso means "oblivion" and Odysseus means "pain." Pain, he said, is a value. We are born to travail, born for trouble. To be born is to cast one's name in the teeth of a hostile universe in order to win one's psyche, which means, loosely, one's life. To live means deliberately to expose oneself for the purpose of being somebody rather than nobody (Odysseus calls himself "Nobody" in order to deceive the Cyclops). Our exposed position admits the necessity of pain as suffering but also of pain as what we cause for others. We are going to plant evils. We are going to be the bane of many people's existence. We receive pain; we inflict it. And this existential condition, the necessity of pain, is the secret of life. On the other hand, permanent engulfment in the womb means that you have calypso'd yourself. If you want no trouble, want merely cover and concealment, you are not a real person. Authentic existence rooted in life establishes your identity with the nature of things. Pain, given and received, snatches a value from death—your humanity.[52]

Mother brought me painfully hither. Shakespeare: "We came crying hither."[53] I came crying hither.

Wordsworth and the English and American Romantics and Transcendentalists who came after him liked to employ the idea of childhood in the service of immortality. Doing so they created a myth that celebrates childhood's visionary privilege in the vocabulary of innocence, wonder, and virtue. Emerson believed that the simplest of objects is God's palimpsest. Whitman praised naivety.[54] Once in a while, I admit, a child may be seeing details with dazzling freshness and clarity, but the notion that this capacity puts a child directly in touch with divinity is, it seems to me, sentimental and arrogant. When wonder is introduced to complexity, is it not swamped, bewildered, indecisive? Not original innocence but the "fine hammered steel of woe" that Melville admired in the words of Ecclesiastes is, I believe, what gives life durable structure.[55] Of course, children may develop a generosity of assimilation, an unselfish curiosity, and a mystical sense of wholeness.

‡ ‡ ‡

Mother named me after her uncle, Dr. Alexander Lambert (1861-1939), who practiced medicine at Cornell Medical College in New York and served as an attending physician at Bellevue Hospital. He was Theodore Roosevelt's lifelong friend and personal physician. During the First World War he was in charge of the American Red Cross in Paris, and in 1920 he became president of the American Medical Association. His advocacy of a compulsory national health insurance program got him in political trouble—and earned my respect when I read about it in a series of articles published in 1966 in *The New Yorker*. At first, in 1917, he had a positive influence on the AMA:

> The A.M.A.'s position at that time reflected the influence of Dr. Alexander Lambert, Theodore Roosevelt's personal physician and a figure of great prestige within the medical profession. As chairman of the A.M.A.'s Social Insurance Committee, Dr. Lambert reported to the Association that his group had looked into the possibilities of voluntary health insurance under private control and, having found it unworkable, recommended adoption of a compulsory system under government control.

Support for that recommendation evaporated by 1920:

> By 1920, the outcry against the model bill had become so clamorous that the A.M.A.'s House of Delegates reversed itself and passed a resolution declaring its "opposition to the institution of any plan embodying the system of compulsory contributing insurance against illness." Dr. Lambert was president of the Association that year, and during the session, a tumultuous one, delegates periodically broke into the chant, "Get Lambert!" They got him by way of their

Dr. Alexander Lambert, Elizabeth Blackburn's uncle by marriage and surrogate father. In fifty years as diagnostician and specialist on internal medicine and drug addiction, he treated many notable persons and was physician to his friend, President Theodore Roosevelt. As president of the A.M.A. in 1920, Lambert introduced a plan for compulsory national health insurance. He died in 1939 at the age of seventy-eight, decades before his plan would become the basis for the 1965 Medicare program.

resolution, and before long most of the names of leading medical scientists like Lambert disappeared for good from the Association's roster of officers.[56]

When Medicare became law in 1965, Uncle Alex was vindicated. Lambert is a genuine, though unsung, national hero. I know now I am honored to bear his name.

At first I rejected it as if it were a transplanted heart. Southern boys, white and black, are permitted names like Beauregard, Roy, Jim Bob, Chuck, and Buddy, seldom the classics like Aeneas, Hannibal, Pompey, Seneca, or Alexander. Teased in kindergarten about "Alexander's Ragtime Band," I developed an aversion to jazz. Luckily I was chopped down to Alex, Alec, or Elleck; only when I went Up North to school and was called "Al," as in Al Capone, did my luck run out. Now I swallow the whole "Alexander" and have given up searching for a pen name such as Mark Twain or O. Henry. I recall that Hamlet traces the noble dust of Alexander until he finds it stopping a bung-hole.[57]

Before I came crying hither, Grandpa Bayne offered Mother a gift of $25,000 on condition she would name me Hugh Bayne Blackburn. Perhaps $25,000 would have yielded my parents enough income to support them for the rest of their lives; perhaps it would have created an estate worth a million dollars. Here was a couple burdened with two children "whether we could afford it or not." The family was not exactly turning the worn-out heels of its shoes toward the nearest church, but Father's academic future looked precarious unless he were adroit enough to avoid the plague of professional jealousy. He was just another Ph.D.-less, scholarly-publications-less, tenure-less professor, neck bared to get the academic ax. As for Mother, if she antagonized her father by refusing his offer, she stood to lose any future inheritance from him but she recognized Grandpa's "gift" as a bribe, a tribute to his ego. She refused his offer without a moment's hesitation.[58]

My baby book is a clothbound portfolio with thick unruled paper. Mother pasted in it photographs, clippings, coats-of-arms, and my stick-figure sketches of Stone Age friends retrieved from the collective unconscious. There are hanks of my hair. Dark at birth, it turned sable as a Shetland sheep dog's and curled itself into Little Lord Fauntleroy ringlets of the kind that Samson died for. When my curls were surreptitiously snipped off, I raged against the rape—and Philistines.

According to my baby book I had more needles stuck in me than a porcupine has quills. Between May 1930 and July 1936, I was inoculated with vaccines against smallpox, diphtheria, tetanus, and typhoid. Although Salk vaccine and penicillin were unavailable and I was plagued by laryngitis, Rosa Infantum, tonsillitis, strep throat, influenza, enlarged adenoids, and fevers in the 103-04 range, I somehow managed to survive. Three times between February 1934 and March 1935 I was hospitalized with flu and again in July 1936 for a severe reaction to anti-tetanus serum. Mesenteric enteritis, at first believed to be appendicitis, paid me visits between May :935 and April 1936. Chickenpox in 1936, measles and whooping cough in 1938, and mumps in 1941: all had a go at me. I was drowned in cod liver oil, purged with enemas, flayed with mustard plasters and tortured with swabs of iodine. Eventually I used illness as a subterfuge, feigning it in order to avoid the boredom of school and to stay at home in bed all day—so that I could write stories and poems and triumph over adversity, like Elizabeth Barrett Browning.

Solitary confinement in hospital gave me nightmares. In a dark room reeking of Lysol, I would lie awake listening to the screams of children in other rooms. This "eternal note of sadness" brought to my mind, as it did to Matthew Arnold's, "the turbid ebb and flow of human misery" and an early conviction that the world hath "really neither joy, nor love, nor light, nor certitude, nor peace, nor help for pain."[59] Intercom systems filled the air with terrifying squawks and blatting: "Doctor Van Deen, Doctor Van Deen, you're wanted in the Cannibal Room." The caterwauling of the sick and dying taught me, long before I read Shakespeare, that hell is empty and all the devils are here.[60] To this day, weather and terrorists permitting, I sleep in a room that has doors and windows open, radio and TV throttled. I dream that all persons with hypodermic needles aimed at me have been rounded up and placed aboard spaceships destined to plant colonists on the Sun.

At the age of two I avenged myself upon the world by flushing Mother's jewels down the toilet. Her rubies and pearls were never recovered. I picked my nose, stuck a moist finger through the bars of my crib, and improved the wallpaper by smearing upon it festoons of snot.

FIVE

Chaotic Splendor

Not long after my birth we moved to a squat red-brick bungalow on the poor end of Vickers Avenue. Doris Duke, the richest woman in the world, maintained a mansion some twenty blocks up the hill and away from us. We had one of Durham's garbage incinerators in our backyard. She didn't know what she was missing.

Ours was a one-story, two-bedroom bungalow with a living room and dining room, each room indistinguishable from the other except by type of furniture, a sofa here, a table there. Uncle Russell's painting of the Cheney Homestead hung over the mantelpiece as a daily reminder of our comparative decline and fall. I don't remember whether Mother's Persian rug had yet been spread over the termite-infested floorboards but believe it may have been stored away until I had successfully completed potty-training. A rotting staircase led to a cellar smelling of mildewed foundations. Mary April and I were strictly forbidden to go down to the cellar: it had, we were warned, a "dangerous" coal-burning furnace.

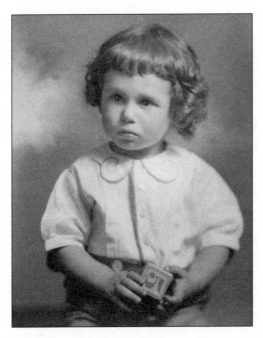

The author with "Little Lord Fauntleroy" curls, considered cute in 1931 (Photograph by Bachrach.)

We played in a patch of woods behind the house, happy to have a sandbox and a swing and to breathe the effluvia of burning rubber tires wafting from the incinerator into our poison ivy and stunted loblollies. A path led from this space to the incinerator. When I was still about two years old, Belle, my nanny, pushed me in a stroller along this path in order to get, every afternoon, the beauty of the incinerator hot.

It was beautiful. Although I didn't know about the salamander that is said to live in fire, being a sort of lizard, myself, I rejoiced in all elements. "Yawl wont t'see the 'cinerator, chile?" Belle had but to ask and I would clap my spiky, scaly hands and scream, "Cinerator! Drips!" Belle would dress me in my drips—pants—and off we would go. Ma-wee Aps (Mary April), being three and a half and too sophisticated for the adventure, didn't go, but Teddy, Jinny, Summer-Boy, and Callula went with us. They were my imaginary playmates. Belle took me to a picket-wire fence from which we could observe an acre of burning refuse. That is my earliest memory.

My second earliest memory is of potty-training. I had a little potty, white-enameled with a hole in it like the one in Segovia's guitar. Thanks to dear potty, by the time I was three tell me to grunt, and I was anal-expulsive. In psychoanalytic terms "anal-expulsive" means you are a generous person. Give me a glass of wart (water) with my metz (medicine), a lunch of nakes (spaghetti) and little dirts (black-eyed peas), and threaten me with a bank (spank) by a pleesum (policeman), and I would deliver gas and related products as fast as an oil tycoon running for president. I disliked, however, performing in front of strangers, preferring to keep them in suspense. Perhaps to this attitude can be traced an Aristotelian lock on dramatic narrative.

Aunt Mallie was another Blackburn with a touch of quixotism. She was idealistic and honorable, impractical but not unwise, fundamentally kind and sweet, occasionally impassioned by a belief that ducks are swans and that rainbows lead to a pot of gold. Although she was far from ever finding one, she made plans to distribute its contents liberally. Her heart was undaunted by misfortune and flooded with the invisible but invincible waves of optimism.

I was about three, Aunt Mallie about twenty-eight, when she came to Durham for a visit. Mother assigned her, a trained nurse with a flair for psychology, to baby-sitting duty but neglected to tell her that I did my best work in private. When my stomach was growling and Mallie had my drips off and was pointing inferentially at my potty, I pretended I didn't know a pot from a hill of beans. She coaxed. I shook my head. She gave commands. I consulted with Summer-Boy and Callula. We tactfully decided to refrain from enlightening such an unworldly grownup. After a while, persuaded that I had never been trained, Mallie got a brilliant idea, the one that is fundamental for creative writers: show, don't tell. Hiking up a skirt as large as a parachute and dropping to the floor the flour sack she wore for panties, she slowly, very slowly, started lowering herself down to my defenseless potty. She was like an atmospheric balloon trying to come in for a landing on a golf tee. She plopped down. My potty disappeared from

Father and son, ca. 1932.(Photograph by
Elizabeth Blackburn)

sight. I watched my dear aunt, during this educational demonstration,
with a mixed sensation of pity and hypnotic horror.

"See, darlin'," she said with an encouraging nod. "Easy as pie."

My third earliest memory can be dated to 1933 when I was three
and a half. It concerns the hobgoblin. For some time Belle had given
me warnings. "Yawl better be good, chile, on account the booguhmans
git you, sho nuff."

This booguhmans, it seemed to me, was worse than the conjure
people she'd told me about. Conjure people roamed the Carolinas from
the Atlantic Ocean to the Blue Ridge Mountains. They carried bags
filled with hair, fingernails, lizard tails, ground-up puppy claws, and graveyard dirt. To boys they gave candy coated with a love powder in order
to make them love girls. I figured to have a sporting chance with conjure people. This booguhmans, though, had me worried. I had flushed
Mother's jewels down the toilet. I was a liar, too, far-gone. I had told
Mother that a burgum (burglar) had stolen Ma-wee Aps's dick (stick).

One afternoon while I was supposed to be taking a nap, I heard a thumping, rasping noise coming from directly under my bed, from the cellar. It was the sound of a giant with chronic asthma. I went and opened the cellar door. The noise stopped. Shafts of an evil-smelling light drifted up to my eyes and nostrils. The cellar had an outside door. It was open. There was a pile of coal on the floor next to the dangerous furnace. I gingered myself up to martial prowess and ventured halfway down the stairs.

All of a sudden the silhouette of a giant blotted the light. His eyes—cross my heart and hope to die—were seashells on a scarecrow. His teeth—I swear to goodness—flashed in the dark like a flung-open piano keyboard. Lordy, he was the booguhmans sure as shootin', and he was a-coming to git me! The blood drained from my head. I let out a scream. I ran back upstairs and across the living room and out the front door. I reckon I would still be running to this day—I do declare—but for the fact that I sprawled on the gravel driveway and "skint" the palm of my left hand. Howling did no good. Nobody came to my rescue. I had little power left to push myself up.

By and by, I peeped down the driveway. What did I see next to the cellar door but a Depression-driven human being in bib-overalls who was shoveling coal out of a pickup truck. The coal had blackened his face as if for a minstrel show. This disenchantment gave me the Sancho Panza crap-detector I would later need as a writer.

‡ ‡ ‡

Childhood is the border country between wonder and judgment. Wonder itself, combining terror and awe, gives life its "chaotic splendor," described by Patricia Hampl:

> The artist's work, it is sometimes said, is to celebrate. But really that is not so; it is to express wonder. And something terrible resides at the heart of wonder. Celebration is social, amenable. Wonder has a chaotic splendor. It moves into experience rather than into judgment. It zooms headlong into an act of perception where the lyric is bred of awe.[61]

Shrouded by society, its power diminished with time, the chaotic splendor of admiration lingers as a conjure-trick to fuel the long endeavor of art. A scene, long forgotten, springs to mind. You see again the glitter of light on an ocean after a violent storm; you un-see urban sprawl, power grids, strip-mined mountains, dead rivers. You recall with Indian eyes the pristine, inviolate nature that you had almost forgotten always will be there:

> The beauty of things was born before eyes
> and sufficient to itself; the
> heart-breaking beauty
> Will remain when there is no heart left to break for it.[62]

The "Credo" of Robinson Jeffers is childhood's religion.

The Eno River has never been navigable for practical purposes. It is shallow, strewn with boulders. It meanders through narrow gorges where willows bow low as if in obeisance to whisperings from the old gods. Above the river, bluffs beetle with thick eyebrows of trembling pines. Once, the Occaneechi Trail snaked alongside the Eno. A trade route stretching from present-day Virginia into Georgia, this path linked tribes as diverse as the Catawbas and the Cherokees and brought the Mississippian mound-building culture into contact with the Southeast. Strategically located on the Roanoke River, the Occaneechi tribe controlled the fur trade. Then in 1676 Nathaniel Bacon, infuriated because the governor of Virginia profited from that trade, assembled a militia and led a rebellion against the Virginia government; he attacked the Occaneechi's island stronghold as well. Defeated by Bacon, the tribe fled south along the trail to an area near present-day Hillsborough and established a community by the Eno River.[63]

Father's friends included professors outside his department, among them Douglas Hill, a chemist whose stepson Robert would marry my sister, and Karl Zener, a psychologist and colleague of the parapsychologist, J.B. Rhine. I was always especially excited when my parents took me on visits to Karl and Ann Zener's home because it was perched on bluffs overlooking the Eno. Father and I descended to the river by way of a steep switchback trail. The sound of ancient water grew louder the nearer we came to it. This was a place of wonder.

When I was in prep school Up North, the invisible feathers of eagle-bonnets by the Eno drifted across my mind and inspired my first short story, published in the school's magazine. A few years later I revised the story and published it as "The Golden River" in *American Vanguard* 1956. Then again, this time in 1965, I worked the story into the opening scenes of my first novel. The lyric that is bred of awe rose out of the lost chaotic splendor.

Thus:

> Down by the river, Chris looks for stones. On mudbanks of the river are stones flat and smooth and bigger ones where the water is shallow and bigger ones still where water turns dark orange getting deep. Where water is deepest there are boulders, big round brown rocks like cows sitting in heathaze. From the rocks come sounds of silent water, whispering water, the muddy hush and stillness that rushes forever. Where willows let down their long green hair, in pines sundappled, in the trembling of spring—birds, squirrels have vanished. Only crickets rasping, only bugs whining on; leaves shake and sigh. A breeze arises from nowhere. It will rain.
>
> Plunk!
>
> The first stone refuses to skip. Chris aims the next at a dragon-fly. This stone skips low across the river. "That was a good one," Chris tells his dog. One by one he throws the stones and they plunk or skip away. The dragonfly remains hovering. "Wish I had a dog." He has spoken aloud.
>
> Down by the river, Chris looks for sticks. Finding a stick that's short and smooth, he slips it in a pocket of his corduroy trousers. Down by the river are sticks short and smooth, pale and green in the mud, and down by the river, in trees around, things feel sad filling up with breezes. Chris and the dog he does not see are listening.
>
> "Awright, Pharoah, watch. . . fetch!"
>
> One by one the sticks are thrown. After school there is not much to do.

The river seems timeless, almost motionless. The boy is restless, lonely, and imagines a dog for companion; he gives the dog a bookish name he has learned at school. He is at the border country where civilization—society, history, judgment—encroaches upon wonder. The narrative continues:

> Christopher Stebbins heard somebody laughing. Wheeling, he spied a pair of skinny brown legs poking from frazzled dungarees and rolled down lady's silk stockings. A fishing rod appeared, and then, popped around from behind an uprooted tree that was lolling branches in the river, a wizened face with unlidded eyes came up gleaming. It was the little old Indian man.[64]

The old fisherman, we soon learn, is part Indian, part African American, formerly a wrongly convicted felon in a chain gang. He wears silk stockings to conceal ankles hideously deformed by the chains.

I never premeditated the appearance of this character on the scene. He manifested himself in imagination out of the spirit of place. An Occaneechi? Once he appeared he brought with him the sense of the past. My story evolved as a search for the sources of contemporary violence in the past. The "little old Indian man" became a representative figure whose suffering calls into question the pastoralism, the wonderment, with which I had begun.

‡   ‡   ‡

The family had by 1933 moved into a two-story duplex at 1028 Gloria Avenue. Father could now, instead of driving in his Ford, walk to his office on East Campus. Mary April and I could now, when ready, walk to George Watts School about ten blocks away.

Across the street lived Ernie Chick. We jumped off twenty-foot concrete embankments together and raided the cherry tree that belonged to the parents of Elephant Ears, a pale, flabby boy who appeared to our cruel eyes to have ears like spinnakers on a cabbage head.

At one end of Gloria Avenue stood a Piggly-Wiggly where Mother took me to shop for groceries. Outside the store were yams and golden corn in pale green shucks and perspiring watermelons and Virginia apples assaulted by tippling wasps. Inside, the floor was saw-dusted, and there was a delicious aroma of freshly baked bread. Stacked high against the store's plaster walls were cereal boxes that I coveted for their coupons ("Free picture of Tom Mix!"). If I wanted a box of Corn Flakes or Rice Krispies, a clerk in a white apron would pry it loose with a long pole and, as the box toppled down, catch it with gentle dexterity as if it were a sparrow's nest. He would then lick the end of a pencil and tote up purchases on a scrap of oily paper, the same paper used for wrapping the bloody hump of our unfrozen, decapitated chicken. Because computers had not yet been introduced to civilization, and because our Piggly-Wiggly was too small to be one of today's supermarkets, the clerk never made mistakes in arithmetic.

At the other end of the avenue stood the King's Daughters Home. On the top story shadows flitted behind windows edged with black palings like metallic flowers. From the slate roof pigeons dropped and rose again as if dangled by strings of an invisible yo-yo. I entered the establishment but once. That was many years later, when Father, at wit's end as to what to do with widowed Grandma Amy, installed her there. The queer odor in her room, I discovered, emanated from her batch of homemade, unrefrigerated yogurt.

It was really a wonderful neighborhood. Sun-gritty foliage would strike the fire of a redbird down and across the street into a garden where it would cool among roses and lilies, honeysuckle and bee-hatted clover. Against a swift wash of semitropical light, full of the shifting, melting, diaphanous effects that give Carolina its drowsy charm, one sensed the energy of the land and felt comforted by clapboard houses over whose trellised porches wisteria cascaded in lavender waves.

Next door to our duplex, qualifying for the Southern Gothic ink-slinging competition, rose a hulking white clapboard house four stories high with screened-in sun porches on the upper floors. It had been used, I was told, as a hospital for Confederate soldiers, but now seemed abandoned.

From my bedroom window I spied on everything that happened in or around the holy hospital. Nothing ever seemed to happen there. No milkman parked his rattling truck on Watts Street, adjacent to

Gloria Avenue, to deliver bottles at the front door. No paperboy floated the *Sun* or the *Herald* onto the front porch. No garbage was put out or collected. A four-story wooden fire escape zigzagged down to a sunken garden out of which wildly sprouted an unclipped privet hedge. Although in my imagination I seemed to hear the screams of boys having their legs amputated without anesthesia and to attend burial of their corpses in the garden, I never noticed any twentieth-century movement related to the hospital.

But once. Somebody lived there. Somebody turned on a light, every night, in an upstairs room. That once, I saw him. He was extremely old, short, stoop-shouldered, and bald. His funereal garments were of the kind I'd seen worn by old-timers who gathered outside the courthouse downtown, sitting beneath the statue of the Confederate soldier and aiming brown tobacco spit at pigeons. This man emerged on the platform at the top of the fire escape. He was gazing about as if to adjust his eloquent remembrance to daylight. Then he went to the edge of the platform, fumbled with his trousers, and relieved himself on the privet hedge.

Although I have little stomach for pontificating about My Generation of Southern writers, I believe that we approach the subject of the Old South with a pinch of irreverence. We align ourselves with Flannery O'Connor, recalling her refutation of our alleged addiction to the grotesque. "I have found," she wrote, "that any fiction that comes out of the South is going to be considered grotesque by the Northern critics, unless it is grotesque, in which case it is going to be considered realistic."[65] Our relation to the Old South makes imitation of William Faulkner unthinkable. Here, for example taken at random, is a passage from his novel *Absalom, Absalom!* that might be comical were it not for tragic irony:

> Because now people—fathers and mothers and sisters and kin and sweethearts of those young men—were coming to Oxford from further away than Jefferson—families with food and bedding and servants, to bivouac among the families, the houses, of Oxford itself, to watch the gallant mimic marching and countermarching of the sons and the brothers, drawn all of them, rich and poor, aristocrat and

redneck, by what is probably the moving mass-sight of all human mass-experience, far more so than the spectacle of so many virgins going to be sacrificed to some heathen Principle, some Priapus—the sight of young men, the light quick bones, the bright gallant deluded blood and flesh dressed in martial glitter of brass and plumes, marching away to battle.[66]

The gone-with-the-wind pieties in this windy passage, we have tuned low or out. We have not sought to purchase pretentious antebellum mansions such as Faulkner's "Rowan Oak" in Oxford, Mississippi; like as not, we have all at one time or another had shacks, perhaps a duplex on Gloria Avenue, without the urge to upgrade to plantations. I, for one, never visualized in Durham anything like the "Fall of the House of Atreus," anything fateful. My chaos was my own, nonderivative, only the burden of history shared with the truly great Proprietor of Yoknapatawpha County.

The lyric that is bred of awe has a twin, the satiric. Satire is bred of desolation whenever one feels the fleeting pulse of Folly.

I had and have, though, the Quixote strain. When I first read *King Arthur and His Knights*, I enjoyed moments of delusion too much to renounce them. I tried to transform Gloria Avenue into Glastonbury, and Ernie Chick, Loring B. Walton, and Elephant Ears into paragons of chivalry pricking on the plains. Although they repudiated the suggestion that we sally forth to perform valorous deeds on behalf of the local damsels in dental braces, they waxed enthusiastic about a bloody tournament. Accordingly, we armed ourselves with six-foot-long dried sunflower stalks from the Confederate hospital's garden and borrowed garbage-can lids from back alleys: spears and shields. Sir Gawain, as I knew, could fight all day without receiving a scratch. I was not therefore in the least bit concerned about injury in battle. When, however, Loring B. and Elephant Ears hurled their first spears at me, an enchantment came over me and permitted one of the spears to glance off the top of my shield. It pierced the flesh in the corner of my left eye, coming—as the doctor soon informed Mother—within a millimeter of blinding me forever. After that episode I distanced myself from romances of chivalry and became a satirist.

The cherry tree that belonged to the parents of Elephant Ears was chopped down long ago to create a parking space for somebody's recreational vehicle. In the spirit of Quixote it would be righteous warfare to sweep so evil a windmill off the face of the earth.

‡ ‡ ‡

I loved words, the sound of words, before I could read. The experience is probably a universal one. Dylan Thomas, for example, loved just the words of nursery rhymes, what they stood for or meant being of very secondary importance. After he began to read for himself it seemed to him that the most important things—"love and terror and pity and pain and wonder and all the other vague abstractions that make our ephemeral lives dangerous, great, and bearable"—came to life. "And as I read more and more," Thomas declares, "my love for the real life of words increased until I knew that I must live with and in them, always. I knew, in fact, that I must be a writer of words, and nothing else."[67]

The compulsion to live with and in words validates writing as a vocation. Otherwise one's desire to be a writer, to write as a career when it involves hardship and sacrifice and seldom reaps financial benefit, has probably been influenced by the dazzling notion of one's becoming a celebrity. As for myself, I aspired to be "a writer of words" because Father was a wizard in that world and because Mother introduced me to the nursery rhymes, the nonsense verses of Edward Lear and Lewis Carroll, the fairy tales of Hans Christian Andersen. I am indebted to my parents for infusing me with the love of words.

When I was three and a half, Mother noted some attributes of a lover of words:

> He has an unusually good memory, but not Mary April's manual dexterity. He is absent-minded and, like her, will not sit still long enough to be read to. He has a keen ear for music, picking out the separate instruments in a symphony orchestra record the first time he hears it. His rhythm is unerring and his pitch, in singing a scale, perfect. He has a sense of the ridiculous and a sense of drama.

In 1935, Mother noted more attributes of a lover of words:

> He is sharp-witted, original, and has a great sense of humor. He is demonstrative and affectionate, adores his Daddy and imitates him. He shows off in front of children and with adults whom he knows. . . He tells lies, sometimes too clever to be detected. His memory is remarkable. He has no sense of the value of money: he will work to earn a penny, then give it away to any child who asks for it.

She went on:

> He is so absent-minded, I have seen him walk into furniture and climb into the bathtub in his shoes and socks, or take off his pajamas before getting into bed.

On May 2, 1935, while Mother was recovering from her nearly fatal bout with pneumonia, I dictated to her these verses:

> I had a bear
> And didn't care.
> I didn't care
> If I met a bear.
>
> . . .
>
> Alex's soldiers like to fight
> But they go to bed at night.
>
> . . .
>
> I went in the pond
> And came up again,
> Then jumped in the pond again
> And saw a snake
> And came up with a belly ache.
>
> . . .
>
> Would you think it was funny
> If I had a lot of money?
>
> . . .
>
> Try to be good,
> I'll give you some pudd'.
>
> . . .
>
> I stuck a pin in Daddy's seat
> To see him jump was such a treat![68]

"It is necessary for the author in his work to be like God in the universe, everywhere present and in nothing visible," Flaubert said.[69] I probably learned this Modernist axiom during the summer of 1935 when Mary April and I opened a "theatre" in my bedroom at 1028 Gloria Avenue, price one penny for admission. Mother describes the enterprise:

> They make new scenery and devise new tableaux every day—work which involves the use of paper, paint, nails, crayons, blocks, string, flowers, and even sand and toy boats for beach scenes. Each night, after supper, Bill and I pay a penny for a ticket to the theatre; we are guided to Alex's bedroom by signs, saying SHOW. Alex has made a long narrow table (for he is a master carpenter!) which blocks the entrance to the room; Mary sits behind this with the cash register and passes out the tickets; we grope our way to seats in the darkness, after the gate-table has been swung aside. Then Alex, crouching behind the theatre, which is an orange crate, up on the bed, turns on a flashlight, directing it through a crack in the top of the box, onto the stage; Mary reads the title of the tableau from a paper which she has typewritten; Alex pulls a string which raises the pretty curtain—a Greenwich Village arty affair, made of sugar sacks stencilled with crayon. Last night they had a circus scene, with Japanese dolls riding on ivory elephants, a lady on a tightrope, paper animals in paper capes, one paper doll standing on tiptoe on a paper horse. . . and a row of tiny dolls on tiny chairs, banked up steeply on tables like a real grandstand.[70]

‡   ‡   ‡

Sooner or later we move into judgment as well as into experience. We become acquainted with what Montaigne calls "that sad, deaf, speechless stupor which seizes us when we are overwhelmed by tragedies beyond endurance."[71] The discovery of our own mortality, while it is not a tragedy in the usual sense, stuns our souls into stupefaction and signals the disappearance of childhood.

In a letter to Grandma Bayne dated 10 January 1934, Mother places that moment in my autobiography, as follows:

I'm surprised by the sympathy you extend to me in your New Year's letter, hoping 1934 will be better than 1933; I must have acquired the gloomy letter habit, if you think last year was a bad year; on the contrary, I like my life just as it is, lived where it is, with the people I live it with; ill health has awfully little to do with enjoyment, provided one is not nauseated, and provided invalidism sneaks upon one gradually, so that one gets used to feeling lousy bit by bit. Poverty cuts out some fun, but only really intrudes if one is a chronic worrier. I like my husband better than anyone else's, my children better than any I have ever met. . . I like being thirty-five better than any other age I have ever been; and live almost totally free of any bickerings and quarrels. I will never be of any use whatever to the world in general, but I am of tremendous use to Bill, and am conscious of it every time I sew on a button or add up a column of figures or administer big doses of praise. Alex also is in need of this medicine, and I think will go far in life if he gets enough.

Speaking of Alex, the latest problem we have had to handle with him is a horror of death. Fortunately, I have had the handling of it alone, because my own attitude toward it is perfect indifference, whereas Bill is morbidly terrified at its very mention. A few days before Christmas, Mary April came home from school excited by the wonderful story of the birth of Christ; she told it to us several times and we read it to her in poems and stories; then she asked me about the rest of Jesus's life and I told her; meanwhile, Alex was looking through an Outline of Art, containing all the famous paintings; suddenly he came upon a primitive picture of the crucifixion and asked me to read the title; not realizing what I was letting myself in for, I told him it was the way Jesus died; his eyes blazing with horror, he pointed to the nails and the blood; I explained that it was not a photograph but a made-up picture by a man who didn't really know how Jesus died; that I had read in a book that he was tied to the cross, not nailed to it at all. But nothing did any good; there were other pictures and they all had nails and in one he was a corpse being put in a tomb; so then they wanted to know if they would die, and if we would die and so on; Alex would talk of nothing else; the Christmas hymns and stories, the very mention of the word Christ, brought up the subject time and again. Alex asked Helen [the cook] about it and she said Christ was still alive, so then he was hopelessly mixed up and even dreamed about it. We hid the book and brought out maps of the Holy Land and stories about the star and the lambs and the fishermen, but he always came back to death and would he ever die too. Each day he asked each member of his family if he or she was going to die, and even asked each caller. All answered truthfully in the affirmative, but with perfect cheer and no mention of heaven or hell. Mary April is full of curiosity about everything but not emotionally upset by anything, but Bill and Alex are alike in all things. He has calmed down but not forgotten.[72]

Curiously, the anguish of one's discovery of old mortality is usually depicted in literature as an occurrence in life later than the age of five, as late as early manhood (Hamlet), even as late as middle age (Tolstoy's Ivan Ilyich). The hero of the Babylonian epic *Gilgamesh*—a story with origins going back to 2500 B.C., close to the invention of writing itself—is already a king when he finds out that he is not a god, not immortal.

SIX

Whiskey-Wow-Wow!

Grandma Amy proudly boasted at the age of ninety-three that she had gone wading in seven seas. Taking her record on faith, I surmise that her toes had touched the Mediterranean, Marmara, Black, Caspian, Dead, and Red—and the Atlantic Ocean. And if it's true what Aunt Bessie told me, namely that she and Amy traced their ancestry to John Howland, then we have the grave testimony of Governor Bradford in *Of Plymouth Plantation*:

> . . . as they thus lay at hull in a mighty storm, a lusty young man called John Howland, coming upon some occasion above the gratings was, with a seele of the ship, thrown into sea; but it pleased God that he caught hold of the topsail halyards which hung overboard and ran out at length. Yet he held his hold (though he was sundry fathoms under water) till he was hauled up by the same rope to the brim of the water, and then with a boat hook and other means got into ship again and his life saved.[73]

Members of the William Blackburn family, it seems, have never been able to resist the sea.

Ishmael says in the opening pages of *Moby-Dick*:

> Whenever I find myself involuntarily pausing before coffin warehouses, and bringing up the rear of every funeral I meet; and especially whenever my hypos get such an upper hand of me, that it requires a strong moral principle to prevent me from deliberately stepping into the street, and methodically knocking peoples' hats off—then, I account it high time to get to the sea as soon as I can.[74]

Father was Ishmael. Although he avoided coffin warehouses and funeral processions, whenever his "hypos"—his famous insecurities plus the piles of papers and bluebooks that required his red pencil—threatened to get the upper hand, he got to the Atlantic as soon as he could. Once at the beach he doffed professorial attire. Off came baggy suits, starched shirts, blocked hats, thin socks, the gaiters he held them up with, and leather shoes he had polished, himself, with many a breathless sigh. On would come Bermuda shorts, a singlet, a pair of sandals. Bare-headed, half-blind without spectacles, nostrils quivering and tongue stuck out like a hound dog's to lick ice cream, he strode manfully down many a mighty strand, leaning eagerly forward after the manner of his mother.

He wanted a cocktail, whereas she dreamed of giving high-fives to angels.

At the beach he swam, ate, drank, and sang with a gusto that revealed the true inner life of The Professor. He collected driftwood and seashells, for once a connoisseur of the cosmos instead of a Grand Inquisitor of those unconsidered trifles, Freshman Themes.

The mental picture that I cherish of Father at the seacoast I can place and date with precision. It is September 4, 1935, two days before my sixth birthday. We are at Cherry Grove (now North Myrtle Beach), South Carolina. We are out swimming in the ominous surf. As a huge wave thunders in and begins to curl, he picks me up and with a great shout—"Whiskey-Wow-Wow!"—tosses me into it to sink, swim, or be rescued. He is my Mayflower, distributor of freedom, my Providence, too, sudden lifeline.

One of the most compelling images that Americans have of a wholesome father-son relationship is that of Playing Ball. In a stereotypical film version of the image, Dad is a weary, bald, potbellied Loser who had never Made It in the Major Leagues but who will realize his Dream of Success through The Kid. Glued to the American soul, this image is apparently intended to inspire us boys to become drug-and-skullduggery-free, heterosexual billionaires.

Whatever the ball—base, foot, basket, golf, tennis, or pin—my father never played it with me. Although he claimed to have set at Oxford a record in the pole-vault—he squeezed his six-foot, one-inch skin and bones over the bar at eight feet—he had retired from competitive sports by the time I came along. I loved sports, but I did understand that in Father's opinion all jocks were morons. We didn't bond with balls and gloves. Moreover, he never beat me, nor did he motivate me to think of myself as a Victim. All he had to do to assure posterity of my moral excellence, whenever I strayed from the primrose path, was to heave a heavy sigh of despair in my direction. Fool, the sigh said. Try leaving this foolishness out.

So I can't quite explain why Father was usually, not always but usually, exactly where and what he should be. I guess it was the Falstaff in him. I don't mean the bad Falstaff, the debauched, unscrupulous, sanctimonious, cowardly rogue. I mean the good Falstaff, the boon companion and clown, the one who never loses the gaiety of youth, the one who warms the heart. Perhaps his having this Falstaff element explains why Father's game of Whiskey-Wow-Wow sufficed to cement the bond between us.

There was also that September of 1935 at Cherry Grove an exhibition of what a son typically seeks in a father—namely, courage.

Our rented cottage was a flimsy, tin-roofed shack perched on little more than two-by-fours and unprotected by sand dunes from the ocean, even at low tide only fifty yards away. On September 5, the day before my birthday, a red sun had water in its eye, a Carolina folk-saying verified by torrential rainfall and by tide that did not go out at all but stayed as near the cottage at low as it had been high. Salt grass in nearby dunes had a brilliant, almost electric hue. White jellyfish like bloated blisters appeared on the beach, strewn there by merciless tides beneath screeching seagulls. In order to find out what kind of storm we should anticipate, Father drove his old Ford to Myrtle Beach where he was advised not to worry: the Weather Bureau had telegraphed that a Florida hurricane would be passing out to sea between Savannah and Charleston, missing the beach resorts. So Mother went right ahead with plans to desacralize my birthdate and have a party that very afternoon.

As waves ramped up the beach and swished underneath the cottage, and as rain pelted the roof and window panes with a sound like drumfire, a couple of little girls arrived for my party at four o'clock. The wind continued to howl. Rain now was coming through the roof and under the walls of the two bedrooms. Mother set the lighted birthday cake on a table in the only dry room. She dressed us up in masks and paper hats and taught us to play her own childhood games, Black Spider, Miss Ginia Jones, and All the Great Men. When the children's father came for them, the wind was blowing so hard they could not stand up in it and had to be carried by Father to the waiting car.

About six o'clock, lightning was irradiating the ocean, revealing collisions of twenty-foot waves. Out a window I observed a churning avalanche of waves rising high above spindrift and slouching toward the cottage. Waves broke thunderously beneath us. A mass of spray splattered against the window as if hurled there by the flick of a sea-monster's flukes. The local cook served supper while weeping and moaning and wringing her hands. When she threatened to run off into the woods to get away from the beach, Father decided to drive her home. I watched anxiously as their shapes disappeared into a rain blowing horizontally through violently swaying palmettos. Tail lights of the Ford made red dots on a palimpsest of parchment-yellow sand clouds.

At 8:30 Father rushed into the cottage and commanded, "We're getting out damn quick!" While driving the cook through the forest, he had seen great trees crashing, some across the road. Cherry Grove had almost become an island, the tide having begun to fill up the surrounding swamp. Mother gathered Andy, the cocker spaniel, in her arms, and we all ran out into whirling rain and sand and got into the car. Father started it all right but had to plunge it through deep pools and around fallen trees to reach a highway. We had evacuated the cottage just before a tidal surge like a range of blizzard-blurred mountains rose from the ocean. On the way to the highway I watched as a privy blew away, leaving a hole the shape of Ohio; it fluttered and spun off, crashing into palmettos hundreds of feet away from the distressed newspaper wads and corn cobs in the hole.

Swish-swop, swish-swop, went the windshield wipers. Father crouched forward over the steering wheel as limbs of trees somersaulted over our car. Giant trees were snapping and crashing on both sides of the road.

He decided to make for Conway, inland via Myrtle Beach about forty miles away. Suddenly we saw the lights of a car on the highway ahead of us, flashing on and off. It was a signal to stop. Luckily, Father stopped. He had not seen the big tree blocking the highway until our car was almost touching its branches. Father jumped out in the rain, and he and the man in the other car—who was fleeing *from* Myrtle Beach where we were trying to go—surveyed the ground with flashlights. The tree was too big to move; there was deep ditch on either side of the road. It took Father some time to get our car turned around and headed north on the last road left open.

After two hours of virtually blind driving, Father got us safely to a tourist home at Little River. When he appeared in the living room, the refugees gathered there burst into laughter at sight of him. On his head was Mother's red bathing cap. He had been driving the car barefooted. His face was ashy pale, and rain dripped off his nose and ears. He had on a soggy yellow leather coat, dark blue cotton shorts. His hairy legs were glistening and ended in muddy toes.

Never at a loss for self-mockery when confronted by an audience that was roaring with laughter at him, he made a long, sweeping bow.[75]

‡ ‡ ‡

Because my childhood and the Great Depression coincided, our family's budget was tight as a matador's trousers. This fact made vacations on the coast especially inviting because the littoral from the Eastern Shore of Maryland to Jacksonville, Florida, had suffered little commercial development. One could find along it cheap accommodations, including jerry-built cabins produced by the CCC (Civilian Conservation Corps) of Roosevelt's New Deal. Of expensive resorts, the Cavalier Hotel at Virginia Beach is the only one that stands out in my memory; Myrtle Beach was in its infancy and Hilton Head did not exist. Apart from Norfolk, Virginia, the one great seaport was Charleston, but the dreary years of recovery from the Civil War deflated its reputation as "the city where the Ashley and the Cooper join together to form the Atlantic Ocean": she was an impoverished old lady down on her luck and knees. Apparently unknown to vacationers commuting from New York to Miami there stretched the magnificent beaches of the Carolinas which could be reached chiefly by motor car over plank bridges or by ferryboat. We spent our vacations on the Outer Banks—Nag's Head, Kitty Hawk, Ocracoke Island, Cape Hatteras—or on the sea islands such as Pawley's and Edisto. These beaches were always plentifully supplied with jellyfish, sting rays, and sharks from the Gulf Stream, and with hurricanes.

I remember the beaches well. Our cabins had kerosene lanterns, wood-burning stoves, and dangling flypaper; outside the cabins there were two-holers furnished with buckets of lime, cut-up newspapers, and wasps. When off-shore fishermen dragged heaving nets onto the beaches, we saw specimens that the New York Aquarium would have rejected for public display, weird creatures with teeth so razor-sharp a dentist would have averted his eyes. We had John-Henry's-hammer waves to pound any boy's head into the sand or propel him, like Tarzan, on a torpedo course into shallows. I could run barefooted at water's edge for ten miles without seeing another person or any signs of previous habitation except the bleached boards of storm-shattered shacks. Society was represented by a Coast Guard station at ten-mile markers.

Today, one can drive up and down the coasts of yesteryear. Strung out for hundreds of miles are tract houses, motels, marinas, yacht clubs, luxury hotels with tennis courts and golf courses, neon-lit pizza, crab, fried chicken, and hamburger emporia. Today, most of the inlets are dredged-out harbors and waterways for motorboats and sea-going yachts stocked with Jack Daniels and *Playboy* centerfolds.

After the family fortunes improved, Father made Pawley's Island his favorite retreat. Located about twenty miles south of Myrtle Beach and about seventy miles north of Charleston, this island is separated from the mainland by a short bridge over a tidal inlet. Dunes with twisted pines rise for a couple of miles on the island, forming a barrier against the ocean. In those days there were a few dozen weather-beaten cottages and houses tucked in to the dunes. We stayed at Miss Daisy McGregor's, a colony consisting of her big house and outlying two-room cabins with screened-in porches for protection against mosquitoes. Our cabin stood on a dune about a hundred yards from the ocean and featured a hammock on the porch. We could read or sleep in the hammock and feel blissfully surrounded by sounds of surf-boom and seagulls.

Or we could go crabbing in the inlet. Father drove his car, by now a "Thrifty 60" 1936 Ford, to an inland store and purchased a crab net, a ball of twine, and a 10¢ hunk of fatback. Back at Miss Daisy's he borrowed a bushel basket and a rowboat. Thus prepared, he rowed Mary April and me out in the inlet at high tide, just when the water was calm as glass and reflecting the sun. We tied fatback to strings and dropped this bait into quiet water. Then we waited silently, almost motionlessly, so as not to spook the crabs. By and by they sashayed into view and sank claws into fatback. Lines suddenly tightened. Slowly we eased them toward the surface, biding our time, making no sound, casting no shadow. And then when a crab was so close to the boat we could see his mean little eyes lit up by the sun like tiny balls of tapioca, Father scooped the creepy-crawly critter into the net with one swift motion, and plopped it in the basket. The basket would be full in less than half an hour.

Always addressed as Miss Daisy, our proprietor seemed to me so old she might have learned how to live during the heyday of the Roman Empire. The cornucopia of her dining table at the big house, like that at Aunt Bessie's, was imperial Carolinian. Once her guests were seated, in would come from the kitchen a jolly crew of gladiators bearing trays of steaming-hot goodies. For breakfast we had a fry-up of eggs and bacon, grits, biscuits, fruits, and coffee. Members of our family worked off the effects of breakfast by walking, swimming, crabbing, or falling asleep in the hammock, then responded with alacrity to the bell rung to announce the next Trimalchio's feast: crab on the half shell, corn on the cob, fried chicken, grits, hush puppies, biscuits, apple pie, and iced tea. We worked off the effects of lunch by taking tours: Anna Hyatt Huntington's Brookgreen Gardens, a restored rice plantation and outdoors museum of modern sculpture, or the Waccamaw River country with its antebellum plantations. Or we fell asleep in the hammock. At five o'clock a relaxed and contented Father, emperor of highballs, served drinks on the porch while cooling sea breezes played in the salt grass. At six the bell rang again. The clams had been roasted in sand pits on red-hot coals. The mackerel or mullet had been caught in the surf that very afternoon; unhusked rice had been brought in from inland paddies.

After dinner, under a canopy of stars, we gathered on the porch and sang. Father's tenor-bass led us in "Sweet and Low" and "Drink to Me Only with Thine Eyes." His imitation cockney accent, learned from attending music halls during his Oxford days, was bathos at its most sublime:

> She was pore but she was honest,
> Pure, unstighned was 'er nighm,
> Till she met a bluddy bishop,
> And she lost 'er nighm in vighn.
>
> It's the sighm the 'ole world over,
> It's the pore what gits the blighm,
> It's the rich what gits the grighvy,
> Ain't it all a bluddy shighm!

And then we went to bed.

‡   ‡   ‡

The first European who is known to have explored the coast of the Carolinas was Giovanni da Verrazzano, a Florentine navigator in the service of France. He explored the Cape Fear coastal region in 1524 and sent to Francis I a description of the country with its "faire fields and plains," its "good and wholesome aire," its huge and beautiful trees—"greater and better than any in Europe"—its great bounty of game and fowl of every kind, and its natives who were "charmed by their first sight of white men." Verrazzano concluded that the country was "as pleasant and delectable to behold, as is possible to imagine."

Inspired by this propaganda Sir Walter Raleigh in 1584 dispatched Captains Philip Amadas and Arthur Barlowe to explore the country and to recommend a suitable site for settlement. After sailing along the coast for "a hundred and twentie English miles" before they could find entrance, the explorers entered Pamlico Sound at Wococon, present-day Ocracoke Inlet, on July 4. A few days later Barlowe and seven of his men "went twenty miles across the sound" to an island "which the Indians called Roanoke." One of the native chieftains, Granganimeo, received the whites cordially and "made all signs of joy and welcome, striking on his head and breast and afterwards on ours, to show wee were all one, smiling and making shewe of the best he could of love and familiarities." Barlowe regarded the Indians as a "very handsome and goodly people. . . well-featured in their limbs. . . broad breasted, strong armed, their legs and other parts of their bodies well fashioned." When Barlowe returned to England with his report, Raleigh enthusiastically christened the New World "Virginia" in honor of Queen Elizabeth.

Raleigh's second expedition, led by Richard Grenville and Ralph Lane, arrived at Roanoke Island on August 17, 1585; but having endured starvation for ten months, they returned to England. His third expedition is the one that has captured the imagination of countless authors as "the lost colony." It was led by John White and consisted of about one hundred and twenty settlers, including seventeen women and nine children. Leaving them to establish a "colonie" at Roanoke Island in July 1587, White returned to England for supplies. Threatened by Spanish attacks, however, White had to delay his voyage back to the new colony until August 1590. Upon his return to Roanoke, all that he found pertaining to the colonists were a few pieces of broken armor.[76] Although the fate of the colonists remains a matter of conjecture, I believe that they were taken captive by Indians and traded as slaves to various tribes.[77]

Mary April and I spent the summers of 1938 and 1939 at Camp Seatone on Roanoke Island. From high sandy bluffs overlooking Albemarle Sound, one could see in the distance the Wright Brothers National Memorial at Kitty Hawk—erected on the sand dune from which they launched the first successful airplane flight—and the plank causeway connecting the island to Nag's Head. On a clear day one could see the ocean. I often sat on the bluffs and tried to imagine what feelings the sight of Elizabethan ships must have stirred in Granganimeo. I don't remember the names of the ships. That's just as well: a schoolboy in Colorado recently identified the ships of Columbus as "the *Niña*, the *Pinta*, and the *Diarrhea*."

Camp Seatone, directed lovingly but firmly by Mrs. Mabel Evans Jones, was segregated according to sex, the boys and girls assigned to separate cabins under the supervision of junior counselors. The age of most campers ranged from six to twelve; anyone older, it was rumored, was given doses of Ex-Lax to offset the ravages of puberty. There were games and horseback riding and toy sailboat races and Mrs. Jones's storytelling and all the watermelon you could eat. Best of all, we went swimming in the sound, which was shallow, and boating if a counselor were present. Campers were forbidden to use one of the five rowboats without the presence of a counselor. These were rope-tied to a long dock. Anchored near the dock was a twenty-five-foot sloop for the exclusive use of Paul, my sixteen-year-old junior counselor.

A veteran camper at the age of nine, packing sixty-nine pounds on my developing bones, I could swim underwater for twenty feet and recite from memory many of the lines in Paul Green's outdoor symphonic pageant, *The Lost Colony*, performed nightly a few miles from Seatone. The toy sailboat I had carved, planed, sanded, and painted had won the 1939 boat race in a favorable breeze out in the sound. My failure as a horseman offset this triumph. One day I rode a tame horse alone to Manteo and back, a total of six miles, but it took me all

The author as toy sailboat prize-winner, summer 1939, Camp Seatone, Roanoke Island, North Carolina

day because the horse ignored my commands and munched grass at the side of the highway. I hadn't the heart to impose my will upon the animal. I did get in some practice using the cuss words I had learned while serving as a batboy for the Duke baseball team.

Another day Mrs. Jones told me to expect visitors next morning. Aunt Mallie and Uncle Archie had driven down from Washington for a vacation at Nag's Head. I had always had a soft spot for Mallie and for her husband, the writer Archibald Robertson.[78] He had a Wilkins Micawber personality—I had already begun reading Dickens's *David Copperfield*—and a glass eye. I was wildly excited at the prospect of showing off my winning sailboat. So excited was I, I slept fitfully that night and woke up a full hour before reveille.

I rose in the dark, stripped off pajamas, put on swimming trunks, and tip-toed barefoot out of my cabin without waking other campers and Paul. The sand, usually blistering hot, was cool in predawn darkness. A breeze played through wind-twisted cedars. Off in the corral a horse was stamping feet and snorting. I was possessed by a tranquilizing belief in the perfect harmony of the world. Aimless, without any intention of disturbing it, I went for a walk and soon came to the bluffs. The silvery, glimmering sheen of the sound was, as I watched, rippled. Sun-tongues licked purplish ribs of a mackerel sky over the ocean. As I peered down the long stairway to the dock, I thought I saw swells rolling in and sloshing against pilings.

Then I heard a faint cry. I held my breath, heard the cry again, the mewly, whining supplication of a child. It had come from far down below, down by the dock. I dashed down the stairs. And, incredulous, paused. Misty the light but by it I saw a rowboat some twenty yards from the dock, in it a little boy in pajamas who was standing up and waving. His oars were drifting away from his boat. He had somehow managed to lose them. Now he and his boat were being swept away from shore by a quickening breeze that could only mean one thing: squall. I looked up at the bluffs. Seeing no one there, I calculated the time it would take me to run and wake up Paul and realized that at any moment the boy could lose his balance and fall overboard into water over his head. He was a Lost Colonist! Everything was on my shoulders.

By now I had recognized him—one of the new six-year-olds whom the older boys called "Retard." He didn't, I felt sure, know how to swim. He knew how to break rules, untie a rowboat without supervision, place oars in oarlocks, and bawl for help, but he didn't know expletive, as baseballers did, from Shinola.

"I'm coming," I yelled to the retard. "Sit down and shut up!" I didn't cuss him out for fear of spooking him. I had to speak gently to him as if he were a suicidal maniac who was threatening to jump from the window ledge of a skyscraper. I'd seen that procedure used in the movies, lots of times. I figured that if I rowed a boat out to where I could tie our boats together, I could row both boats back to dock before reveille.

Ten minutes later I had our boats rope-tied, but we were now some seventy yards from the dock. The retard just sat and cried. He had a powerful itch, I surmised, to be home with his mommy. Obviously, he had never played "Whiskey-Wow-Wow" with a father who knew how to toughen up a boy's spirit! His puffy, freckled face had the featureless complexion of a jellyfish. "Please shut up, please," I said to him gently.

I rowed my boat for about twenty minutes and made some headway against the current. Pull the right-hand oar, skim the left-hand oar, rotating blade. Reverse this action, then heave with both oars. All was going well, we were only about thirty yards from dock, and all of a sudden I had cramps in both arms and shipped my oars quickly lest I lose them as the retard had lost his. I would, I decided, jump overboard and pull the boats behind me. I did that. Swells were now coming at intervals during which I lost contact with oozy muck. I was on a treadmill to nowhere, only twenty yards from dock one moment, thirty yards from it the next, then forty. . . . I pulled myself into the retard's boat and pointed at some toothpicks about a mile away in the sound. "See those poles? We'll drift over to them and tie up," I said in a confident tone. What I didn't say was this: if the squall drove us past the poles, we would drift to the Nag's Head causeway; if we hurtled past the causeway, we would soon be in the ocean, well-known locally as the Graveyard of the Atlantic. The retard, who had stopped crying, said nothing. I respected him for his deference to my age, leadership, and stupidity.

An hour later we were tied up to one of those long wooden poles that fishermen wrapped nets around to create a pen. In gale-force wind our boats tilted up and down. My teeth were chattering like a runaway telegraph transmitting the news about Jesse James. Way, way off in the vicinity of Camp Seatone, a puny sailboat, seemingly no bigger than my toy one, loomed into view. That must be Paul, I reckoned.

Paul took us in tow an hour later. At first, because he asked no questions, I believed he had a perfect understanding of the courageous behavior I had copied from Father. After a while, as we approached the dock crowded with campers, I pondered matters such as fate, justice, and the confusion of reality and appearances. If I told the unvarnished truth, I would get the retard in trouble; anyway, my excuses would not be believed. I whispered in the retard's ear, using my best James Cagney imitation, "Don't squeal, you little rat."

We docked about one in the afternoon. The squall had passed out to sea. The sun was out. Mrs. Jones was out, too, out on the dock with her arms akimbo and some serious fury inscribed on her face. "Do you realize," she raged as soon as I stood on dock, "that I had to call the Coast Guard?" She pointed in the direction of the Wright Brothers National Memorial. I looked and saw a sleek white cutter hugging the shore a couple of miles away. She panicked, I said to myself with a feeling of relief. No skin off my nose. "Do you realize," she went on, "you've kept your kinfolks waiting all morning?" Uh-oh, I said to myself. I had forgotten all about the visit of Aunt Mallie and Uncle Archie. If there was one thing we didn't tolerate in the William Blackburn family, it was rudeness. I deserved to get a "what-fer."

From the bottom of the stairway, I looked up. Mallie and Archie were on the bluff, looking down at me. I looked back toward the dock. The retard, squatting in pajamas and rubbing his eyes, hadn't squealed on me. What a good boy! I mounted the stairs, head bowed low.

Mallie had always tried to look on the bright side of things, like Father but with more success than he. Indoctrinated with Freudian psychology, she believed it was healthy and natural for children to hate their parents. Therefore, I reasoned, since I didn't hate my parents, I could count on her for double security: (1) her kindness, and (2) my unnatural virtue. As for Archie, his one eye, like that on the Masonic pyramid, guaranteed wisdom.

Mallie rushed forward, hugged me. "Isn't this the most glorious day you ever saw in your born days, darlin'? Isn't it wonderful, Archie?"

"Wonderful!" Archie repeated in his sweetly formal voice. He was dressed in a rumpled seersucker suit and wore a Panama hat. Removing hat, wiping brow with a folded handkerchief, and glass eye blinking rapidly, he declared with authority, "You're absolutely right as ever, Mrs. Robertson."

I glanced away. From the middle of the sound the big house had been but a white speck. Big again, it now had a different, Lost Colony look. One day it would disappear along with the cabins and the corral.

One day the only traces of us campers would be a few rusted jack-knives and a bunch of glass marbles, like eyes.

"Let's go to Nag's Head for refreshment," Mallie proposed. "What do you think, Archie?"

He cleared his throat, blinked the eye. "Excellent idea, Mrs. Robertson. . . .May I suggest that our friend excuse himself to put on, er, some clothes?"

"Would you like to see my sailboat?" I asked brightly in the Blackburn tradition of non sequitur.

A few days later I wrote to Mother and Father a letter which the Professor neglected to criticize for choppy sentences and lack of emphasis:

Tuesday, July 17, 1939

Dear Mommy and Daddy,

I hope you are well. I received the shoes you sent me. I enjoyed the pageant a lot Sunday. Saturday I saved a boy from drowning in a hard spot. I have the sty I think rather I have something wrong with my eye. I am the best baseball player except Paul Crull a junior counselor. I can swim under water 20 feet. Mallie & Archie have visited several times. Mallie gave me some citronella and invited me to visit them in Washington sometimes. . .

Lots of love,

Alex

SEVEN

Home

I left Durham schools in 1944, ten years before the Supreme Court's decision in the case of *Brown v. Board of Education* banned segregation in public education.[79] In September of 1962 two black children were assigned to George Watts School, and after a period of "white flight" racial integration was achieved there. By the mid-1970s Durham Central Junior High School (now Carr) and Durham High School implemented the integration policy. Having attended George Watts from third grade in 1937 through sixth grade in 1941 and Central Junior from seventh grade in 1941 through ninth grade in 1944, I knew no black children my own age. Life would have been richer and better had someone like Martin Luther King, Jr., my exact contemporary, been my classmate. I didn't know that then. I couldn't.

The long aftermath of slavery had covered with a mask of pretense the coexistence and equality of races. We children lived in an atmosphere of falsehood, trapped by its inertia, capable of an enlargement of consciousness but paralyzed by the power of habit. Montaigne tells the tale of a village woman who had grown used to cuddling a calf and carrying it about from the time it was born; she grew so accustomed to doing so that she was able to carry it when a fully grown bull. "Habit," Montaigne says, "is a violent and treacherous schoolteacher."[80] Segregation was one bull Durham could live without.

Let me mention a few African Americans with whom it has been my privilege to strike up some acquaintance. Claude Daniels was the young nephew of my mother's sometime housekeeper. Along with others he staged a famously defiant "sit-in" at a racially segregated lunch counter in Greensboro. He was in my mind when I created the character of Manny Branch:

> You would go down many dark roads, you would pass through many a city's wilderness, you would be wandering now for many years among many nations and peoples, and always it would be slow— glacier-slow, Buck McKay had said—man's movement toward kinship with his kind. It would be slow, slow and burdensome, but a change in the human weather was coming and, little by little, wherever the evening suns went down, wherever he would be, just then, appearing and being at one with his brothers, the people would kindle their fires and strike off their chains and arise, in a new dawn, free.[81]

Levi Jackson was captain of the Yale football team and starting guard on the basketball team, Ivy League champions in 1948, while I was a member of the freshman squad. We exchanged few words, but he, too, set me an example of courage. Then there was Ralph Ellison, author of a great novel, *Invisible Man*. When he visited the campus of the University of Pennsylvania for a few weeks, I was selected by the department of English to accompany him on his rounds of lectures and luncheons. One day, as we were having lunch together at a deli on Walnut Street, an agitated student burst through the door with news of the assassination of Malcolm X. "You predicted it in your novel," I blurted out. Ralph said thoughtfully, "If your imagination works at a certain depth, you are bound to predict certain things, though you don't know what." I would remember his words when I wrote a novel about a Hungarian boy driven into exile during the revolt against the Soviets in 1956. No one will recall that revolution, I was thinking, but before *Suddenly a Mortal Splendor* was published in 1995, the Soviet empire had collapsed and the Hungarian revolution was indeed remembered as a bloody first step in that direction. It was Ralph Ellison whose words had helped me to keep going. Ralph also told me, "A good writer is paranoid, a bad writer isn't paranoid enough," a wise observation. I met John Edgar Wideman when he was at Oxford in 1965-66, a Rhodes Scholar and a Marshall Scholar; we renewed acquaintance when he was teaching at the University of Wyoming, at the time he won the Faulkner Prize. Finally, I might mention my friend and former student at the University of Colorado, Yusef Komunyakaa, who in 1994 won the Pulitzer Prize for Poetry.[82]

Durham in the 1929 to 1944 period had a population of about forty percent African American. Most lived in a section of town called "Hayti"—a derogatory term never used in my family. I saw "them" in the back seats of buses, in the balconies of theaters, in the segregated public bathrooms. Black men were visible—Ralph Ellison would say "invisible"—as janitors, garbage collectors, gardeners, porters at the railroad depot, bellhops at the Washington Duke Hotel. Black women, who were not invisible to our family, often served as cooks, nannies, laundresses, seamstresses; a few became Mother's friends.

Father once took me to to "Hayti" to hear a concert performance by Marian Anderson at the North Carolina College for Negroes (now North Carolina Central University). Upon arrival at the auditorium, we were escorted to seats in the back row of the balcony where we soon realized we were the only whites in the audience. That was a delightful, reverse segregation joke, gracefully played on us and accompanied by shy smiles. Father enjoyed it as much as I did. For years afterwards we would sit together and listen to recordings of Anderson's incomparably beautiful contralto voice, especially her rendition of the Brahms "Alto Rhapsody." I was lucky to have a father who had taken me to hear her sing in person.

Once, when Mother on a Caribbean cruise stopped at one of the

Yusef Komunyakaa, a student in my creative writing classes, 1973-76. Yusef contributed remarkable Vietnam War poems to early volumes of Writers' Forum. *Winner of the Pulitzer Prize for Poetry in 1994 and subsequently a professor at Princeton, Yusef spent an afternoon with us in September 2001 in New York.* (Photograph by Inés Dölz Blackburn.)

Virgin Islands, she was met by Susie Christmas and given a royal tour, with military escort, of the island. Susie's son was the highest ranking American officer there. Susie had been one of my nannies and Mother's seamstress in Durham.

It is sad to reflect, though, that Durham was home to so many people whom I couldn't know.

George Watts School, built in 1916, is the oldest school structure in Durham that still serves its original purpose. Without a fondly conceived book about the school by Betsy Holloway, I would not be able to fill out a description of it as it was in my day. I am indebted to her for details long forgotten. I merely embellish her account. Quite recently the City Board of Education saved the school from destruction, evidently in part because it has a literary connection with Hollywood: Mrs. Lorraine Pridgen, fifth-grade geography teacher and principal of the school from 1945 to 1962, is widely believed to have been the inspiration for Frances Gray Patton's best-selling novel, *Good Morning,*

"Andy" and I and the Cannon Cup on graduation day from Watts School, 1941 (Photograph by Elizabeth Blackburn.)

Miss Dove, the basis for a movie of that name, starring Jennifer Jones. It is the story of a strict disciplinarian teacher who expects a great deal from the children she really loves and who ends up earning the respect of the adults she once taught and of, ultimately, the whole town. Fanny's daughters had been subjected to Mrs. Pridgen's tutelage. But, then, so had I. More about that in a moment.

Lily Nelson Jones, known to parents and children alike as "Miss Lily," was principal of the school from 1924 to 1940. Tiny, rotund, sweet-faced, her white hair pulled back into a bun, Miss Lily belonged to an era that simply ignored the separation of church and state. Although I owe to her Palmer Method of Penmanship whatever legibility persists in my handwriting, her religious enthusiasm impressed me as what Mark Twain has Huck Finn call "soul butter." At all times except outside classrooms and cafeteria, we had to be separated by sex. Each morning we boys entered school by the left-hand front entrance, while girls used the right-hand entrance. Once we were inside, Miss Lily would greet us at the head of the stairs, behind her in the hall a

George Watts School, Durham, North Carolina, ca. 1918. Mary April and I attended this racially segregated school, remembered for its geography teacher, fictionally transfigured in Frances Gray Patton's best-selling novel Good Morning, Miss Dove, *later adapted into film.* (Courtesy of Durham Historic Photographic Archives, Durham County Library.)

portable blackboard with the week's maxim on it in her perfect handwriting, for instance,

> Reputation is what men think you are; character is what God and the angels know you are.

Then when we were assembled in the auditorium, she sang her favorite hymn—we children reluctantly mumbled through it—the one about the glories of persecution "in spite of dungeon, fire, and sword":

> Faith of our fathers' holy faith,
> We will be true to thee till death.

As she sang she swept us with a look so keen that it filled me with a feeling akin to depression.

Thanks to Miss Lily's more worldly efforts, a silver loving cup was, starting in 1934, awarded at graduation each year to the outstanding sixth-grade boy. She had persuaded Dr. and Mrs. James Cannon III to establish the award in memory of their son Jimmy. I won it in 1941, evidently while God and the angels were distracted by youngsters with better character than my own.

Miss Lily believed that children needed to be surrounded by dull, nauseating colors in order to behave themselves. Accordingly the interior walls of the school were painted with a mixture of vomit green and tobacco-spit brown. The unwashed children, with an odor permeating the hallways like rancid peanut butter, would have produced the same demoralizing effect. Classrooms, fortunately, had fresh air and sunlight. We put our galoshes, raincoats, book sacks, and pornography in a cloakroom behind a row of blackboard-covered doors.[83] Large pull-down maps were hung close to a teacher's desk, and high on the walls an alphabet in cursive script flowed menacingly around the room. When a teacher left the room, we had to put our heads on our desks. Spitballs flew anyway.

Mrs. Pridgen had rules of her own. She required us to enter her classroom in an orderly, quiet fashion and greet her with "Good morning, Mrs. Pridgen"—the origin of Fanny Patton's title—as she stood at the door. She inspected our fingernails to see if they were clean and demanded that every child bring a clean handkerchief to class. Urgent requests to be excused to go to the bathroom were always denied. Our bladder-control skills improved dramatically, and I'm sure if we graduates had been condemned to face a firing squad, she would have had reason to be proud of us for our dry underwear. According to Betsy Holloway, "the worst punishment offered at Watts School was being sentenced to stay after school in Mrs. Pridgen's room, cleaning the blackboard and suffering her cool, measured gaze."

On the other hand, if she called upon a child to answer a question and the right answer was given, she would say, "Hoo-rah for you!" Such praise was tantamount to free admission at heaven's gate—unless she said it sarcastically.

Fanny Patton's first "Miss Dove" short story, "The Terrible Miss Dove," had been published in 1947 and greatly admired in the Blackburn household.[84] It was undoubtedly circulating in my subconscious when, before I read *Good Morning, Miss Dove* (1954), I submitted my short story, "The Golden River," to my creative writing teacher at the New School in New York. I had had my own experience of Mrs. Pridgen and Miss Lily, and so I used a child's point of view in portraying a fifth-grade geography teacher named "Miss Huff":

> "Christopher Stebbins!" roared old Huff next day.
>
> "Yes, ma'am?"
>
> "Suppose you tell the class what we learned yesterday."
>
> "Yes, ma'am. You said the Nile was a dirty old river in Egypt. You said it was full of crocodiles. The Nile flows past the pyramids. They buried Pharaoh in his mummy"—giggles erupted in the classroom, but Miss Huff's eyes were like slate so everyone shut up; Chris, who had been gagging his mouth with his hand, continued—"and they put this and his treasure in a boat inside the pyramid. You said the Nile is not as nice as the Tigris."
>
> "Anything else?"
>
> "Yes, ma'am. The Tigris has a twin river, Euphrates. On the map the Tigris and Euphrates look like a wishbone. There's this swamp in the middle of the wishbone where there's this Cradle called Civilization. Noah found the animals there before this flood."
>
> "The Flood," Miss Huff corrected him. "Approximately 3,765 B.C. . . . That will do. Hoo-rah for you." Chris raised his hand. "Miss?"
>
> "Yes, Mr. Stebbins?"
>
> "Do they have catfish in the Nile?"
>
> "No, Mr. Stebbins, they do not have catfish in the Nile."
>
> "Well, ma'am, what about the Tigris and Euphrates? They have catfish there, don't they?"
>
> "Mr. Stebbins, the class does not care whether they have catfish in the Tigris and Euphrates."
>
> Someone tittered. Miss Huff puffed out her lower, pencil-blackened lip. The noise stopped as though sheared off by invisible scissors.
>
> "What kind of fish do they have there? Bass?"
>
> "Yes, they have bass. The best kind of fish only. They have bass and trout and salmon, and they have the whale that swallowed Jonah."
>
> Chris frowned. "A whale ain't a fish, ma'am."
>
> "That will do, Mr. Stebbins."
>
> Chris kept his hand raised. "But, ma'am, do they have catfish in the Jordan we studied about?"

"Mr. Stebbins. They do not have catfish in the Nile and the Tigris and the Euphrates. Certainly such an ugly fish would not be found in the blessed River Jordan. Now, Mr. Long, you have your hand up?"

"Please, ma'am," said the small boy in a dry voice, "can I be scused? I got to."

The Huff-Puff stood up slowly, brushing creases from her black dress. . . She stepped off her platform and placed herself before the door, her arms folded. "Well, hoo-rah for you, Mr. Long. We did not hear from you yesterday. We shall hear from you now."

"I got to, ma'am, please?"

No one giggled. "Mr. Long," said Miss Huff the way she did when she wanted to scare you, "what shall we do with you? The only thing you got to is tell us where the Pharos Lighthouse was located."

The last hour always dragged. Chris stared down at Miss Huff's legs. On one of them were two meandering stripes of purplish blue. They joined where her ankle was; they looked like the wishbone of the Tigris and Euphrates. . . .[85]

I felt the impact of radio long before the advent of television. Jack Benny, Fred Allen, "The Lone Ranger," "The Shadow," and other radio programs stirred my imagination, as did the commercials with which they were interrupted. Local products, Betsy Holloway recalls, typified the soft sell of the day. Chesterfield cigarettes were "Like Getting Back Home for Thanksgiving—They Satisfy!" and BC Headache Remedy was "Never Fails to Cure! Never Dopes!"

While rapidly switching stations with a hand-operated dial like today's TV remote control, I discovered that a sentence unfinished on one radio program was often completed, incongruously, on another program. With that discovery in mind, I wrote a skit that was performed by my homeroom classmates on the stage of the George Watts auditorium:

ROY: Men and gentlewomen! This is station URAZ, Thirdrow, North Carolina, bringing you the Crunchie-Wunchie program. You "can't-get-the-right-breakfast-cereal" housewives should know about the delicious Crunchie-Wunchies. It comes in five appetizing flavors: Avalon, Old Gold, Lucky Strike, Pall Mall and Camels. Yes! It is guaranteed to be a kick to the whole family. Now, station URAZ brings to you through Crunchie-Wunchies ——

(dial turned)

ALEX: —— "Pepsi-Cola hits the spot/ Twelve full ounces, that's a lot,/ Twice" ——

(dial turned)

HARRIET: —— as many people have been buying ladies' guaranteed undies this year. There has been such a popular demand for them this year that ——

(dial turned)

ROY: —— Rudy York pounded out his eleventh homerun of the baseball season. Just look at the Philadelphia Athletics! They are now in ——

(dial turned)

NANCY: —— the State Pen, awaiting trial. Several little tough guys have been rounded up by Durham police squads, the best in the State. They deserve ——

(dial turned)

LEAH: —— to have Uncle Happy's birthday party back on the air at five o'clock. Everyone wants to listen to them sing ——

(dial turned)

ALEX: —— "Pepsi-Cola is the thing for you." This next ——

(dial turned)

ALICE: —— book which she shall write is about "Household Worries When the Baby is Still Young." She has already written

——

(dial turned)

HARRIET: —— how the special elastic has helped to make ladies undies popular this year. Why, even yesterday, I saw ——

(dial turned)

CHARLOTTE: —— Wallace the Magician swallow ten cakes of Lux Toilet Soap. Why, everyone uses this swell soap. Even Wallace the Magician likes ——

(dial turned)

ROY: —— Crunchie-Wunchies. Now, let's see how the kiddies do. Try this ordinary cereal, kiddies!

EVERYONE (spitting): Bah!

ROY: Now try these Crunchie-Wunchies.

EVERYONE (happily): Yum! Yum! Yum! more!

ROY: See there? Be sure and get Crunchie-Wunchies!

‡ ‡ ‡

After Mother received a small inheritance from Grandma Bayne, she decided to be, in her vocabulary, "extravagant" and to have a house built for Father that would put a poor professor on the same gentrified footing as football coaches. She purchased an acre of land on Anderson Street, originally a part of Duke Forest and only a few blocks away from Duke's West Campus. After she hired an architect with the splendid name of Willy Sprinkle, this small red-headed man soon gave us in 1938 a home at #713. It was a Jane Austenish parson's cottage minus rigid decorum, chambermaid, and horses. Father scavenged crepe myrtle bushes from Duke Gardens and pine saplings from Duke Forest. These pines, sixty-five years later, are ninety feet tall.

Home!

We had a house and we had lawns and we had in the backyard a pine forest with a creek polluted by sewage! There was more: the vacant lot adjacent to our lot yielded a gray weed known locally as "rabbit tobacco." Rolling this possible cousin of marijuana into joints made with toilet paper, Mary April and I enjoyed many an innocent smoke of grass.

It was now my responsibility to mow the other grass, those lawns. Because Father considered physical exercise as an insult to his intelligence, I was volunteered as grass-cutter at 25¢ the job, whatever the hours. The thing was, cutting grass in North Carolina is not a sport but an accessory to the crime of planting grass in the first place. Give grass Carolina's 100-degree heat and humidity and it will grow faster than Jack's beanstalk. Neglect it for a week and it will need a herd of goats or a bulldozer to be brought under control. Father, bless him, equipped me with a rusty, dull-bladed, ball-bearing-less push-mower that, whenever it encountered a blade of grass more than one inch high, would have the mechanical equivalent of a grand mal seizure. I often trimmed our lawn by getting down on hands and knees with a pair of scissors or a short-handled scythe. Father, at times one of the gloomiest men in captivity, always taught us in the family, "Don't take the gloomy view." I didn't. My 25¢ empowered me with a 10¢ roundtrip

The William Blackburn home, 713 Anderson Street near West Campus of Duke University. Pine saplings planted by Father in 1938 had grown to enormous height in this 1993 photograph. (Photograph by Inés Dölz Blackburn.)

bus ticket into town and with a 10¢ ticket to an air-conditioned movie theater, and I still had a nickel left over with which to purchase a *Batman's Comics* or a Baby Ruth candy bar.

Father's big adventure as a caretaker occurred that time he tried to rid our pine forest of poison ivy. He cut the ivy down, he did, and then raked it into an enormous heap, he did. Then he set fire to it. Of course he didn't know that poison ivy loves smoke the way Br'er Rabbit loves the briar patch. The smoke blew all over me. The next thing I knew, I had scabies-like pustules over my entire body. I itched so much I was confined to bed for a week and was treated with so many applications of a soothing lotion that I looked as if I'd been dipped in a vat of Pepto Bismol. After that episode, if I had outdoor work to do, I first made sure that Father was a long way from home.

We had a wonderful home, me, Father, Mother, Mary April, and Andy!

I'll begin with the back porch, 50 feet by 15 feet, brick-floored, screened-in. Andy and I liked to sleep there summers, getting the cool of the night, the sound of rain on the roof and of crickets in the forest, the sight of heat lightning and the scent of wet pine needles. Small and full of years, Andy, if he picked up the scent of wild dogs in the forest, shot through wire-mesh screening, leaving a hole, and absented himself for many days and nights. When he returned from battle he was so scratched and bloodied he could hardly walk.

Andy made veterinary medical history in North Carolina. Following one of his amorous adventures he was diagnosed with dumb rabies and quarantined at a kennel in Chapel Hill where the vet gave him no chance to survive. The family went to Duke Hospital for the Pasteur treatment. It consisted of a shot of vaccine between the shoulder blades once a week for twenty weeks. Father disliked the sight of a needle as much as I did, but I pitied myself, not him. At least his co-ed students didn't whack him on the sore back, whereas the devils at my school, once they discovered the spot between my shoulder blades, regularly pounded it with their fists. Andy survived. That's the history part.

Ours from a realtor's perspective was a two-story brick house with living room, dining room, kitchen, bathroom and study downstairs, with upstairs a master bedroom, three small bedrooms, two bathrooms, no claw-footed tubs; porch, one-car garage, basement with coal-burning furnace. Unique features: the living room had a French window and was papered with Japanese grass cloth; an iron spiral staircase, lighthouse type, connected Father's study with his bedroom above. Our single telephone, located in the front hallway, resembled a shiny black Donald Duck with one monstrous earring. We dreaded to hear the catarrhal whine of an operator's "Long distance," because we didn't know anybody outside of Durham who had something interesting to say, unless it was to announce a catastrophe, in which case a letter or a telegram seemed to us the more civilized mode of communication.

Victor Hugo's four-story house in St. Peter Port, Guernsey, Channel Islands, which I have seen, accommodated Madame Hugo on the second story, Monsieur on the fourth, and from the fourth he could escape via an outdoor staircase to spend the night with his mistress, who lived in a little house just across the garden. I mention this arrangement because my parents slept in separate rooms with a

Professor and Mrs. Blackburn looking contented outside their new home in 1938.

connecting door—not a blueprint for hypocrisy. When Father wanted sex, he placed a bottle of Toujours Moi on Mother's dressing table.

The living room was our Carnegie Hall, Roseland, Reading Room of the British Museum. Here it was that Mother played her Steinway piano while I lay on the floor beneath it, watching hammers strike. Here it was that Father kept his Magnavox and pre-LP records: Beethoven, Brahms, Mozart, Schubert (especially the Quintet). Here it was we gave parties and dances for faculty friends and spouses; students such as William Styron came for beer, talk, music. When Mary April had girlfriends over for a dance, I was usually the only boy. To the cloying balm of Bing Crosby I placed my head under a girl's chin and against her sudden bosom. Some of our favorite guests were the Fletchers from Elon College. Accompanying themselves on guitar or dulcimer, they sang the old, haunting ballads, "Lord Randall," "My Love Is Like a Red, Red Rose," "I'm Goin' Down That Road Feelin' Bad," "Black Is the Color of My True Love's Hair," and, above all, "Barbara Allen." Inspired by the Fletchers, Father purchased a cheap guitar with nylon strings, taught his fingers to find C-major and D-minor, and began entertaining—I choose the word tactfully—his students by plucking a string or two as backup to his ballad singing. Because LPs of Susan Reed, John Jacob Niles, and Burl Ives were not yet known and cherished by students, The Professor may have come across to them with the aura of Abélard, who more than 800 years ago at the University of Paris sang his way into Helóise's heart.

There in the living room we heard poetry readings by Newman Ivey White and his wife Marie, by Fanny Patton and by Helen Bevington, both then publishing in *The New Yorker*. And there in the living room we hosted the Play Readers. Once, the family performed in Lillian Hellman's *Watch on the Rhine*. I played Bodo (one line in German), Mary April played Babette, Mother played the stern American lady, and Father played the leading role, Müller. An audience of fifty professors and wives applauded us wildly. The highballs they were drinking helped, but Father, though denied drama lessons at Furman, was as good an actor as Spencer Tracy.

Reading was best. We had at least a thousand books in the house. I memorized most of the titles. I am considered to this day something of a bibliographical resource.

Proximity to the university meant attendance at concerts: Yehudi Menuhin, Artur Schnabel, Kirsten Flagstaff, New York Philharmonic Orchestra, Budapest String Quartet. I had been captivated by the dancing of Leonid Massine with the Ballet Russe de Monte Carlo even before we moved to 713 Anderson Street. After watching his effortless leaps and twirlings at Page Auditorium in March 1936, I wrote to Grandma Bayne in the decided voice of a seven-year-old artist:

Massine was one of the Russian dancers; he did a funny clown dance; he dances like me when he tries to show off. When I am eight I want to go away to Massine's school.

Proximity to the university meant that a faculty brat, entitled or not, could use its facilities for sports—tennis, swimming, track, basketball. I taught myself to play basketball in Cameron Indoor Stadium before the varnish dried on the floor. Nowadays, whenever I watch the Duke team play there on TV, I think I know the exact arc needed to hit the net with a corner jump-shot.

In the spring of 1939 "Colby Jack" Coombs, baseball coach, let me sit in the dugout and serve his team as batboy. He had pitched, I was told, for Connie Mack, this grizzled veteran of a bygone era. He

The Blackburns entertaining students. Duke undergraduates frequently were invited for dinner or an evening of listening to classical music on phonograph records. In this photo originally published in the Durham Morning Herald *(23 February 1947), Father, Mother, and Miss Margaret Feathergill of Ecuador are seated on the sofa while William Styron, then a senior, looks on.* (Reprinted, by permission, from Charles Cooper/ *Durham Herald-Sun.*)

inadvertently taught me how to cuss. "You g_d d____d son of a b__h!" he would explode at the umpire, then peer sheepishly toward the bleachers in hopes that his wife hadn't heard him. Eric Tipton was the star. He had played on Duke's "undefeated, untied, and unscored-on" football team in the Rose Bowl. Now he was clean-up batter, and when he stepped to the plate, a wad of chewing tobacco wedged in his cheek, the score tied in the bottom of the ninth inning, I just knew that a home run would be in the cards. In his final collegiate game before he went into major-league baseball, Tipton did in fact hit the home run that defeated the Carolina Tar Heels, splintering his bat in the process. Retrieving the pieces of that Louisville Slugger, I noticed that it had a reddish color. "That, son," said Colby Jack with a sage look in his eyes, "is f____kin' iodine." I could only surmise that the secret of Tipton's prowess had been revealed: he had soaked his lucky bat in iodine.

European refugees trickled into town before and during the Second World War. One of them was Kai Klitgaard, a stocky Danish sea captain with a wild mane of gray hair. He and Georgiana, his American wife, opened an art school on the second floor of a five-and-dime store. Pretty soon they had all the art students they could manage, including bored housewives from the Hope Valley Country Club set and faculty brats. Every Saturday morning Loring B. Walton, his sister Eleanore, Gray Patton, and I would gather at the school, but since we were not allowed to sketch nudes, Kai took us out into Durham County for landscape painting in watercolor or gouache. There and then landscape painting became my hobby. Weary valleys melted into bright yellow ochre and somber burnt umber. Corrugated tin rooftops of farmhouses and tobacco-curing log barns created highlights like trapezoids sifted with a powder that was blue. Chimneys made of rocks mortised with red clay evoked a feeling of antiquity, and the giant hardwoods surrounding them were the many-armed Shiva. It was a brooding great country of soil red as blood; it evinced splendor and annihilation and the honor that men die for and the wrath of the terrible swift sword.

Frame, squint, compose, sketch, paint: Kai's elementary instructions got me going. To frame a subject, I cut a window in a three-by-five-inch index card, peered through, eliminated unwanted detail. Squinting, I discovered the lights and darks that really mattered. Composition meant rearranging the handiwork of Creation. "You dew not haff to draw all der trees, dear boy," Kai said as he bent over to inspect what I had been laboriously drawing on my twelve-by-sixteen-inch sheet Movlin à Papier d'Arches. "Moof der trees vhere you vant them. Geometry of der mind, dear boy, geometry of der mind." After a while I learned to sketch quickly. I looked for bare outlines and ceased to rely upon art-gum to erase mistakes. Then I squeezed gobs of Windsor & Newton colors on my palette, moistened sable brushes in an old mayonnaise jar filled with water, and began to paint. Hours passed, it seemed, in a minute.

When I was old enough to own a bicycle, I loaded its basket with painting equipment and went alone into the countryside on all-day excursions, stopping only at a fugitive store to get a Coke and a packet of Cheese Nabs to go along with my peanut-butter-and-mustard sandwich. As soon as my soul locked-on to an irresistible scene, I settled down to dazzlement like

> some watcher of the skies
> When a new planet swims into his ken.[86]

A lonesome world would suddenly become populated with art critics. They approached me cautiously at first, as if I might be a conjureman's apprentice freshly fallen from the sky. Here would come the gap-toothed farmer in his faded blue bib-overalls, hobnailed boots, straw hat, his unshaven cheeks a mass of black stubble against sickly white skin; with him would come barefooted children.

"Mind I have a look?" a boy would ask with the courteous deference of the truly poor.

"Okay," I'd say.

The boy would look at my painting. After a while he'd say, "Purdy."
I would thank him.

"C'moan's over s'here," the boy would say to the other children.
"Hit's right smart."

‡ ‡ ‡

We went to Duke Forest to cut a small tree for Christmas. We put
it in the living room and draped it with lights and baubles; we surrounded it with boxes wrapped in last year's paper from Woolworth's.
We assembled on the coffee table a crèche: Madonna, Babe, baffled
Joseph, shepherds, a bunch of sheep with broken legs.

Come Christmas Eve we neighborhood children gathered at the
home of Dr. Julian Ruffin. When he finished tuning his guitar and
drinking his mint julep, he shouted, "Time to go, chi'ren!" Mrs. Ruffin
passed out candles and mimeographed song-sheets, then we piled into
cars, drove a few blocks, and stopped at some Duke administrator's
mansion, the girls in the most angelic costumes standing in front of
our semi-circle of carol singers. We lit our candles. Dr. Ruffin rang the
doorbell, stepped back, found C-chord on the guitar, whispered the
title of our first number, and, when an opened door revealed some
merry old gentleman and his blue-rinsed mouse, we sang:

> Good King Wencelas
> Last looked out
> On the feast of Stephen. . .

Or,

> We three kings of Orient are,
> Bearing gifts we travel a-far. . .

Then Dr. Ruffin bellowed, "Merry Christmas!" and we screamed,
"Merry Christmas!" and we ran to the cars and went to some more
mansions, and so on. Later on Christmas Eve our family went to
Cranford Road to the home of Loring and Suzanne Walton. Because

Suzanne was German and celebrated Christmas on the Eve, she always had ready a feast of cakes and cookies; Loring, a professor of French, laced his eggnog with brandy. Still later on the Eve, once home, Father lit logs in the fireplace and read passages from Luke, after which I read passages from Charles—Charles Dickens. With Tiny Tim's blessings ringing in our ears we embraced and kissed one another for the first and only time all year![87]

Come Christmas Day, Father put on a blue Cossack tunic —booty collected in Iran by Grandma Amy—and plugged in the lights on the tree. Then Mary April and I raced downstairs and tore open our presents. Andy licked the glue on the wrappings.

It was like this....

It is the Christmas after the bombing of Pearl Harbor. Hours have passed since the opening of presents. Mother is in the kitchen, roasting a chicken for lunch....

Now, between the living room and the study wing there was a closet for firewood. . . a bathroom next to that....

I go to collect firewood. Instead, I open the bathroom door and burst in—but stop, stunned. Is that old, bleary-eyed, plumb-wore-out man sitting on the toilet and puffing on a cigarette Father? Looming out of thick smoke is a face—not yet surprised—of a stranger, desperate, lugubrious, inconsolable. I excuse myself, back out, close the door behind me, go to my room.

I have a new Erector set. I have built a bridge between two stacks of blocks and have laid toy railroad tracks that lead up to one stack, cross the bridge to the other stack, and come to a dead end. I wind up my Lionel engine. I send it on a suicide mission, up the gradient, across the bridge, over the precipice at the dead end. It flip-flops, spins its wheels in futility. . . .It is time for lunch.

Father is cheerfully slicing the chicken by the time I am seated at the dining room table. "White or dark, Master Alex?"

I ask for dark meat—and the wishbone. He piles my plate up with chicken, yams, lima beans, stuffing, and cranberry sauce. "There," he says with a tight smile as he adds the wishbone and passes me the plate.

"That ought to hold you," Mother says with a laugh. It is her idea

Mary April Blackburn at eighteen, 1946

of food that it is the only thing that keeps children from floating away into space.

"Mommy?"

"What's wrong? You don't look well."

"I'm not hungry."

"Remember the starving Chinese."

"May I be excused, please?"

"Clean your plate first."

I am still picking at my food after everyone else has finished eating and left the table without feeling guilty about the Starving

Chinese. Mother appears from the kitchen, wiping hands on a dish-cloth, and says gently, "You can go now. It's Christmas."

I put the wishbone in my pocket and go upstairs to my room. I knock the blocks down and throw the Erector set into the closet. I take out the wishbone, nibble it clean. I go to the bathroom, find a bottle of iodine in the medicine cabinet, and soak the long side of the wishbone in iodine, giving it extra luck. Returning to my room, I decide upon a rule: the long, lucky side of the wishbone, the one that makes wishes come true, must be permitted to "win" only if it is still the longer piece at the end of the contest.

I close my eyes, make my wish. "Please make Daddy happy." I have spoken aloud. With eyes still closed, I grip the wishbone with the thumb and forefinger of each hand. I pull until the wishbone snaps. I open my eyes.

What had been the longer, iodine-lucky bone is now the shorter bone. It has lost the contest. I have lost my wish. Father is doomed.

EIGHT

Away School

Our family had for generations had little contact with or predisposition toward the peoples and cultures of the Hispanic world. We were oriented toward England, France, and Italy, in that order; we did not peep over the Pyrenees or show more than the slightest interest in Latin America. For history and literature, we looked to Great Britain primarily, for art and architecture to France and Italy of the Renaissance. Like many other Americans—like, for instance, Henry James, who exiled himself from what his brother called "the skinniness and aridity of America"[88] —we deplored the crudity of our native land, though we loved it passionately. The warmth, the vitality, the sheer poetry of Spanish and Latin peoples, much that we "Anglos" need to enliven our phlegmatic, don't-show-emotions, don't-touch-me temperament, went largely ignored.

I discovered the Hispanic world by accident. While I was taking a course in the history of the English novel, I was curious as to why the so-called *novela picaresca* of sixteenth-century Spain—a category that does not include Cervantes's *Don Quixote*—was regarded by English scholars as an inferior precursor of the novels of Defoe and Fielding in the eighteenth century. I read *Lazarillo de Tormes* (1554) and was astonished. It was not an embryonic novel at all but a masterpiece of fictional art. It was, I realized, the first modern novel, distinct from narratives of antiquity in its temporal disposition of events and thematically closer to late-nineteenth- and twentieth-century novels than almost anything in the eighteenth century. This discovery, already made by Hispanic scholars but new to English studies, led me to a doctoral dissertation at Cambridge University and later to the publication of a book that revises notions of the origins of the novel, *The Myth of the Picaro.*[89]

In 1961 a beautiful young graduate of the Universidad de Chile came to the United States to teach Spanish language and literature at Saint Mary's College, University of Notre Dame. Inés and I met and married in Colorado Springs in 1975. My warm impressions of Chilean life and culture appear in *Suddenly a Mortal Splendor.*[90]

The point I wish to make here is a small but important one. People in Hispanic and Latin culture express their emotions without hesitation or reserve. They allow no wounds to fester. They engage in dialogue. Anglos, on the other hand, hold their emotions in, sometimes until it is too late to mend a strained or broken relationship.

That is what happened in the marriage of William and Elizabeth Blackburn (and to some extent in my own first marriage), no infidelities, no violence, nothing of a sensational nature, but characterological conflict, suffering caused by historically created cultural values and exacerbated by the show-no-emotion posture. They quarreled behind closed doors. They made secret trips to Philadelphia to seek the counsel of an eminent psychiatrist. Eventually they decided to send us children to schools away from home in order to "work" on their marriage before we became aware of the tensions within it. Not being Murdstones, at least where this Copperfield was concerned, they did not coerce us, I am glad to say, into accepting a fait accompli nor campaign with conspicuous zeal on behalf of its benefits. On the contrary, they presented "away school" as a choice, should an opportunity

Inés Dölz Blackburn from Santiago de Chile and author, 1984. We married in 1975, she a professor of Spanish language and literature, I a professor of English and creative writing at the University of Colorado at Colorado Springs. (Photograph by Ximena Chacón de Leeper.)

arise. At the age of fourteen, when I took the road less traveled by, I never at first doubted if I should ever come back. Mary April went to school in Pennsylvania; I went to school in Massachusetts.

There was a wildness about me, a restless intensity, a ravaged quality, a need for independence. Whatever my parents' personal agenda, they fostered this spirit, understanding that freedom is not a lack of requirement but the release and flourishing of a state of collective human consciousness. The jealously guarded achievement in isolation of one's own individuality is freedom without love, whereas the union of heart and spirit, as Teilhard de Chardin says, "far from diminishing the individual, enhances, enriches and liberates him in terms of himself."[91] A fierce devotion to becoming, which is to say growth in consciousness, had determined the lives of my parents in their youth, and they had inspired in me the same devotion. They had given me both the security of a home and the strength to depart from it.

In the times of which I speak, the time of my boyhood and youth, wars flickered over the face of the earth to such an extent that they became part of the air one breathed. Long before I was born they had seemed to my family inevitable and their terror responsible for the poisoning of that air. Warings, Baynes, and Cheneys had been involved in the Civil War on both sides. Grandpa Bayne and Cheney relatives had served in France during the First World War. Father survived the brutality of basic training. One of Father's colleagues at Duke, Professor Herbert Sugden, had suffered a mustard-gas attack in the Ardennes; as a result his eyes protruded from their sockets like billiard balls. On any excursion into the countryside I might find a bridge that had been destroyed by retreating Confederate troops. By the time I was old enough to understand broadcasts over our Philco radio, wars in Manchuria, Ethiopia, and Spain confirmed my impression of almost unimaginable horrors. Newspaper reports put the Rhineland, Austria, and the Sudetenland on my map. By the age of ten I was distressingly familiar, at ocean's length, with Dunkirk, the Battle of Britain, Vichy, Tobruk. Then came Pearl Harbor, Bataan, Guadalcanal—all that—and a barrage of newsreel and propaganda films. The divergence of races, peoples, nations, clearly the cause of conflict, seemed like an established proceeding of Nature.

On the other hand, this culture of war—a culture because it was more than an atmosphere, all this world upheaval, all this mass movement, violence, and tragedy, all this testing of values—stirred opposition to the falsehood of inertia, of immobilized habits, of pessimism, of the passionless common sense of traditional order. It was a time of revolution, one that opened new fields of thought to children. Especially to children with visions of convergence.

I support egalitarian education. At the same time I resist the vulgarization produced by democratic society, not least in public education. The conflict between inclusiveness and exclusiveness remains unresolved in my mind—and, I think, in the nation.

Central Junior High School in Durham had outstanding students in the 1941-44 years. Although I think of all of them with affection, I'll here recall two in particular, Nick Galifianakis and Roger Craig.

Nick, a swarthy boy of Greek descent, was our "most popular" and "most likely to succeed" classmate. We appeared together in the ninth-grade class play, *Brother Goose*, with Nick carrying the show while I was the "romantic" jerk mortified because the *ingénue*, Sister Cobb, surprises me with my—heavens to Betsy! galloping goldfish!—shirt off. Nick went on to high school, to Duke, to Duke Law School, to the Marine Corps, rising to the rank of lieutenant colonel in the Reserve; he served North Carolina as U.S. Representative in Congress, 1966-72, and was the Democratic nominee for the U.S. Senate in 1972.

Roger was not popular: on the playground he gave us skinny boys a "hickey," meaning the blow of a knuckled fist to the tender flesh of a shoulder joint. But he was already a major-league prospect in the ninth grade. He went on to pitch for the Dodgers and to manage the Padres and the Giants. As recently as the World Series of 2001 Roger was being praised on TV as the tutor of winning pitcher Randy Johnson of the Arizona Diamondbacks.

The academic side of Central was unfortunately somewhat incidental to its function as a quasi-custodial institution for children held to be in some sense uneducable. There was little attempt to educate any of us in serious subjects or to sponsor the ideal of mastery of any subject. This environment, boring to children seeking to develop their minds for intellectual or imaginative achievement, was not unique to Durham. The values of traditional education had been eroded over several decades throughout the nation, according to Richard Hofstadter, historian of the decline:

> The old academic curriculum. . . reached its apogee around 1910. In that year more pupils were studying foreign languages or mathematics or science or English—any one of these—than all non-academic subjects combined. During the following forty-year span the academic subjects offered in the high-school curricula fell from about three-fourths to about one-fifth. Latin, taken in 1910 by 49 per cent of public high-school pupils in grades 9 to 12, fell by 1949 to 7.9 per cent. All modern-language enrollments fell from 84.1 per cent to

22 per cent. Algebra fell from 56.9 per cent to 26.8 per cent, and geometry from 30.9 per cent to 12.8 per cent; total mathematics enrollments from 89.7 per cent to 55 per cent. Total science enrollments. . . fell from 81.7 per cent to 33.3 per cent. . . English, though it almost held its own in purely quantitative terms, was much diluted in many school systems. The picture in history and social studies is too complex to render in figures, but changing enrollments made it more parochial both in space and time—that is, it put greater stress on recent and American history, less on the remoter past and on European history.[92]

These data put my experience of public education into perspective. Latin, though taught pleasantly by Miss Isabel Arrowhead—so pleasantly that on graduation day in May 1944 I received the uncoveted Morris Plan Bank Latin Prize—was reduced to a study of the etymology of English words such as "republican." Although Miss Minnie Delamar strove valiantly to give us Homer's *Odyssey* in English class, it was diluted into a story of a "good" bourgeois whose family values withstood the challenge of cannibals and witches.

One afternoon in the late spring of 1944 Father casually mentioned to me that a "prep school" called Phillips Academy in Andover, Massachusetts, was offering scholarships to a few boys to enable them to attend its summer session.

"What's a prep school, Dad?" I was truly puzzled.

By the time he had finished explaining the phenomenon of a single-sex school where "masters" prepared boys for entrance to college, I thought I had a clear picture: Andover was a place whose schoolmasters were like Washington Irving's Ichabod Crane, the credulous scarecrow on whose head Brom Bones had smashed a pumpkin. They would, like Ichabod, be "exceedingly lank, with narrow shoulders, long arms and legs, hands that dangled a mile out of his sleeves, feet that might have served for shovels."[93] Because schoolmarms had vaccinated me against the idiocy virus with 95 in English, 95 in Math, and a cool 98 in Latin, I figured to find Andover masters equally and habitually indolent. I filled in and mailed an application form. A few weeks later I received a letter from the admissions officer at Andover. The formal note of congratulations was accompanied by a slick brochure with photographs of a large and magnificent campus. For the first time I had misgivings. I was getting into something way over my head. I was amazed and terrified.

Mother threw her arms about me in the grand and dizzying manner of a Miss Peggitty. "You've won the scholarship!" she exclaimed.

"I be doggone," I muttered, quite flabbergasted.

‡ ‡ ‡

One hot summer day I board a Southern Railroad coach train. As it lurches out of "Durms," I go to a platform between cars, pull a pack of Luckies out of my pocket, and light my first-ever cigarette. I inhale deeply. Suddenly church spires tick-tock like metronomes and the Washington Duke Hotel sways and gyrates like a belly dancer in Pompeii. I grab a railing to keep myself from falling into the clickitty-rack clackitty-rick of wheels on tracks. My head clears. I flick the cigarette into Tobacco Road. My throat feels scratchy. I am catching a cold.

At Greensboro my coach is coupled to a choo-choo bound for Points North. The coach's temperature is about 100 degrees, mine is about 101. Windows are sealed shut. Steam leaks through floors. My fellow passengers look already dead. They are soldiers on their way to war. In seats, aisles, lavatories, in the overhead baggage racks, soldiers are sleeping, their features gray, creased, and lumpy as dough. I fall into feverish sleep, myself. Once in a while a door is flung open, fresh air rushes in on waves of journey-noise, the screeching of wheels, the wailing of whistles, the chanting of a peddler—

Pea-NUTS!
Pop-CORN!
Apple pie
and
CRACKER-JACKS!

I change trains in Washington, again in New York, again in Boston. I have been traveling for two days and a night, my temperature is still about 101; I am as hungry as one of Mother's Starving Chinese. After a delirious ride on the Boston & Maine—twenty-five miles in two hours—a conductor sings out, "An-DOUGH-vah! AN-dough-vah!" I pick up my suitcase and alight onto a small platform.

"Excuse me." I am speaking to a big boy who is wearing what I will soon learn to recognize as a Brooks Brothers suit. "Can you-all tell me whereabouts yonder I might could find the 'cademy?" These are my famous last words.

As I recover my senses, I am lying on the platform, gingerly feeling my jaw and watching the dandy boy climb into a taxicab. I remember that, just before he sucker-punched me with a left jab to the solar plexus and a right upper-cut to the jaw, he had smirked and said scornfully, "Johnny Reb."

‡   ‡   ‡

I trudged up the Hill, located and registered in George Washington Hall, learned to my consternation that I would be taking Math and Latin classes six days a week for six weeks —whoever heard of classes on Saturdays?—then went to the Beanery and feasted on leftovers from what seemed to be the Pilgrims' first Thanksgiving: Brussels sprouts and creamed dried beef on toast. Then I went to my assigned dormitory and met my assigned roommate, Bill from New Hampshire. He was friendly. I refrained from balling my fists and assuming a crouching position like Joe Lewis. His Yankee accent, however, required studious concentration on my part. I managed to pick out a few words that we use in the South for religious purposes, like "Jesus is lowered." Bill had a neat box by means of which, he explained, he would mail laundry to his mother and she would return it nice and clean. I recognized Yankee ingenuity right off the bat and felt homesick and stupid just thinking about my lack of foresight, because I didn't have such a box or such an arrangement. But Mother, I realized, wouldn't have washed my clothes unless I'd been rolling in a mountain of dog poo, and I wasn't planning on doing that, not yet anyway.

My first night alone in the Kingdom of the Yankees I slept on a rusted iron cot that probably had some tradition going for it, like the War of 1812. Next morning, fever gone, I strolled about campus. Georgian brick buildings served as dormitories and classrooms. The spire of the enormous chapel soared above elm trees. One felt in the Addison Gallery of American Art and in the large, oak-paneled library the happiness that comes when knowledge is delight. How beautiful this academy among the pleasant lawns that I would not have to mow! There was one drawback: no girls. Apparently the only girls who lived, it was thought, anywhere near my new world of welcome were just down the Hill in a place called Abbot Academy. But they were protected by a high, spiky, iron fence. A former Phillipian, a movie star, had succeeded in climbing over the fence in pursuit of fugitive and cloistered virtue, only to be kicked out of school, all the way to Hollywood.

Six weeks later, the glamorous fate that seemed to await me was that mountain of poo: I flunked Latin. Back in Durham I had won the Morris Plan Bank Latin Prize because Miss Isabel Arrowhead liked my jokes, for instance, "Achilles's mother dipped him in the River Stynx until he was intolerable." Up North at Andover, I discovered that I didn't know Cicero from Kickapoo. My master, "Zeus" Benton, had covered in one week everything I had learned from Miss Arrowhead. When he introduced me to subjunctive and indicative verb moods, my grades fell into a sort of coma from which I could not recover them in spite of the fact that I loved Latin and had an ambition to read Virgil's *Aeneid* in the original text just to square accounts with the Yankee who had sucker-punched me. I hated Zeus Benton with Promethean rage, hated him because he was bald as Daddy Warbucks and had triple chins sloshing like a pink jellyfish over his Adam's apple, hated him because when he thundered, "Black-BURN!," his voice came, like God's to Job, out of a whirlwind on my left flank, my gaze being fixed upon the blackboard. Little did I know that he had written on my report card that I had promise to outweigh poor preparation.

My life seemed to be over at the age of fourteen. I stuffed all my unwashed clothes into the suitcase, then, with wandering steps and slow, through Eden took my solitary way. Whereas I could accept disappointment, I could not live with dishonor. I had brought disgrace upon the family of William Blackburn.

When I arrived home, I found a letter awaiting me. Mr. James Adriance, Dean of Admissions, Phillips Academy, was pleased to inform me that I had been awarded a generous scholarship to enter Andover as a lower middler, beginning in the fall semester.

‡ ‡ ‡

I live in Stowe House. It had once belonged, I am told, to Harriet Beecher Stowe, author of *Uncle Tom's Cabin*. The association pleases me. I am not Johnny Reb anymore. I pass all subjects, including Latin, sing in the choir, do daily calisthenics in case Roosevelt wants me to kill Hitler, and wait on tables at the Beanery. I smoke only two cigarettes all school year, both in a "permitted" area.

Roosevelt dies on April 12, 1945. His death wrenches my viscera. He has always borne a resemblance to Father. When I hear some of the rich kids cheering about the death of the President, I seek sanctuary in the chapel. It is empty, silent. I have sung, there, "For Those in Peril on the Sea" and Bach's "Christ lag in Todesbanden." I slump in a pew and weep. Later at the permitted area I smoke my second cigarette.

‡ ‡ ‡

I fell in love. First love. Marilyn. Marilyn Goodman.

It happened at the end of the summer of '45, a tad before my sixteenth birthday, after the atomic bombing of Japan, after the end of the Second World War.

In the vestibule of the Addison Gallery of American Art, a nymph of marble, Psyche, forever gazed into a pool. Often on my way to art classes under the tutelage of Patrick Morgan, I had paused to contemplate this beauty and been filled with longings both sacred and profane. I dared not hope to meet her in real life.

One of Father's brightest students lived with her parents and younger sister at the seacoast near Wilmington, North Carolina. She and her father, Siggy Goodman, invited me to come for a visit, which I did, and the family, like all Jewish families I had known Up North, welcomed me with great kindness and warmth. As soon as I laid eyes on younger sister Marilyn, who was my same age, I reckoned I had met Soul in real life.

> O she doth teach the torches to burn bright!
> It seems she hangs upon the cheek of night
> As a rich jewel in an Ethiop's ear. . .[94]

For three days my head swam with incandescent feelings akin to Romeo's. I lived inside the miracle of usual things. At high tide in the inlet near the cottage, we waded out, Siggy, Marilyn, and I, and dragged a seine net for shrimp. It took but a few minutes to capture a bushel of them. Mrs. Goodman cooked them. All of us peeled and ate them. In the cool of the evening, while Marilyn's older sister was reading *War and Peace* by lamplight in the kitchen, Marilyn and I went out to the porch and lay side by side, wordlessly, breathlessly, in a hammock, not kissing, just holding hands.

At the end of my visit, but not until then, I recognized the hopelessness of our love, she going to high school in Wilmington, I going to away school, a faraway school. And,

> knowing how way leads on to way,
> I doubted if I should ever come back.[95]

Previously, when leaving home at the now-distant age of fourteen, I had not doubted the return of the native; now I doubted. I had drifted on another high tide far from the shores of home.

Oh, we promised each other we would write letters. When I returned to Andover for upper middle year, Marilyn sent me her photograph, as I had requested. I placed it on my desk in the dormitory and gazed at it for dreamy hours. Upon reading in advanced Latin class Virgil's *Aeneid*, in which the hero abandons Queen Dido in order to found an empire, I learned, too late, the fruitlessness of elitist and imperial enterprises.

A photo taken in an Andover studio in 1946. I remember thinking it would please my parents. In retrospect I wonder why a teenager would choose to wear a double-breasted, pin-striped suit.

I never saw Marilyn again.

‡ ‡ ‡

Nowadays, Joseph Campbell, thanks to a series of TV programs in the late 1980s, is a household name. I discovered his great books on mythology in 1968 but hesitated to extract from them a personal philosophy. I am nevertheless drawn to what he says about following one's bliss:

If you have the guts to follow the risk, . . . life opens, opens,

opens up all along the line. I'm not superstitious, but I do believe in spiritual magic, you might say. I feel that if one follows what I call one's 'bliss'—the thing that really gets you deep in the gut and that you feel is your life—doors will open up.[96]

Not all teachers follow their bliss. I have observed, perhaps, a thousand of them, and it seems to me—as it did to Father before me—that far too many of them have no calling, or have a calling and neglect it. Some devote their energies to narrow specialization. Others succumb to the lure of power and try to emulate by political means the dubious success of corporate executives, in which event they place administrators at the top of the ladder, professors in a hierarchy subservient to these, and students at the bottom, more or less an irrelevance. While all protest their allegiance to vague generalizations about "academic freedom" and "the pursuit of excellence," few seem to realize how precious even in academies the academic spirit really is, still fewer the danger of confusing excellence, which is self-validating, with what is deemed "relevant" to students and society.

The true teachers are risk-takers in Campbell's sense. They eschew the world of money and power and lead the mythologically grounded life of their Call. Following their bliss, they find a life that opens up. Like as not, they have the gift of opening life up for their students. Father was a teacher of this kind.

My teachers at Andover were of this kind. True, the weakness of the private, nonsectarian secondary school lies in its catering to the rich, but it gains strength when it tries to follow the Jeffersonian ideal of an aristocracy of the virtuous and talented. Then the charge of "elitism" becomes for the most part moot. And since the teachers in such schools are not public officers, they are free to fit students, in Hofstadter's words, "to become a disciplined part of the world of production and competition, ambition and vocation, creativity, and analytical thought."[97]

I had at Andover, then, fine and true teachers, never a one whom I did not learn to respect and love, not even such an Olympian as Zeus Benton; but the decisive teacher for me was Walter Gierasch, a member of the English faculty from 1941 to 1970.

Gierasch was a native of Concord, Massachusetts. His field was American literature at a time when it was just beginning to gain ground in academic prestige. He was neither charming nor popular. Slender and clerkish in appearance, with thinning sandy hair and wizard eyes darting nervously about behind his horned-rim glasses, he exhibited a prickly personality and a brusque manner. His earnest attempts to put pupils at ease—he called me "Al," the name I hated—failed. He had little patience, suffered fools not at all, scorned shoddiness, verbosity, and unnecessary stupidity, and insisted on the importance of informed discipline and of independent, critical thinking. He was a great and great-hearted teacher.

I never told him so. I owe him a letter.

Dear Mr. Gierasch:

Former pupils usually begin by writing, "Sir, you probably don't remember me." I won't begin so. You remembered all of us.

You made the literature of our country come alive. You introduced me to Hawthorne, Emerson, Melville, Whitman and, above all, to Thoreau, your fellow townsman whose keen perception, freedom from the tyranny of things, devotion to idea and ideal, passion for simplicity and wry humor were part of your heart's blood. You introduced me to literary criticism at its greatest when you read aloud from Matthiessen's *American Renaissance*. You introduced me to the mythological mode of thinking when you encouraged me to read on my own the works of Henry Adams. You threw big stones in the shallow waters of our civilization.

From you, as from my father, I learned that to study literature is to perform a literary act, and that to create is an act of liberty. From you, sir, I learned that the positive merit of the historical spirit is the liberation of judgment and that the fact of literary excellence is what the study of literature seeks to examine, not its utility. From you, sir, I learned that those who know liberty are least likely to be confined within systems of established values, unquestioned assumptions, and naive acceptance of habitual ideas. You opened up for me the quest for truth, and the quest became part of my identity.

Thank you.

Love from Al

Walter Gierasch, my English teacher at
Phillips Academy. He kindled in me a love
of American literature and of literary
criticism. (Photograph courtesy of
Phillips Academy)

‡ ‡ ‡

I was growing fast, moving toward the six-foot, three-inch height
and 175-pound weight that I would reach in college and that I remain
today. In spite of this growth, I seemed destined to be a Prufrock in a
jockstrap. In order to follow my bliss, I needed to prove myself a champion. But Frank "Deke" DiClemente, basketball coach, didn't know that
boys from Duke and Durham are practically synonymous with
hoopsters. He had cut me from the Andover team in both my upper-
middle and senior years. I seemed to be thwarted in a personal rite of
passage as well as discriminated against on the basis of region of origin. Then in the spring of senior year I turned my attention to track.
The most individual of "major" sports, track could be pursued outside
the coaching culture. No coach, not Penrose Hallowell, coach of JV
track, not Steve Sirota, coach of varsity track, could stop me from

running for honor and dear life. I had no one to please but myself, no teammate save solitude.

Father took me to Pawley's Island to train during my spring vacation. There I sprinted twenty miles a day in bare feet along the strand. I wasn't strong but I was fast. When I returned to school, I focused my efforts on the half-mile, the 880-yarder, and "walked on," as they say, to compete in that event for the JV. After winning the event in four meets, I was approached by Coach Hallowell.

"Take off four seconds," he told me, "and you'll have a record."

Would he promote me to the varsity, so that I could earn a letter in its up-coming meet with Phillips Exeter? I could run a 2:06, something like that, I would win, I was ready—one chance?

Hallowell, a chain-smoker, had a problem: he was not only my track coach but also my theater director. I had a problem, too: I had the habit of vomiting after every victory. As he sucked on a cigarette, I understood what he was thinking. If I ran in the Exeter meet that Saturday afternoon and appeared in a leading role in *The Devil's Disciple* that Saturday night, there was a chance I would puke all over George Bernard Shaw.

"Suppose," he began and stopped for a fit of coughing. "Suppose," he began again, "you wait for the JV meet in Exeter on Monday. If you equal or surpass the winning time in the varsity meet, I'll recommend to Coach Sirota that you receive the major-A letter."

"There won't be any competition," I countered.

He nodded. "You'll have to set the pace. You'll have to decide when to kick. I'll have someone call out your time at the quarter-mile."

That Saturday afternoon, our varsity half-miler won the event in what I'll call, for lack of exactitude in memory, 2:07. That Saturday night, playing the part of Reverend Anderson, I kissed Mrs. Anderson, played by a faculty wife, on stage. I didn't throw up. We'd had some awkward rehearsals.

On the following Monday our JV track team arrived in Exeter, New Hampshire, to find a cinder track swept by a nor'easter, winds about 40 mph blowing rain in gusty slants. Coach Hallowell couldn't light a cigarette. I could tell from the grim look on Coach Sirota's face that anyone running a winning time against that wind had to be either Mercury or a knife. He didn't know that I had had hurricane experience, that I was, thanks to Father's game of "Whiskey-Wow-Wow," a character Atlantean.

I won the race in some sort of record time and lettered. After I had relieved my stomach of its contents, to my astonishment a man I didn't know, Coach Sirota, came over to me and said, "You did that on guts. You're a champion." He also said something about training for the Olympics when I matriculated at Yale.

I knew I wasn't really a champion. I knew that if Father had been a spectator of my performance, he would have graded it a C. I seemed to know all this because the father-part of myself considered everything I had ever done a flop. On the other hand I had discovered that bliss has a taste. It was sweet.

‡ ‡ ‡

In the following piece, running is depicted as a mystical experience. Paul is an eighteen-year-old Hungarian refugee who lives in London and attends school under his adopted name, Woolpack. He is still grieving over the loss of his mother, Terézia, murdered in 1956 by Soviet soldiers at the Austrian border. In Budapest the statue of "Soul" had represented for him a power similar to Shelley's Ideal Beauty.

Mr. Simonini was a stockily built man with the leonine visage of a Roman emperor and round-rimmed National Health Service glasses. In addition to teaching Latin and Romance languages, he coached athletics at Hurtfield. Early that year of '62, after Latin class, I asked him if I could run for the school's club in a meet to be held with North London clubs the next Saturday afternoon. He lit his pipe, shook his head. "One must train, Woolpack. Tanta est animi beatitudo," he said, blowing out the Swan Vestas match.

"The more of it the better?"

"Very good, Woolpack." He removed the pipe and squinted at me, then puffed again.

"I can run, sir. I feel it."

"How fast are you, Woolpack?"

I told him I didn't know.

"Can't put the clock on you before Saturday. Still," he nodded to himself. "We need someone for the 800 meters. Just follow the pack. Forget about winning."

"I intend to win, sir."

He squinted, puffed. "Marcus condidit imperator, Woolpack."

"I didn't mean to be ostentatious, sir."

Simonini cracked a smile. "Very good, Woolpack. . . Here." He went to a closet, removed a box full of muddied track shoes. "Find a pair that fits. Remember. Festaene lente."

"I'll make haste slowly, sir. Thank you, sir," I said. He left the classroom while I sorted through shoes.

Saturday afternoon arrived, gray with gusts of rain, a few puddles on the cinder track. A hundred or so of the school's boarders had turned up for the occasion wearing blazers and scarfs. Dozens of runners were warming up or competing in their events. I went behind the bleachers in order to prepare myself mentally.

For I had learned to play tricks with my mind. I seemed to have two minds, one that reasoned about things and one that related them according to a sense of wholeness. By concentrating thought upon a power outside myself, I partook of that power, albeit fleetingly. Thus it happened on the occasion of my first—also my last—competitive race. Opening my mind, while physically present in one of the great benighted cities of the world, I found myself by the strand of a sun-bright sea, by the uncoiling crash and sough of surf where seagulls screeched out of the immeasurable silence. I would run upon that coast. My legs would sing of the sun and the wind and the sea.

The 800 meters was announced. Soon the starter's pistol cracked. My legs sprang forward of their own accord. The sound of scuffed cinder receded. I was free and the invisible sun fueled my body and the invisible ocean echoed my breathing.

At the three-quarter turn of the first lap I glanced back and laughed in my heart, the nearest runner about 100 meters behind me. . . A sound of applause rippled like waves. A face leaned from the track: Simonini. "Fifty-six," he said. "Mind the headwind, save the kick!" Words, meaningless words! I was free in the song of the sun, the wind and the sea! What did the creature say? Headwind. I could feel it now separating me from the rhythm of my will. Not the wind my undoing, I thought and picked up the beat of my legs and lengthened their stride until I rounded the one-quarter turn of the second lap and had the wind behind me.

With half a lap to go, thighs were on fire, legs loosening. The seascape of my dream had dissolved into the ever-closer pounding of feet behind me. A sensation akin to terror grazed my heart. Heavy breathing ever closer, then one runner, then another could be felt beside me, overtaking, and my legs churned on beneath me, their song all but spent, and my head spun as Terézia screamed in snowy blur, incandescent flares bursting like disks in my eyes, and suddenly—suddenly on a far-off surf returning—the statue of Soul lifted her gaze to me from the seaweed of her hair. The pain was gone.

I kicked. My legs sang once more. Like a bird in flight on the wind soaring to the sun, I lifted from my heart. First one runner over-taken, then another. The last wave over, I breasted the tape, slowed for 100 meters, wobbled to a wire fence, and vomited until tears streamed from my eyes. I didn't need another race, ever.

In the gray distance, some women pushed prams, a couple embraced on the grass.[98]

NINE

Things Fall Apart

Father was raised in his parents' expectation that he would pursue a career in the Christian ministry. They named him after the grandfather he never knew, the minister, church historian, and college president who died in South Dakota before he was born. Another relative who was held up to him as a model of purity was a cousin, George C. Stebbins (1846-1945).[99] Devotee of the evangelists Moody and Sankey, Cousin George on at least four occasions was in charge of organizing and leading the singing for choruses numbering over 2,000, at, for example, Madison Square Garden in 1892 and Carnegie Hall in 1900. Of the nearly 1,500 songs that he composed, many are still known and sung all over the world, among them "There Is a Green Hill Far Away," "The Gray Hills Taught Me Patience," and "Throw Out the Lifeline, Someone Is Drifting Away." "Green Hill" is quoted by Charles Ives in *Serenity*, though probably as a musical cliché.

Then of course the Reverend Charles Blackburn was himself a faithful worker in missionary and evangelical work. And no one entered more whole-heartedly into the spirit of the Gospel message than Father's mother. She hammered into the boy's head, via the Bible, *Pilgrim's Progress*, and *The Youth's Companion*, all the nails necessary for vocational piety—and dread of Old Nick.

It must have been SIN, writ large, that drove Father initially away from the ministry. Then INTELLIGENCE, exemplified and nurtured by his Waring grandmother, prompted his quest for bliss. By sending him to Furman College, instead of to a seminary, she enabled him to discover his true path in a kind of secular religion, CULTURE.[100] The moral orientation of culture involved imagination and a spiritual attitude whereby truth is something which the intuition can grasp and the analytical reason can scrutinize. Whereas literal interpretation of the Bible put an exclusive emphasis on merely a few powers or even on only one, the moral, the ideal of culture, as defined by Matthew Arnold in *Culture and Anarchy*, went beyond religious literalism in that it conceived perfection as the "harmonious expansion of all the powers which make the beauty and worth of human nature." Culture begins with the realization, Arnold contended, "that the sweetness and light of the few must be imperfect until the raw and unkindled masses of humanity are touched with sweetness and light"[101]—a kind of ministry without the sense of sin, without the objections available to intelligence.

Father at some point came across Arnold's highly influential conception of culture, probably at Yale. One of his graduate professors there, Chauncey Brewster Tinker, was a prominent Arnoldian scholar who may have steered Father, early on, to the study of *Literature and Dogma*.[102] Certainly Father's years at Oxford confirmed in him a devotion to Arnold. Father, I believe, instinctively realized that the Bible is a work of literature and that the study and teaching of literature—the diffusing and humanizing of culture—satisfied the spirit, though not the letter, of evangelism.

A key to understanding Father may be found, I believe, in any number of Arnold's pronouncements. For instance,

The great men of culture are those who have had a passion for

William Blackburn and students at picnic. He and his creative writing students met with journalism students from the University of North Carolina for an occasional picnic in Duke Forest. In this photo published in the Durham Morning Herald *(12 May 1946), he is top left, Philip Russell of U.N.C. is standing center, and William Styron is in the back row immediately behind and to the right of him.* (Photograph courtesy of Duke University Archives.)

diffusing, for making prevail, for carrying from one end of society to the other, the best knowledge, the best ideas of their time; who have laboured to divest knowledge of all that was harsh, uncouth, difficult, abstract, professional, exclusive, to humanize it, to make it efficient outside the clique of the cultivated and learned, yet still remaining the best knowledge and thought of the time, and a true source, therefore, of sweetness and light.[103]

Inspired by the vision of "sweetness and light," Father was no longer pretending to have experienced certain religious sentiments and commitments. He could feel intellectually satisfied with an emphasis on the ethical rather than on any metaphysical significance of scripture. For him as for Arnold, however, lost faith carried with it a dark vision of the dissolution of modern civilization. "Dover Beach" was one of Father's personal touchstones:

> And we are here as on a darkling plain
> Swept with confused alarms of struggle and flight,
> Where ignorant armies clash by night.[104]

From Arnold's poem to Yeats's "The Second Coming" was but a short commuter hop:

> Things fall apart; the center cannot hold;
> Mere anarchy is loosed upon the world.[105]

Indoctrination in the mythology of sin, damnation, heaven and hell had staying power, nightmarish staying power. Deviation from the prescribed spiritual life could lug with it a feeling of marginalization, a sense of failure, of helplessness, of frustrated energy. Father, though influenced by Arnold, felt especially drawn to the English writers of the Renaissance and seventeenth century, from Shakespeare and Donne to Milton. Many of them, as he, looked simultaneously at the natural world and at the supernatural other-world of God, belonging to neither in spite of the powerful professions of faith. The result of this wall-eyed baroque consciousness was anguish, solitariness, and confusion. Whether Father dreaded disintegration, as many of the seventeenth-century poets did, or found the spectacle of anarchy merely distasteful, as Arnold and Yeats apparently did, I can only conjecture. Connotations of both attitudes are suggested by the word *flight,* and this word appeared often and emphatically in Father's vocabulary.

Two of his publications, *One and Twenty* (1945) and "Flight to Firenze," a personal narrative in *The American Oxonian* (April 1946), convey in spite of subtle restraint an elegiac or a tragic sense of a blighted world in which culture is failing to advance the cause of full humanity. Ostensibly an anthology of Duke writers, *One and Twenty* gives pride of place to servicemen killed or wounded in action, numbed by frontline duty, or still in harm's way (William Styron, published here for the first time, had been in Okinawa). The title from a poem by

A.E. Housman sets the tone of the volume: life is fleeting, promise is cut short, belated recognition has little more to offer than pity and admiration.[106]

"Flight to Firenze" is a tersely written account of Father's experiences in Italy where he was sent in 1945 to serve as an instructor in the University Training Command in Florence, the G.I. study center for the Mediterranean theater. He registers his admiration for the valor of the Fifth Army and his chagrin at the ruin caused by war. But the narrative swerves into a contrast of Italian culture and American arrogance. It is a kind of "Dover Beach," beginning with illusory enchantment and ending with a premonition of future catastrophe.

Here are samples from that essay:

> Just down the hall from my quarters I found that night a little balcony from which I could peer out on the rooftops of the city and see looming up in the moonlight, seemingly almost within arm's reach, Brunelleschi's great dome on the Cathedral, his dome on San Lorenzo, and the tower of the Palazzo Vecchio.

> All the bridges except the Monte Vecchio are down, including the S. Trinità, often called the most beautiful in the world. . . The Ponte Vecchio was spared at the request of the Florentines, but the approaches to it were obstructed. . . Thus some of the old medieval guild buildings and some of the finest houses by the riverside were reduced to rubble. It is an ugly wound, and the lover of Florence becomes reconciled to it, and to the other damaged spots, only when he recalls the great monuments which have gone unscathed—to name but a few, the Duomo, Giotto's Campanile, and the Baptistry, San Lorenzo, Santa Croce, San Miniato, Santa Maria Novella, the Pitti Palace, and the Uffizi. The Florentines are artists even in defeat. In the Palazzo Strozzi last fall the commune sponsored a large exhibit of paintings and sketches of the destruction.

> There is no cut-out like a conqueror's, and G.I. truck drivers roared through narrow streets packed with people as if they were still winning the war, let the "guineas" scatter for cover as well they might. If

one didn't manage to get out of the way, well, that made it one "guinea" the less.

Thousands in Florence would be looking forward to the primavera while the snow was on the mountains. The homeless boys warming themselves over fires at street corners, the pianist I had seen stomping his feet and wringing his hands between movements in the concerto, the little girl running barefoot through the streets with a battered camouflaged helmet half filled with coal dust under her arm, the mother on the trolley with two children tugging at her skirt and the Negro lieutenant fondling her possessively—these and thousands of others in Florence and millions of others in Europe will be glad when spring comes round again this year, if they live to see it.

"The American soldier," one of my GI friends once remarked to me, "is the most arrogant in the world. Absolutely nothing in Italy pleases him—except the women." I had been alarmed to find so many of my students asking who dragged us into this mess anyway and what business of ours was it anyway. To some of them it seemed a just criticism of the British to damn them because they drank tea on the line every afternoon at four o'clock. Or again: the whole Italian race can be disposed of quite easily by noting that some of them have filthy habits and cannot resist a wall. The main thing to remember is to get the hell out and rush back to God's Country. It was after the First World War that we discovered God's Country, settled down to selling each other gadgets, and let the rest of the world go by. There is many a Columbus in our midst ready to make once again the same happy revelation. That would be comfortable, if there were time. But the next war is in the making now—or the next peace.[107]

The New World—not of Columbus, not of the All-American doctrine of innocence, but of terror—was discovered on July 16, 1945, in the New Mexican desert. Witnessed by only a few scientists, government officials, and military personnel, the event remained secret until the atomic bomb was dropped on Hiroshima several weeks later. Then for a brief period of time people throughout the world woke to a realization of the apocalyptic nature of the Atomic Age. The death of mankind could now be envisioned as a technological possibility. Not a retreat from culture into anarchy and barbarism but a prospect of annihilation of life on the planet loomed on the horizon. The only question of profound significance was whether Man could temper his will to use his new power and find in his heart a fundamental inner impulse of sacrifice and of union.

By the bomb's early light, the sheer magnitude of the terror led not to an enlargement but to a numbing of consciousness. Paul Boyer, a historian, puts the situation this way:

> If a scholar a thousand years from now had no evidence about what had happened in the United States between 1945 and 1985 except the books produced by the cultural and intellectual historians of that era, he or she would hardly guess that such a thing as nuclear weapons had existed. We have studies of the evolution of nuclear strategy and some superb explorations of the political and diplomatic ramifications of the nuclear arms race, but few assessments of the bomb's effects on American culture and consciousness.

It is as though, Boyer continues, "the Bomb has become one of those categories of Being, like Space and Time, that, according to Kant, are built into the very structure of our minds, giving shape and meaning to all our perceptions."[108] The memory of the bombing of Hiroshima and of Nagasaki is almost extirpated from the American conscience!

My family shared in the collective atmosphere of the Atomic Age. We at a repressed level of consciousness dreaded the brimming vials of wrath, the worldwide drift into frozen relationships, the feeling of powerlessness against the forces of dehumanization.

Things fall apart.

At dawn on October 29, 1951, I along with some 5,000 other soldiers witnessed the testing of an atomic bomb in the Nevada desert.[109] Incredibly beautiful was that sight, not terrible—terror was an extrapolation from films and John Hersey's *Hiroshima*—and the vividness of the scene deliquesced as if it had been a tourist attraction. If the military brass who deployed us troops to demonstrate a "tactical" use of nuclear weapons had not expected us to feel outraged, they would not have converted Operation Desert Rock into a wild orgy, as they did. A convoy of trucks loaded with cases of whiskey had, before the test, snaked its way out of Las Vegas, and these, upon arrival in our tent city, were distributed free of charge. For two days and two nights the rootinest-tootinest habitat in the West would have been found in the middle of a lunar landscape.

I have written a trilogy of novels about the Atomic Age, its effects: frozen relationships brought about by generations of violence, dread of disappearance, and evolution of conscience. All were inspired by that experience in the desert, as here described:

Eastwards toward dawn, Earth is like an old crone with sawnoff breasts. Across the eye of the heavens there pass, obscured by the advent of light, all the indecipherable glances of the stars. The desert valley is cold. Soldiers have waited in that valley that lies between ranges of mutilated mesa. When, up the valley, dynamiting started a fire, when the fire held out erotic promise like the spurt of a match behind a windowpane, the soldiers had briefly flickered into view, thousands of them seated on the sands like devotees of a mad religion.

The valley is flanked by high mesa and blocked to the north by recessed columns of basalt. Indeed there is a resemblance to a kind of basilica: nave and apse the floor of a Genesis sea heaved a mile up, dome the undeceived sky, altar the zero-point of a mile-wide dustbowl. At zero-point the fire becomes a thin S-plume, like incense. Soldiers in combat fatigues, weapons slung, wait for the truth of the morning to march on.

And it is marching on. Already the sun bleaches the flame of snow on far off mountain peaks. Blood of dark barrancas begins to flow like molten ore from crucibles. The lunar chill is gone.

Then a voice blats through throats of amplifiers: twennynine, twennyeight. . . The mesas bleed from rims like old crones with sawnoff breasts. Mountains lag shadows into eternity. The soldiers turn about, facing away from zero-point.

Three, two, one.

Dawn.

There is no dawn like this dawn. For a moment the light is infi-
nitely, massively complete, and every valley is exalted. Mountains
are baroque, sky is magnesium white. In the next moment the land
fulfills the promise of that early, simple fire: it achieves the volup-
tuous quality of inner thighs. Men are salt. The truth of the morning
marches on. At an unspoken signal, soldiers turn and face zero-point.
There is no sun like this sun, this sun cradled in the valley between
rocking and nurturing motherland. This sun is a prodigious serpent-
writhing feather-gorgeous flame.

Casual groups of soldiers form, light cigarettes.

There is a sound rising and falling before it appears no sound at
all but the beating of the heart of solitude and apathy as when snow
swirls and whirls through cones of arclight along deserted streets, as
when fire blackened trees, candelabra-limbed, reproach the wind like
clumsy giants blinded by stars.

Time bends the cyclone stalk toward the surprising morning.
Soon there will be coffee and then the soldiers will be herded into
trucks in order to tour the perimeter of zero-point and inspect the
smouldering of uniformed straw effigies aflame, the vegetable kings.
Across the eye of heaven a small tempest mushrooms.

On the soldiers descends a dust as fine and lascivious as cos-
metic powder.[110]

‡ ‡ ‡

For graduation from Andover in 1947, I received two presents:
Father gave me a Swiss watch, Mother gave me a trip to Europe, one
sponsored by American Youth hostels (AYH) headquartered in New
York. I would join a group of college students for a cycling tour of
France, Switzerland, and England; we would also donate our labor for
construction of a hostel/school at an undisclosed location in France.
For about $230 we would have roundtrip passage by ship, New York-
Le Havre, Southampton-New York; for about $200 we would have
board and lodging at hostels; $200 was supposed to cover miscella-
neous expenses. A sleeping bag could be rented from AYH.

Mother and I went downtown to purchase impedimenta for my
adventure. These consisted of a gear-less, thick-tired Schwinn bicycle

that not even Hannibal could have used to cross the Alps; army-surplus khakis, a rubber poncho, a Gillette razor, a bar of Ivory soap. As an economy, she drove me to Henderson, North Carolina, from which point I could hitchhike rides, bike and all, then left me in a rainstorm. When motorists or truckers stopped to pick me up, I addressed them as "Sir" and took care to speak in a drawl with Southernisms such as "might could" and "I reckon so" and absolutely no agreement between subjects and verbs or distinction of pronouns between cases. Thus disguised, I arrived safely in Baltimore, but there my luck almost ran out: a fat man in a Cadillac fell in love with me and put his hand on my knee. But it turned out all right because, remembering Grandma Amy's method for discouraging strangers, I asked the fat man if he was Saved in the Precious Blood of the Lamb. While he was chewing on that unlikely prospect, I politely requested to be dropped off at the next stoplight. He did that. I got to New York by and by and cycled to AYH headquarters and met the members of my group, some ten men and women from Harvard, Vassar, and other moral institutions.

I took one look at the college girls and scratched Love off my list of hopes for the summer. After my years in a single-sex prep school, I expected college girls to be all beautiful, smart, and randy, so it puzzled me a little bit when these girls started scraping their knuckles on the sidewalk. In one respect, though, everyone in the group was donkey's years ahead of a Blackburn: all had come equipped with racing bikes, nylon parkas, and lightweight sleeping bags. The sleeping bag I had rented from AYH, a heavy canvas tarpaulin with horsehair insert, mortified the flesh just to look at it. In fact, as I later learned, a night spent inside this relic was like sleeping in a sauna bath full of chiggers.

We crossed the Atlantic in a reconverted troop ship, the *S.S. Falcon*. When the *Queen Elizabeth* overtook us in mid-ocean, the waves that hit us broadside sent our rusty screw-propellers momentarily flailing to the surface. I slept on "D" deck in an Auschwitz-style tier of bunks. My bunk, top of the tier, could be reached only by means of a rope ladder and only during intervals between pitching and rolling. So it must have been for some American boy scarcely older than I a couple of years or more back, except that I had no fear of being torpedoed by a German U-boat or of being stitched by a German machine gun on a beachhead in France. There are all kinds of ways to learn humility. This was one of them.

Did someone neglect to inform AYH about food shortages, inflation, and disease in France?

The good ship *Falcon* provided us with fruit and sandwiches when we disembarked at Le Havre. I was immediately surrounded by a swarm of little children with bloated bellies. I wrote home:

> Those Children of Paradise whose minds are just as cold and foggy as the sorry weather from which there is no relief for them chilled me inside. . . It was shameful to eat in front of beady little eyes which stared at us and seemed to see us in Hell. I divided several sandwiches with one little fellow. "Demi pour vous, demi pour moi," I said trying hopelessly to erase the accusation in his eyes. He ran off in a corner where his friends would not steal his prizes away from him. "Bon?" I asked, and I cannot forget his smile.

As memories recede they often return in the historical present....

Upon arrival in Paris we are accommodated in tents erected on a bombsite on Rue Barbet de Jouay near the Invalides. Here we learn about a national disaster: the Americans who were supposed to send shiploads of *blé* (wheat) had sent *maïs* (corn). As a result of mistranslation, French bread, that traditional long thin loaf, is as tasty as shoe leather and as hard on the teeth as a Louisville Slugger. Traditional *café* is made from chicory and tastes like a finely ground rattlesnake. Because *déjeuner* costs an astronomical 350 francs, I seek a favorable exchange rate at the *marché-noir* near the Opera. It doesn't occur to me until afterwards that the pock-faced Algerians who take my dollars could have slit my throat with ease. There being no nonpotable sign, I fill my canteen with water from a pump at the bombsite and am soon plagued with dysentery. The cure for this, I learn from a pharmacist, is a Gallic shrug of the shoulders. As I cycle about Paris in almost deserted streets—there is a severe petrol shortage—I keep myself within short running distance of Turkish latrines even though the toilet paper seems to be made out of glass. I am a champion in this event.

Our group attracts the interest of a short, bald American photographer who wants to do an article on "Students Abroad" for a popular New York magazine. He promises to pay all expenses. So on Bastille Day, after a million Communists have finished marching down the Champs Elysées, we decide to demonstrate to the world the attractions of freedom and democracy. We do this first by dancing the Virginia reel in the streets of Montmartre. Then about midnight we are driven in a limousine to the banks of the Seine where there is a night-club deep inside ancient catacombs called "Caveaux des Oubliettes," dungeons of the forgotten. There in a smoke-filled, claustrophobic cave, I drink my first-ever snifters of cognac and listen to a bunch of actors in peasant costumes singing *chansons provençaux*, one of which I memorized and translate thus:

> Knights of the Round Table,
> Let's taste the wine to see if it's good!
> If it's good, if it's agreeable,
> I'll drink as much as I like.
>   Oui oui oui, non non non.

> I drank five or six bottles,
> My old woman was on her knees,
> If I die, I wish to be buried
> In a cave full of good wine,
> My two feet against the wall,
> My head under the tap.
>   Oui oui oui, non non non.

Songs such as this one are so edifying, so anti-communist, that the American girls suddenly seem to be wrinkling their brows as if to reconsider the evolutionary value of preserving their quaint virginity— and mine. We stagger out of the caves and are driven to "La Cygne d'Or," a restaurant recently vacated by Nazi officers. As we are about to enter the Golden Swan, a burly American, so drunk he can't see, is tossed out the door and into the gutter. I recognize him from book-jacket photographs at once; he is a famous writer, destined to win the Nobel Prize. We go inside, bottles of red wine are already opened for us Students

Abroad. I stand on a table, precariously holding a flashbulb. The photographer takes pictures, his French mistress jots down in a notebook each and every immortal shot, and I am about to fall in love with our beautiful American girls when, my head like a run-on sentence, dysentery calls the whole thing off. I am sure Mrs. Pridgen is cooing, "Hoorah for you!" and Father is muttering, "Try leaving this out."

On July 21 we arrive in Raon l'Étape, a village in the Vosges Mountains not far from the Rhine. Here we assist two masons, a communist and an anarchist who despise Americans, in building the hostel/school. Of 5,000 pre-war inhabitants, 1,000 departed and another 300 were tortured and executed as members of the *maquis*. Following American occupation of the village, the Germans in the surrounding hills bombarded it for fifteen days. Two hundred citizens were killed during the bombardment. Most houses were reduced to rubble. The remaining houses have no roofs. We sleep on the stone floor of the former *mairie* beneath the vault of heaven. As soon as American tanks left the village, I learn, the citizens hanged the mayor from a beam just above the area where I sleep on top of my itchy bag. Our group donates eight hours a day of hard labor, felling trees, moving rocks, wheeling barrows of dirt, eating wormy plums. The commie keeps us happy with anti-American lectures spiced with quotations translated, he says, from Arabic proverbs; he smiles and smokes his pipe and I am the only one who understands a word of what he is saying. Indeed, because I speak Andover French, I am dispatched one morning to buy vegetables from a lady who lives in the ruins of a townhouse. I knock on the bullet-riddled door. Apparently pleased by my preppy politesse, she lets me into the house and I follow her to the garden that is walled-in behind it. As she gathers vegetables I am appalled to see great gaps in the stone walls.

What caused the terrible damage? I ask.

The tanks Sherman, is her reply.

I am very sorry, I say, apologizing for the tanks.

She brings me a basket full of vegetables and says gently, "Tout le monde était très content à voir les Américains." Everyone was very glad to see the Americans.

I love this lady. She has the magnanimous heart of the French at their best.

A few weeks later I go to Nancy to obtain a visa from the Swiss consulate. Out in the street I am approached by a fat Charles Bovary in a three-piece suit, who hands me a note. I read: "Si vous êtes français, nous vous desirons, mais si vous êtes américain, retournez chez vous." If you're French, stick around, if you're American, go home. I say nothing and give the frightened little man back his note.

I believe that it is the destiny of individuals, tribes, and nations to converge. The compression within the limits of the Earth's surface of a living mass, a fact of "overpopulation" that for many people seems to spell Doom, to me means a transformation of the human condition not unlike the paradox I have been exploring, namely, the union of freedom and love.

Before the *Falcon* is permitted to dock in New York, we are interrogated by our government agents. Some passengers, not AYH-ers, have been in Prague for a "Peace" hootenanny, singing folksongs about union organizers who got shot by bosses, and there is apprehension lest we have all come back from Evil Europe believing in the overthrow of all governments. Maladjusted in a nonpolitical way, I've been coming down with a bad case of Existentialism. But I pass inspection. After we dock, after we go through Customs, I suffer my first doubt about God's Country: some New Yorker has stolen my bicycle. It had toured France and climbed the Alps, been tossed into trains and boats without a scratch, and not even the meanest commie in Europe had laid a hand on it! The American scoundrel has class, I figure: he has recognized my bike's historical value and will pedal it and peddle it to the Smithsonian.

I'm really a lucky fellow.

First, I have survived until my eighteenth birthday. Second, I have gifted and caring parents. Third, Mary April is engaged to marry Robert M. Hill, captain of the Cornell swimming team and a promising physicist. Fourth, I am going to Yale.

Mr. James Israel, a New York philanthropist, wanted to memorialize a brother killed in action and accordingly set up the Andover-Yale scholarship. Out of the blue and probably influenced by Walter

Gierasch, my teachers at Andover have awarded it to me. Grandpa Bayne promises additional funds. Sheer good fortune, very Dickensian.

I had a friend, too, someone I could talk to, listen to, Dr. D.D. Holt. He had been a poor sharecropper in eastern North Carolina until one day he read Darwin's *Origin of Species*, dropped his hoe, lifted his gaze to heaven, and found his bliss. Somehow he entered Duke Divinity School and also studied under Duke's most famous professor, J.B. Rhine, Jungian psychologist and the scientifically minded investigator of E.S.P., extrasensory perception. When I met Dr. Holt, he was pastor of Trinity Methodist Church in downtown Durham. Always his door was open to me, and that door was the world. As we talked in his book-lined study, he demolished the barriers between science and religion, posited that mythology precedes religion, and, above all, combining evolutionary theory with Jungian psychology and Rhine's parapsychology, pointed the way to the future, a new world of the mind. It would take me many years to digest all his teachings, but it is clear in retrospect that he, like my parents, laid some of the foundations of my future philosophy.

Years later, Dr. Holt's son would be killed in Vietnam. Not long afterwards his outspoken views against the war and in favor of civil rights caused a stir in his congregation. His bishops transferred him to the presidency of a Methodist college in Tennessee.

At Yale in the fall of 1947, I made friends my own age, two of whom especially kept me on even keel.[111] One was a six-foot five-inch geographer from Seattle whom I'll call Mountain Man, and the other was a rosy-cheeked New Englander whom I'll call Goodthought. Mountain Man and I were teammates on the Yale freshmen basketball team— I had the pleasure, by the way, of starting against and of defeating Coach DiClemente's Andover team—and took long hikes together in the Connecticut countryside. Credited with a number of first ascents, he was already a member of the American Alpine Club and slated for an assault on Mount Everest; he spent summers doing geological research on the Juneau ice cap. It was Mountain Man's westernness in general, not just his rugged individualism, that I found admirable. He lacked the despair, hostility, and alienation then in vogue in the East as it had been in France. Like the West, itself, to borrow a phrase from Wallace Stegner, he had a shine on him and wasn't tired.[112] Up in the stacks of the library I had cut the pages of and read *Le Mythe de Sisyphe* by a little-known author, Albert Camus, and was steeped in Existentialist angst, in the near-absurdity of life. A bull session with Mountain Man made me realize I didn't know what it means to be licked. I could never be a nihilist. As for Goodthought, he was a thinker who never brooded. He greeted everything from the trivial to the tragic, from a touchdown in Yale Bowl to a poem by Eliot, with the same expression: "Perfect!"

Because Mountain Man didn't have enough Christmas vacation time to drive to Seattle and back, I invited him to come home with me to Durham. We both served as ushers at Mary April's wedding in Duke Chapel, then served as factotums for the reception Mother held at 713 Anderson Street for the various clans. While Mountain Man shuttled guests back and forth to the railroad station, I distributed cocktails and kept a wary eye on my grandparents, lest Grandpa Bayne have too much to drink and try to dominate the proceedings by singing bawdy French songs to a Born Again young librarian, lest Grandma Amy corner a Cheney—gentle, silver-haired Uncle Cliff, for instance, that rare breed of Yankee industrialist whom 10,000 factory workers knew by name and loved—and urge him to be Saved in the Precious Blood of the Lamb. All went well, and Father, I noted, displayed his usual fine mixture of pride, invincible gravity, and genial gaiety. When Mountain Man and I drove back to New Haven, I hadn't fully realized that I would never, in Thomas Wolfe's sense, go home again.

During spring semester I was too preoccupied with studies and too naive to read between the lines of Mother's letters from home.[113] Father, who was on sabbatical leave, was living in a boardinghouse in Beaufort, South Carolina, evidently for the purpose of finishing a book on the English poets. A textbook under contract to publishers in Boston could net him the tidy sum of money he craved.[114] He could do his best work, I knew, at the coast, especially with elderly ladies present to serve him meals. I invited Goodthought to come home with me to Durham for Easter vacation. I figured Father would be home by then, too.

We arrived at dusk. Father's car was not in the driveway. "Mom?" I called, flinging open the kitchen door. "We're here." Seeing a light in the living room, I went there and found Mother sitting stiffly on the sofa with a half-empty pint of whiskey on the coffee table in front of her. She gave me a kiss and hug and greeted Goodthought with sincere warmth, only asking that he make himself at home in an upstairs room while she and I had a quick chat. As soon as he was gone and I seated, she burst into tears. I had never seen her do that before. I had never seen her drinking alone before, either. She stopped crying, became her stoic and patrician self again. "Dad has left me," she said.

"I knew he left for Beaufort," I said, puzzled by her meaning, "to work on his book."

"The publishers rejected it," she said. "He's going out of his mind. One day he sends me orchids, the next day he insists upon a divorce. . . . I won't give him a divorce because he's confused. He believes love is impossible."

A chill ran through me. "Is he all right?"

"Of course he's not all right!" she snapped but went on in another tone. "He writes that he's on the verge of a moral collapse. . . . Oh, he won't do anything! He's afraid of going insane, like his father, but he won't. . . . My lawyer believes there's another woman. Nonsense! He sent a spy to Beaufort against my wishes, and the spy confirmed there is no other woman. Daddy isn't like that. I know that. You know." She paused. "He wants to see you."

"When?"

"Tomorrow."

"Where is he?"

"Pawley's."

"Miss Daisy's?"

Mother laughed in her throat. "You know his obsession about money. He contributes almost nothing to your support. Yet he lives for months at expensive beach resorts. . . ."

I felt a warm flush in my cheeks. "Mom?"

"What?" She poured a shot of whiskey into a tumbler and drank it neat. I'd certainly never seen her do that before!

"Stick to the point. Tell me what happened. Tell me what I'm supposed to do."

He had been planning to leave Mother as soon as my sister got married. He wanted a divorce to be finalized on September 6, 1951, my twenty-first birthday, because he would then no longer be legally responsible for my support. Mother wanted me to tell him that he should come back home. "I'm sorry you see me this way," she concluded her story with a sigh. "Let's have a drink."

"I'll fetch two more tumblers," I said. In the kitchen, my head in a whirl, I resolved to put on a cheerful face, be a detached and feckless Great Gatsby, not a victim. I called upstairs to Goodthought, returned to the living room, and poured three shots in the tumblers. "Mom? Put on the glad rags. Goodthought and I are taking you to dinner at the Wash Duke. You may have a bourbon old-fashioned with two cherries in it. You can save this rot-gut stuff for the old man. He'll come back, I'm sure of it."

Mother—flapper from the Zelda Fitzgerald era, early advocate of women's liberation—perked up. "I'd be delighted! You do understand that I didn't want my children to know what was going on. . . It's my fault. I've glorified Dad. He is the most wonderful —"

"—Okay, okay, Mom. Here's Goodthought." And there he was, rosy-cheeked, bright-eyed. "Have a drink, old bean. We're taking Mom to dinner, and tomorrow we're going to the beach."

"Perfect!" he said with a grin.

We were expected at Miss Daisy's and shown to Father's cottage. Not finding him there, I left Goodthought to settle in and started for the beach. A cool wind whipped through dunes and created a frenzied clink-clack in the metal chain on a flagpole. It was March, too early for tourists, not a soul to be seen on the beach. Since my last visit to Pawley's, engineers had erected groins to prevent sand-erosion. The thick piles of heavily creosoted timbers had the look of transient things.

I saw him at the bottom of a bleached staircase. He saw me. He put his arms over a railing and hung his head on his arms. His unbuttoned white shirt fluttered in the breeze. I descended the stairs, stood before him. He lifted his countenance. His glasses slipped to the bridge of his nose. Tears streaked down his cheeks. In the squinting look of his eyes the reflected surface of his mind was one of unbearable anguish.

"Hi, Dad."

He tilted glasses back in place. He cleared a constricted throat. "Can you still love me?" I heard him say.[115]

No Cordelia, love more ponderous than tongue, could hope to calm the little wrenching movements of my father's body. For a few seconds I could think of nothing to say in response to the love test

It is winter on the range at Camp Gordon, Georgia, in 1952 shortly before I receive orders to go to O.C.S. in New Jersey. A thousand recruits are being qualified, before they go to the combat zone in Korea, in the discipline of throwing fragmentation hand grenades. Previously the recruits have received instruction with dummy grenades and know the drill: pull pin, prepare to throw, throw. It is understood that, once the pin is pulled from a real grenade, unless one grips the releasing arm, the grenade will explode in three to four seconds. I, an instructor on the range, am standing in a sand-bagged pit about the size of a broom closet. I face each recruit as he jumps into the pit. It is my job to make sure that he has a grenade in hand and carries out the procedure exactly as and when ordered over the Range Officer's loudspeaker. I have been doing this job for hours. My ears are half-deafened from hundreds of explosions. An acrid smoke drifts over the line of pits and into the forest toward which grenades have been tossed. A big blond kid jumps into my pit. Range Officer orders: "Pull pin!" The kid pulls the pin. "What am I s'posed to do now, sarge?" he asks me. His ungripped grenade is dropped at my feet. I bend, pick it up, flip it over the sandbags. It GA-BOOMs! Many hours later, as I am reaching for a bottle of beer at the NCO club, my hand begins to shake with a kind of exquisite palsy. I begin to realize just how short a time it is when one has three, perhaps four, seconds to live.

"I love you and Mom equally," I said, speaking the truth with no more time to think of words, or think at all, than I would one day have on a firing range in Georgia. "Let's take a walk, Dad."

His face brightened. Thrusting hands in pockets of rolled-up seersucker trousers, he fell in stride with me, his bare, penguin feet turned outward, as usual, after the manner of Charlie Chaplin—he who moments before had been Lear.

This is what I wrote to Mother a couple of weeks after the love test:

> Dad and I did not plot anything against you at Pawley's. But I knew when I saw him that he was emotionally going through a worse hell than ever before in his life. He had to discover whether his own children would be alienated from him. His condition (understand I am speaking of the first five minutes of our meeting) was almost hysterical and I have never felt so overcome with pity before in my life—pity and love. I had hoped when I left you to persuade Dad to go back on his decision. When I got there, I did the only thing I could do: I relieved him. I told him, not taking any sides, that I, as his son, would stand by his decision either way—provided that the greatest good would in the end result from his choice, whichever it might be; that, if this decision were not his but Miss Greig's, then I would feel justified in questioning his decision. I was thinking fast and talking fast. The effect was one of the most touching things in my life, for Dad seemed to brighten and seemed infused with new strength. He wrote me soon after from Washington that I had in many ways saved him from complete collapse. He seemed to look forward with something of eager anticipation to writing his books. So, you can see why I have been suffering from confusion lately, which partly explains my not having written. I feel a bit guilty in not having been able to change Dad's mind but, rather, appearing to approve of his action. I do approve—as I think you do—if the sum result is Dad's happiness and greater energy.[116]

Goodthought and I are driving in his Ford back to New Haven.

We have been talking about Father. "Unsure of love," Goodthought remarks. "Don't get me wrong. He is every bit as remarkable a man as I've met. But he has this occluded anxiety about personal worth, like Lear, as you put it. He cannot give you the moral satisfaction of explaining his behavior because he cannot explain it to himself."

"And?" I urge.

"And he gives you the task of rejuvenating him. And what falls short of blind adoration is to him no longer love. Central conflict of the age."

"Don't be pompous, Goodthought."

"Take Virginia Woolf," he continues after a pause. "Her father felt personally wronged by the death of her mother, so he demanded pity from his children. She felt enraged because no word of her feeling could be expressed. He had control. She couldn't refuse his demand for sweet compliance."

"She was a woman," I counter. "She was expected to owe her father validation and emotional caretaking. I'm my father's son."

Goodthought nods. "And because you're a son, you can establish a common measure."

"Meaning?"

"You have the freedom to act. You've been shocked because your father broke the rules and made himself pitiable. To hell with the impression you make on him."

"You mean, we set each other free?" I offer.

Goodthought grins. "Perfect!" he roars.

TEN

The Education

A whaling ship was Herman Melville's Harvard and Yale. A Mississippi steamboat was Mark Twain's Harvard and Yale. Although William Faulkner attended the University of Mississippi for one year, he dropped out. He had worked at the small post office there and grew tired of being at the beck and call of anyone with two cents to spend. Another great American writer, Frank Waters, dropped out of Colorado College after three years in order to work as a roustabout in the Wyoming oil fields and as a telephone engineer in the vast furnace of the Southern California desert near the Mexican border. Then there are the great men who attended universities far from the Ivy League. Ernest Lawrence, who had never seen the country on the eastern side of the Great Divide until he graduated from South Dakota University, invented the particle accelerator and won the Nobel Prize for physics before his thirtieth birthday. David Bohm, Einstein's protégé and probably the world's greatest authority on quantum mechanics, was educated at Pennsylvania State College. Then there is Shakespeare: the poor chap got his little Latin

Frank Waters and author cosigning copies of A Sunrise Brighter Still: The Visionary Novels of Frank Waters *at the Moby-Dickens Bookshop, Taos, New Mexico, 1991. Father had always hoped to take Mary April and me on a tour of the western United States. The three of us separately discovered the vast spaces, towering mountains, and diverse cultures of the West—he in Utah, California, and Mexico; she in California and Oregon; and I especially in Colorado and New Mexico. The Southern Literary Renaissance, to which a generation of his students has been contributing before and after the death of William Faulkner in 1962, has a counterpart, the Western Literary Renaissance, its genius the Nobel-nominated Frank Waters (1902-1995).* (Photograph by Inés Dölz Blackburn.)

and less Greek at Stratford Grammar School and left the university men of his time, Kit Marlowe and Ben Jonson and Francis Bacon, in his wake. The moral of this story is or seems to be that there is no necessary correlation between college education and creative achievement, and no moral geography that necessarily makes one college superior to another. In fact, the great teacher, the great educator, is not an institution at all but Life, which involves suffering, and "suffering, Rodion Romanovich, is a great thing," quoth Dostoevsky.[117]

All that being said, I still believe that formal education is also a great thing. Having had experience of it in both America and England, I am firmly on the side of the American ideal, education for the many as opposed to the few. We have our vestiges of Puritanism, our emphasis upon an elect who are presumed to have special worth, our disapprobation of the unchosen, who are met with righteousness; but we have established a couple of thousand colleges and universities, and no other nation in history has felt compelled to do that. I reckon, too, with the pride of the poor, those people who will spend earnings of a lifetime on a marriage or a funeral, that their neighbors will think well of them, but also on a son's or daughter's education, that the future may loom bright for them.

I entered Yale College in September 1947. Deep, very deep within myself, deep in the heart below the layers of ignorance and immaturity, so deep I dared not speak of ambition to family or friends, I wanted to be a poet, that is, a maker of worlds (prose will do as well as verse). How could I reconcile such a dream, in America a foolish dream remote from the "real" world of production and consumption, with scholarship, also regarded dubiously? I owe my father yet another debt of praise here. Not only had he mentored writers within an academic environment but also he had insisted that good writers must first of all become good readers. As Professor and Poet—albeit poet manqué—he set an example of possibility. I resolved the dilemma by aiming myself in the direction of a two-fold career as both a poet and a scholar. It seemed to me that the better part of a lifetime might pass before these disparate claims upon the spirit could be mutually accommodated. In reality that has proved to be so.

The first thing I noticed upon arrival in New Haven was that a disproportionate number of undergraduates resembled one another in appearance. I soon learned why: Yalies were divided into a caste system according to dress codes, White Shoe and Black Shoe. If you were White Shoe, connoting the "right" sort, you wore gray flannel trousers, tweed jacket, button-down-collar oxford shirt, regimental necktie, dark socks, and white buckskin shoes. You never polished the white shoes, moreover; if you didn't scuff and soil them until they had the look of a coal-miner's snot rag, you were an imposter. Black Shoe Yalies, by way of contrast, wore two-piece nonflannel suits, Arrow shirts, neckties presumably designed in wallpaper factories, white socks, and polished brown or black shoes. Exceptions existed. Every Thursday night the members of secret societies, at least some of them, put on gray flannel suits, black ties, and black shoes, and marched in military formation from their residential colleges to their doleful mausoleums like Dante's dead souls. Veterans of the war, and there were many of them in 1947, tended to form an unwitting vanguard for today's collegiate muckers: chino pants or Levi's, Ike jackets, loafers or sandals, T-shirts, no ties. Football players wore white sweaters with a "Y" and did without underarm deodorants until after the Harvard game, evidently for the purpose of asphyxiating opponents.

I discovered upon my return from Europe that my old clothes didn't fit. Trousers made high-water marks above my ankles; shirts buttoned halfway up my forearms. Lacking initially the Blackburnian determination to fit style to budget, I sauntered into J. Press, an exclusive haberdashery, and emerged from it a White Shoe. I stood out like a C.I.A. agent in Manchuria.

I began to live, albeit slightly, beyond my means.

There was on the Old Campus in those days, abiding by his pelf, a gentleman known as Fibuck who purchased old clothes. Expecting to sell him my Andover uniform for $50, I bundled it under my arm, raced down the steps of Dirty Durfee, my dorm, and found Fibuck just outside the quad, flapping his arms to keep warm. Grizzled features, a Stonehenge of teeth, a milky eye and a knitted stocking cap gave him a curious resemblance to N.C. Wyeth's painting of Old Pew at the Admiral Benbow Inn. I showed him the blue suit and Arrow shirts. "How much?" I asked.

"Fi' buck," Fibuck said.

"They're worth a lot more, sir."

He shrugged hunched shoulders. "Fi' buck."

I accepted the money—and the worldly education.

Meanwhile, I earn some of my scholarship aid by waiting tables, washing dishes, and mopping floors twice a day at the dining hall of Berkeley College. Disguising my new clothes with an apron, I scurry between kitchen and hall carrying loaded aluminum trays and hoping

Author catching football for Yale's Timothy Dwight College team. Upset about the breakup of the family home and seeking ways to express independence from powers, privileges, and paternal influences, I played low-caste football at Yale wearing what may have been a Babylonian charioteer's leather helmet. (Photograph courtesy of *Yale Daily News.*)

to dodge the embarrassing stares of classmates. It is a relief to leave the hall and return to the kitchen. My buddies are there, the hired help, all Italian immigrants who wear black shoes and feel indifferent to living up to externally defined expectations.

One evening some White Shoes decide to play a trick on me. They fill glasses with water, cover each glass with a napkin, invert the glasses onto a table and remove the napkins so that each upside-down glass remains full of water. On top of these glasses they place a tray; on this tray they invert more glasses, all full of water. The White Shoes eyeball me, grin, fold arms. They expect me, while they are watching, to dismantle the pyramid and mop up the resulting puddles. There is no way that I will give them such satisfaction, even if I have to stay on the job until midnight listening to the mournful tolling of the bells in Battell Chapel and to the bellowing of drunks out in the street singing about the tables down at Mory's and damnation from here to eternity. After a while the White Shoes get bored and leave. I do the chores. I notice that I am wearing old brown shoes instead of my new buckskins. The laces of the brown shoes are knotted where I have broken them.

For some years Grandpa Bayne, my benefactor, had been living in a small room of the Graduate Club across the street from New Haven Green. He had decorated his room with a large Confederate flag, his First World War medals, and photographs of his son dating from the time before Uncle Hughie became a lush and a gambler and still had the looks of a movie star. Grandpa entertained himself by playing backgammon with Skull & Bones cronies, by smoking a dozen Havana cigars a day, and by getting drunk before dinner. Like Nicholas Nickleby's uncle, he kept meticulous accounts of all financial transactions, large and small. He had paid for Hughie's gambling debts, detox hospitalizations, and four divorces. Anyone else must therefore be held to contract. For me, he stipulated $750 per annum for the education and not a penny more.

He had indeed drawn up a contract, lawyer that he was, and I was truly grateful. He had neglected, however, to spell out the strings he attached to it, expectations that were flauntings of power, a means of impressing me or of humiliating me in order to bolster his vanity. Since one drunken night in October 1947 when he had managed to get himself run over by a bus, his thinking became muddled. His egotism was no longer concealed by extravagant displays of Old South and Gallic charm. I was, for example, always to address him as "Colonel." In order to extract from him a check to cover a bursary bill of, say, $40, I had to go to the Graduate Club and play a minimum of a dozen games of backgammon, taking care that he always won them. After each game, as he re-lit a cigar, he drew a mark on a scrap of paper until the fifth game, whereupon he made a diagonal mark across four perpendicular marks. Over a period of years that scrap of paper came to resemble a congeries of off-limits gates, Lilliputian scale. During my sophomore year Colonel formally asked my "permission" to bring my "presence" to the "attention" of the boys in his old fraternity, described in his letter as a "better crowd of boys." When I declined the offer—it had not included payment of dues—he sent Pudge

Hefflefinger, an intimidatingly gigantic football player of the 1890s, to my residence to hustle me into changing my mind. Once the fog of Old Boy persiflage cleared, I gathered that joining the fraternity was but a ploy to get me elected in junior year to Skull & Bones.

Well, I hardly considered myself an acceptable "brother" for the likes of George Bush and William Buckley, then thought to be in Bones. I had no political or professional ambitions and no literary achievement, and I detested the notion of using "pull" to advance myself in *Vanity Fair*. What really got my goat was that Levi Jackson, who by tradition as captain of the football team should have been tapped for Bones, had been shunted off to another society. My own grandfather had busied himself among the powers-that-be to effect precisely that racist insult. I thanked the Old Boy and then, in an effort to put an end to Colonel's games, accepted an invitation to join Saint Anthony Hall, a secret society beyond his control.

That decision almost ruined my budget. By the end of sophomore year I considered dropping out of Yale and enlisting in the army. At least as a private in the army I could support myself and have something left over to send to Mother, who was, I believed, having a hard time.

Two letters from Mother persuaded me to stay in college for the long haul. Here is the first, dated 8 June 1948:

> Your worry about your parents' financially "roughing it" for your sake is utterly groundless. Just forget that from now until graduation at Yale. Compared to what most parents do for their children, skimping themselves to save for their education from birth onward, Dad and I have done nothing for you. We are still living in luxury, sacrificing nothing. There is, of course, nothing for savings out of any teacher's salary. You and Mary were to have been educated out of my capital (which most mothers do not have). What I spent in capital, and thereby lost in yearly income, was to have been made up for by Dad's support of me in my old age. He would normally have been making more, perhaps as a full professor, by the time you graduated. He may yet do so, if he comes to his senses in time. But, as things stand, during his present middle-aged mental confusion, he does not plan to support me at all. That is why I did not get the point of your enlisting in the army so that I could be supported. . . . Simply by not

running the Ford—not selling it, but simply not running it—would supply your needs apart from your scholarship and Grandpa's help. That is not much of a sacrifice... What a very very small sacrifice that is, compared to what most parents make! What you get out of Yale is more to me than any worldly or frivolous pleasure.

Here is the second letter, dated 19 January 1949:

I'm sorry your pride is so involved about taking as much money as you need for your college education from your parents. After all, you've paid your own way pretty heavily, by work and scholarships, ever since you first went to prep school. In the normal course of... fair division of family income, you would have been entitled to four years of college ... financed by Dad alone. Because I had investments of my own, Dad never put aside any fund, except insurance, to send you through college; if he cannot send you enough or borrow any more from his insurance, because of his sabbatical, the cost of living separately, and Mary's wedding, then you should not hesitate a moment to at least borrow from me, if only temporarily. I think our financial picture is shifting and that Dad quite soon may get over his neurotic terror of dependence: I have spent, I suppose, around $10,000 on each of my children and I would no more bat an eyelid at receiving help from them some day than a Chinese parent would.[118]

‡ ‡ ‡

Memory of a lost home bred hope for a promised land. I reserved vacations for myself. I wanted to explore America. That was an education I craved.

Again, now, historical present....

The summer of 1948 at Camp Adventure, Lake Junaluska, in the Blue Ridge Mountains of North Carolina, I am employed as a counselor, teaching swimming, boating, archery, and Sunday school. The camp is teetering on the brink of bankruptcy until twenty Cuban adolescents turn up with money to finance culture shock. Because Dusty and Rusty, hillbilly moonshiners in charge of horses, are entertaining Cuban girls in the hayloft over the stables, I become an expert in breaking up fights among macho-infuriated Cuban boys. The baseball instructor is a half-breed Indian from Texas who is dying from TB. I like his gentleness, his softness; I am sick at heart when one swing of his bat brings on a fit of coughing. My buddy is Lindsey from Jackson, Mississippi, a sweet, quiet fellow who sleeps with his girlfriend at Millsaps College. Lindsey is in this respect—and in the opinion of an accursed virgin— a couple of decades ahead of his time. On Saturday nights we arm ourselves with a pint of Dusty's white lightning, sneak out of camp, walk eight miles to Waynesville over Eaglenest Ridge, a trackless, snaky wilderness, and join a folk-dance group that performs reels, hoe-cakes, and dos-à-dos to the music of a wild bluegrass band in front of foot-stomping tourists. After dancing and drinking, we weave our way through lonesome woods and arrive in time for Sunday school. My text is, "I will lift mine eyes unto these hills." It takes an effort to pry the lids off my red eyeballs.

I remain in New Haven to work as a postman during the Christmas vacation of 1948-49. The worst blizzard in living memory blankets the city for a week. From six in the morning until five in the afternoon I trudge through three feet of snow lugging a fifty-pound leather mailbag. My breath makes cartoon bubbles in frigid air; my toes and fingers may drop off to furnish study for future paleontologists. I deliver smudged cards to the whorehouses down by the railroad tracks. The cards are addressed in penciled capital letters to "Sally" or to "Ginger." I sleep in my digs on the fifth floor of Dirty Durfee. I am the only student on the Old Campus. For a few days the city is silent, no rumble and clang of trolley cars, only the swoop of pigeons on the Green, only the bong-ga-bong from the belfry of Battell Chapel. It is a time of beauty. It is a time of poetry.

When the summer of 1949 looms beyond exams week, I consult with Hank, a roommate from Huntington, West Virginia. We come up with a scheme to go west and earn our way as itinerant laborers in the wheat fields. A friend of his at Princeton, an ex-G.I. from Narragansett, Rhode Island, named Mal, owns a pickup truck and is going along; four Yalies in another car are also going. Hank, an ex-G.I. and a former reporter for *Stars & Stripes* who has actually visited and published an article about Hiroshima, says that writers have to have experience. He is preaching to the choir.

We arrive in Alva, Oklahoma, by mid-June. I take note of pioneer wagons half buried in sand. The town has railroad tracks, American Flour Mills grain elevators, and a teacher's college built by the Works Progress Administration in 1932. It also has a Coca-Cola bottling plant, a few shops, a drugstore and, after sunrise, 100-degree heat. We settle down for the first night on the dead grass of an elementary school, and about two in the morning large creatures with .38 revolvers pop out of police cars and want to know what planet we're from. There is no wheat in Alva, they say.

Hank and other Yalies do a one-day Coke job to get a grubstake and take off for Colorado, leaving Mal and me to work in the grain elevators. After five minutes spent checking conveyor belts inside the explosive 120-degree pressure-cooker heat of an elevator thick with dust, I look as if I've been rolling in a flour barrel. At the end of a day's work I crash in a dorm room rented from the college. Mal goes to the drugstore in hopes of charming a pretty girl who jerks the soda pop. Mr. Woodson, our boss, tells me he had a fine job at a chicken hatchery but lost it "because a lady took a dislike to me." He tells me he kicks his wife in her pregnant belly "because the dust makes me cough all night." I write Mother:

> I guess no place is too bad after you've lived there a while, but Alva, Oklahoma, comes pretty close. There is only one virgin in town and my buddy is trying to make her. "For twelve long years she kept her virginity, which is quite a record in this vicinity." If you want to dress hayfoot-strawfoot, there are a couple of clothing stores in town. Also, if you like popcorn, there are two movies nearby. If you want refreshment, there is a big beer joint originally decorated with signs saying "No Minors Served" and "Don't Stare at the Bartender, You May Be Crazy Too Someday." The dryness of the state is directly proportional to the number of bootleggers and varies inversely with the amount of bribes given the highway patrolmen.

We certainly have a strange crew at the grain terminal. They are what you might call congenial but not genteel. Every one of us has a nickname—"Irish," "Fat," "Big Chief Hitch," "Colonel," "The Kid,"

"Cowboy," "Scales," and I am, inevitably, plain "Slim." All of these are characters in their own right and so make work rather entertaining at times, despite the fact that "son-of-a-bitch" and the like are abused by constant use as adjective, noun, and even verb. "Big Chief Hitch" derives his name from the fact that all he has to do is stand around all day and when a freight car comes in to check to see if it's coupled right. . . ."Irish" came to Alva from Boston during the war and found the women to his liking—almost, at any rate. His story is that he got drunk one night and woke up married. . . "Irish" says he met a homosexual once who visited a man and a woman in one night and afterwards referred to the woman as a "damned whore.". . . ."The Kid" is a toothless 23-year-old bum and delinquent. He has developed a strange affection for Mal and me and favors us with stories about the advantages of fat women. "Cowboy" is getting on in years but is the nicest of the bunch—he's a real cowboy down on his luck and used to be every boy's ideal in his bronco-busting days in this region years ago. I am going in the best circles this summer.[119]

Mal makes two fatal mistakes with the girl at the drugstore. One, he lets her see the Rhode Island license plates on his truck. Two, he reveals to her that he has been a "sailor in the Mediterranean." She says she can't date a sailor who has been in the Mediterranean. It turns out she thinks the Mediterranean is the name of a whorehouse. It's time to cash our paychecks and head north into Kansas.

Kansas is an ocean, a state of unconsciousness. Our first night there we anchor the pickup in the plains and observe gigantic webs of heat lightning spin the enormous sky into sheets of rippled black tinfoil. A cyclone gets its pecker up and it's a picker-up of pickups. I can see Dorothy cruising by at 150 mph about 1,000 feet over my head. After the cyclone passes, the stars come out of hiding from horizon to horizon. A million diamonds sparkle on an ocean of pine tar. For a couple of days, going from hamlet to hamlet in West Kansas, we stop at county courthouses hoping a farmer needs to hire hands but find we are about a week too early for harvesting jobs. Finally one morning we hit dead end in McCook, Nebraska. It is about eighty miles west of Red Cloud, Willa Cather's home, and almost as thrilling:

There was nothing but land: not a country at all, but the material

175

out of which countries are made. . . . I had never before looked up at the sky when there was not a familiar mountain ridge against it. . . . Between that earth and that sky I felt erased, blotted out.[120]

McCook makes us, too, remember mountains.

On the day I graduated from Andover, Bill Davis of Denver introduced me to his mother, Mrs. Margaret Evans Davis. She invited me, should I ever find myself near the Rockies, to drop in for a visit. I kept her telephone number in my wallet. . . .

McCook has a kiosk with a pay phone inside. I have three dollars' worth of dimes to feed into the machine. The operator in Denver rings Mrs. Davis's number, somebody gives me another number, the operator in Idaho Springs puts me through to Mrs. Davis herself. She instructs me as to how to find her "place" in the Rockies. She has, I imagine, a log cabin, perhaps a toolshed for visitors.

All day we drive west. Late in the afternoon I see the Rockies for the first time, a caravan of purple hunchback giants marching across eternity. We reach Denver at night, continue westward, climb into high country. The air is thin and cool. One can dream over the world. We decide to stop for the night in Evergreen, a cluster of shacks by a creek. I fall asleep to the sound of snowmelt in the creek, recalling the physical exhilaration I had once experienced in Zermatt where I stopped to sketch the Matterhorn.

Rising before dawn we rattle up Beaver Creek Road, over a cattle guard at elevation about 9,000 feet, and up to a red-rock ranch house perched on a green hill at the foot of Mount Evans. Evans! It hits me all of a sudden, something Bill Davis had said about being the great-grandson of the second territorial governor of Colorado. Here it is, the Evans Ranch, thousands of acres of pristine wilderness, but I reflect as Mrs. Margaret Evans Davis emerges from a porch with her arms opened wide and a warmly beautiful smile on her face that the ranch is not a property that has ever belonged to anybody but an earthly paradise over which mortals merely hold stewardship. Upon this paradise the sun, ascending in the east, is a light descending from the mountain peaks with a dramatically sudden fall of brilliance. The mountains are snow-patched and scintillant against a sky that is bluer than blue. They arrest my soul.

So it must have been for Wordsworth in the presence of mountains. He writes in *The Prelude*:

> Gently did my soul
> Put off her veil, and, self-transmuted, stood
> Naked as in the presence of her God.[121]

It is said that man's quest to surmount his earthly existence is to be associated with mountain worship or with monuments such as pyramids and cathedrals that carry on the mountain theme of spiritual aspiration. It is said that if there is an influence or quintessence that gives sacredness to mountains, then the devotee desires to share in it by partaking of its flesh and blood—an accession to grace.[122]

As we prepare a few days later to go back to the wheat fields Mrs. Davis invites us to join her at the Aspen Institute to hear a talk by Dr. Albert Schweitzer, whose reverence for life has made him one of the most admired men in the world. We cannot go, but how fitting it is that such a man, the missionary physician in Africa, the biographer of Bach, can be heard in boondocks! The roads that lead away from the East are not, after all, bad roads. I catch the sparkle of a crystalline stream as it meanders among putty-colored aspens.

"I'm coming back some day," I say to Mrs. Davis. I say it vehemently. It is a vow.

‡ ‡ ‡

Old by American standards, prestigious by any, Yale probably had fewer than 4,000 undergraduates at the time I was enrolled there. Compared with public institutions where a typical freshman class might number in the thousands, Yale had the advantage, had it chosen to press it, of offering small classes with a low ratio as between teachers and students. Efforts had been made, moreover, to bring distinguished professors, those who might have preferred to teach graduate students and research associates, into the undergraduate classrooms, thus restricting the number of untenured instructors and teaching assistants (TAs) to be thrown to the wolves. Finally, the mass of students was distributed among residential colleges—Timothy Dwight, Trumbull, Calhoun, Davenport, and the like—in order to create environments in which students and professors could meet informally, dining together, drinking beer together, "shooting the bull" (as was said) together; each college had a Master, whose function was not unlike that of the headmaster of a prep school, and Fellows, professors who were presumably available for stimulating off-the-cuff Socratic dialogues. It was all modeled, albeit remotely, on the Oxbridge system in England, and had Yale College taken the drastic but essential next step of assigning small groups of students to Tutors and of making Tutors responsible in a personal way for each student's academic and even moral progress, it might have worked. Lacking the tutorial system, the college in my day, and of course only in my opinion, seldom actually achieved its goal of making education personal or of providing each student with genuine mastery of at least one subject.

Roughly calculated from my own experience, I took forty courses in four academic years. Of these courses 75 percent were taught by tenured professors, only 25 percent by instructors and TAs. But 75 percent of the courses had enrollments of more than twenty-five students, and six of these courses had enrollments of more than a hundred. Only eight courses could be counted as seminars with enrollments under twenty. Of my teachers (I'll say forty), I met in my four years only two outside the classroom, one an old friend of Father's, the other a TA who really cared about his pupils (and would go on to a brilliant career at the University of California). The Fellows of my college, Timothy Dwight, if they showed up at all, dined with each other, and the Master, who made an effort to know us all by name, could do little more than feel his cheeks ache from smiling. Once designated as an English major, honored in fact to be selected as an Intensive Major, I had a sprinkling of those seminars, a small dose of the Socratic elixir. The one time I met the chairman of the English Department, he denied me admission to Robert Penn Warren's creative writing class. He coldly reminded me that I had twice flunked chemistry. Was my road to Parnassus blocked by vindictive molecules?

An innovative curriculum of high moral and intellectual promise, but boneheaded in execution, had been installed in order to coerce all undergraduates, regardless of aptitude, to take courses in chemistry, physics, geology, and astronomy. It soon became evident that the teachers of these subjects were indisposed to present them for the layman's understanding, which could have been ignited by their indisputably great historical and philosophical significance. We had to memorize "facts." Physics, which had just revolutionized the entire world, was reductionist Newton with no mention of Einstein, Rutherford, Jeans, Bohr, Heisenberg, Feynman, et al. Astronomy, then in the throes of Big Bang theory, was taught in broken English by a German, his incomprehensible sentences beginning with "der ecliptic" and ending with "Zo." Carl Sagan's *Cosmos* it wasn't. The geology professor, who wore diamond cufflinks, had us memorize the names of countless rocks but neglected to mention Darwin. Similarly, the chemist had us memorize the periodic table of elements and lots of compounds—I vaguely grasped hydrogen and salt—and made the insubstantial pageant of earth, air, fire, and water about as interesting as a shot of sodium pentothal. Although I elected to take a course in psychology, I was dismayed to find James, Freud, and Jung dismissed as "mystics" and study of "mind" relegated to something not unlike statistical analysis of pigeon droppings.

The education reflected society's fragmentation. Arts, sciences, technologies, and human work in general were carved up into special disciplines, each separated from the others, just as society has developed in such a way that it is broken into separate groups, tribes, and nations and into religious, political, economic, and racial parts; just as the natural environment has correspondingly been seen as an aggregate of separately existing parts to be exploited by different groups of people. The notion that all these fragments are separately existent—it was the notion prevalent at college—is nevertheless an illusion. To quote David Bohm:

> Indeed, the attempt to live according to the notion that the fragments are really separate is, in essence, what has led to the growing series of extremely urgent crises that is confronting us today. Thus,

as is now well-known, this way of life has brought about pollution, destruction of the balance of nature, over-population, world-wide economic and political disorder, and the creation of an overall environment that is neither physically nor mentally healthy for most of the people who have to live in it. Individually there has developed a widespread feeling of helplessness and despair, in the face of what seems to be an overwhelming mass of disparate social forces, going beyond control and even the comprehension of the human beings who are caught up in it.[123]

The fragmentation in The Education was, then, brought about by the almost universal habit of taking the content of thought for a description of the world as it is. We were led to confuse the forms and shapes induced in our perceptions by theoretical insight with a reality independent of our thought and our way of looking. Had wholeness been perceived as what is real, we might have become aware of our habit of fragmentary thought and started thinking and acting from the point of view of what is one and indivisible.

Two examples. The so-called "New Criticism" prevailed at Yale. At its best, as demonstrated in the lectures of Professor Cleanth Brooks, it was a practical method leading to appreciation of the synthesizing power of the imagination.[124] Two mutually incompatible things might be held in mind by paradox: the seeming death of a thing could be recovered as miraculously alive, the spoil of beauty communicated as eternal love, the silence of an urn fixed beyond human passion in defiance of time. The language of paradox, in particular, transcends an alien world of dehumanizing power. New Criticism, however, tended to celebrate a world in bits and pieces, making T.S. Eliot's poem, "The Waste Land," into the altarpiece of modern art, whereas the poetry of Robinson Jeffers, arguably the only American poet with a cosmic vision comparable to that of Homer, Dante, and Milton, didn't fit the theory and was tossed aside.[125] "The Intellectual History of Modern Europe," a course taught brilliantly by Professor Franklin Le Van Baumer, is my second example. His notion that the modern mind had disintegrated into an "age of anxiety" simply blotted out the holistic possibilities in quantum physics and in Jungian psychology, then-available studies for the making of that mind.[126]

Professors and students at any time and at any institution have the predicament of living between two worlds, past and future. In this respect those of us fortunate enough to study at Yale seldom if ever encountered long-accepted "certainties" that needed to be assailed. Whereas Henry Adams in *The Education* tells the story of a man trained to be at home in Puritanism and in the Enlightenment who yet had to live in a world transformed by the new science and the new technology, our Class of 1951 had no indoctrination to fear and every quest to pursue.

The oddest, the most terrifying, yet eventually the most revealing episode in my life occurred in New Haven one fall afternoon in 1949. Because I tried to erase the memory of the experience for many years and left no written record of it, I cannot now identify the exact date and time. It was time itself, initially exact, that disappeared.

It is, say, 1:07 P.M.; I glance at my wristwatch because my class in Italian has been let out late. Dave, whose family fled the Bolsheviks, and I are strolling down College Street on our way to Timothy Dwight. Suddenly I am possessed by a powerful sensation of imminent danger to Mother. That is, I know with uncanny and preternatural cognizance that she is causing the feeling. Well, my mind has been at ease for many months where she is concerned. I do not even think about her except when I receive her letters from Richmond, Virginia, where she has gone to study occupational therapy at a polytechnic institute and to build a new life. Nothing in recent letters would suggest illness or impending danger. Laughing about our textbook, *La famosa invasione degli orsi nella Sicilia*, Dave and I continue walking. The feeling persists.

I arrive at the college, have lunch, and retire to study in my room— but the feeling does not go away. I am almost in a panic. Am I insane? The question does surface. What can I do? Call Richmond, I decide, though I have been encouraged since childhood to avoid making long-distance calls. Call Richmond. It's an imperative. I ask an affluent student's permission to use his telephone. I call Mother's landlady, and this is what she says: "Your mother was taken by ambulance to the hospital about an hour and a half ago, with pneumonia." Without further ado, I borrow twenty dollars from Goodthought, explaining only that there has been an emergency, walk directly to the Trailways bus station, board a bus for New York, from there board an express bus to Richmond, and arrive about five o'clock in the morning at Mother's bedside in hospital. Astonished to see me, she sits up in bed. She is recovering nicely.

"Mom," I ask, "at what time yesterday, precisely what time, did you call the ambulance?"

"About twelve-thirty."

"When did it arrive?"

"About twenty minutes later. Then I passed out. . . . The doctor told me last night that I was at death's door."

"The time?"

"It must have been just after one."

Jung used the word *synchronicity* to describe the coincidence in time of two or more causally unrelated events which have the same or similar meaning. The coincidence of a psychic state and a physical state means that time and space have been opened to the glare of a multidimensional reality. In short, my experience in New Haven, hundreds of miles north of Richmond, had been one of timelessness, of synchronicity.[127]

Today there are many scientists who are moving in the direction of mysticism, their basic assumption being that the universe is unfolding according to a hidden, dynamic, and enfolded order. Experiments indicating that matter is alive—responsive, relational, and self-modifying in response to the activities of other matter—point to a constant creativity in nature, an external unfolding of the potential of the universe from an all-encompassing background. It seems increasingly likely that in the background's inward recesses both mind and matter have their source. If so, we are ourselves enfolded in a total wholeness and unity of the universe. We already exist in a numinous world and have but to be awakened to the reality.

ELEVEN

Meet the Professor

When last I portrayed Father he was tearfully begging me for an assurance of love. Once assured of my true affection, that of a soul knit close to his own, he transmogrified himself from King Lear to Charlie Chaplin—without real damage to his nobility.

For William Blackburn was noble. Perhaps nowadays we Americans are beginning to have, as the imperial Romans indeed had, a blind antipathy to virtue, but like the Agricola eulogized by his son-in-law Tacitus, Father never sought to glorify himself. We have no reason to deny him just praise.

I begin with a quotation from Gilbert Highet's *The Art of Teaching*:

> In spite of being such relentless critics, the good teachers of this period had another quality which ineffective teachers, however

brilliant as discoverers, lacked. It gave them that power over their pupils which extended to all kinds of young men and women, from different countries and classes, and which continued to work long after they were dead. It is difficult to describe. Indeed, many people, after feeling it, have complained of being unable to describe it. It is still more difficult to acquire. It cannot be taught at teachers' colleges, and not always developed by meditation and practice. Yet it is invaluable for a successful teacher; it is the core of a successful man or woman. Roughly speaking, it could be called largeness of heart.[128]

Whether largeness of heart manifests itself as love of and caring for students or as maturity's welcoming of youth, I cannot swear, but such manifestations have embedded themselves in my affections to such an extent that I recall "the good teachers" effortlessly, as if I were still in their charge, and forget the others as so many faces in a crowd.

It is October 1959. Invited to come for a year of study at Cambridge University, I am hopeful that the book I propose to write after preliminary research will prove of sufficient interest to my supervisor that he will extend my period of residence for an additional two years and enable me to qualify for a Ph.D. in English. Will my proposed subject for investigation turn out to be a publishable book at the frontier of knowledge? That is the criterion for advancement to the degree, not letter grades for "courses"—Cambridge professors give lectures and tutorials but not courses—and not oral and written examinations. All depends upon the production of a typed and bound dissertation of no fewer than 60,000 words, this to be examined by experts in the field. It is common knowledge that fewer than ten percent of dissertations presented to the Faculty of English are approved on the first try. The first step for me is to meet my professor. Mine is formidable: Dr. David Daiches. He is hardly less famous than his colleague, C.S. Lewis.

I purchase the required black gown and mortarboard. Thus properly medievalized, I sally forth on Rocinante, my $5 bicycle, in search of Jesus College where Professor Daiches is a Fellow. Well, "going to Jesus" does not mean here, as it might in Durham, departure from this world, but I have a sense of doom in my heart. It is pitch-dark, and an ice-cold pelting rain, blown on gale-force winds out of the North Sea,

William Blackburn riding a donkey to the Acropolis, Lindos, Rhodes, June 1960. This photo captures his spirit of fun, his Falstaffian comic aplomb in the midst of distress or some incongruous situation.

stings my face and soaks my clothing. Socks squish about in shoes. My hair is a housepainter's dark brush stuck to my brow and flopping over my eyes. I find Jesus College, take a deep breath, mount a flight of stone steps worn down in the middle where generations of wretched boys have trod, possibly including Newton, Wordsworth, and Lord Byron. I pause before an oaken door with a lion's head knocker that could have inspired Marley's in *A Christmas Carol*. I knock: thunk thunk. If all this crummy atmosphere is just part of a picture show, then why is my heart beating rapidly?

The door doesn't just open, it creaks open. There before me stands a small man with a small mustache. He is silhouetted against the blaze of a hearth in a book-lined study.

"Blackburn?" Professor's voice is gentle.

"Sir."

"Welcome," he says. "Have a glass of sherry." He pronounces it *gloss*.

A few minutes later we are seated before the fire with our glasses of sherry. Professor taps with a finger his copy of my research proposal and smiles encouragingly. "It's jolly good," he says. "Go to the library, and I'll see you again in the spring."

For the first time in my life I have been personally welcomed at an institution by someone other than a cashier in a finance office, not only welcomed but also trusted, trusted immediately, made a part of a great conversation.

Father often spoke of teaching as a "conversation." He flourished through togetherness. "Such a man," Highet writes, "is borne upwards and swept onwards by energy which flows into him from outside, from the group of which he is the heart and voice."[129] As such heart and voice Father brought out the best in his students: taste, eager sincerity, admiration for truth and beauty, love of a subject, responsibility. He shared with his students the wisdom and beauty achieved by the human race and explained to them the nobility of that achievement and the sadness of failures. He did not impose his will on students because he knew that, if he did so, they could thwart and disgrace him as Prince Hal does to Henry IV by leaning on Falstaff. He understood that the great secret to helping to create a human being, to transforming Hal into Henry V, lay in one's heart, in one's humanness, in one's willingness to show weakness as well as caring. He was a supreme artist in the sense thus described in *The Art of Teaching*.

His particular kind of magic may not have been art at all. It was, rather, a spontaneous rapture of his soul, one occasioned when he read aloud from the poets and one that was more than the sum of his oratorical and theatrical skills. I made this discovery when, once, I sat in on his class in "Elizabethan and Seventeenth-Century English Literature." There came a moment when with trembling hand he picked up from his desk a little book and after a sigh began to read a little-known poem by Sir Walter Raleigh, that flamboyant venture capitalist who had backed the

Lost Colony and had his head chopped off by the Virgin Queen of Virginia. This poem would not stand up to criticism by New Critics. It was full of trite conceits and of caged-bird sentiments that had lost their freshness when Petrarch lost Laura to the fourteenth-century Black Death. Father's voice transformed the words into a measured, wanton music that arrested time. One simply for the moment forgot the conventionality, what we would nowadays call the poet's "insincerity." I heard an accent of greatness. And midway through the reading Father began to weep unabashedly, touched by the authentic sublime.

‡ ‡ ‡

When Father arrived in Durham in 1926 to begin his long career at Duke, he sought for his exclusive use a classroom that could also serve as his office. He wanted to create the intimate atmosphere of tutorial rooms at Oxford even though his students would be denied views of charming quadrangles and gardens and of scholar gypsies wearing straw boaters and punting on the Cherwell. He found a small rectangular storeroom on the second floor of East Duke Building, an old Trinity structure. Located beneath the balcony of a Victorian auditorium, approached over floorboards that creaked and flapped like a plank road in the wilderness, the storeroom had large, old-fashioned sash windows, pigeons a-flutter on their ledges, and a bucolic vista of elephant-trunk magnolias with waxen green leaves and bridal flower-cones, also of a lily pond with goldfish.

He had the walls replastered and painted a light Botticellian blue. He decorated the walls with brass rubbings, a Persian kilim, lithographs of Parisian scenes, and a Folger Shakespeare Library print of Visscher's "View of London, 1616," South Warke and Globe Theatre in the foreground, in the middle Thamesis Fluvius, Bridge intact, in the distance a Saint Paul's towering over a cramped town. He would later add mementos of brilliant students: a painting by Guy Davenport, a framed dust jacket of William Styron's first novel, *Lie Down in Darkness*. In the center of the room he placed a long wooden table; against the walls on three sides he arranged some twenty-five deskboard chairs; at one end he had a desk backed by bookcases and a portable blackboard. The most unusual item in the room was the Persian samovar from Urumiah. From it, class after class, year after year, he served afternoon tea to students.

Serving tea caused Father no end of trouble, as he recalled in an interview in 1972:

> We had to haul the water in and the only place to throw the dirty water was out the window, which seemed undignified, but I did it nevertheless. I once showed President Few what the problem was; I told him what we needed was a spigot and a drain, and he looked at me as if to say, "I know you are out of your mind," but he didn't say anything at all.[130]

After Father's death this magical room, owing to the renovation of East Duke to make space for administrators, was stripped of everything and used to store reams of paper for laser printers.

Father often complained about a research university that "teaching doesn't count." The first duty of a professor, he believed, was to awaken in human beings an understanding and appreciation of genuinely important things. Not the prestigious research of an institution but its tone concerned him, its prevailing style or spirit of thought and behavior. Sweetness and light—Arnoldian culture—gave priority to a professor's relationship with students. Even though he cringed at the idea of teachers as metaphorical lathes, he aimed, in his words, "to turn out good students." And he did.

William Styron arrived at Duke University near the end of June 1943, a few days after his eighteenth birthday. As part of the V-12 program that enabled U.S. Navy and Marine Corps officer candidates to attend college for several semesters before shipping out, Styron felt free to elect some nontechnical courses. He signed up for Father's English 103, "Literary Composition," one of the first courses offered at a large Southern university in a field that would later be called creative writing. In Styron's words as quoted by his biographer, the desire to be an author was at this point still "vagrant" and "nubile. . . so fuzzy, really, as to border on a whim." But the writing course seemed "attractively undemanding, vaguely educative and entertaining."[131] Styron's encounter with Father changed his life.

The following excerpts are from William Styron's essay, "William Blackburn," in *This Quiet Dust and Other Writings* (1982):

> William Blackburn cared about writing and had an almost holy concern for the language. I realized this the first time out, with a brief theme in which we were required to describe a place—any place. In my two-page essay I chose a Tidewater river scene, the mudflats at low tide; attempting to grapple with the drab beauty of the view, groping for detail, I wrote of the fishnet stakes standing in the gray water, "looking stark and mute." A pretty conceit, I had thought, until the theme came back from Blackburn covered with red corrections, including the scathing comment on my attempt at imagery: "Mute? Did those stakes ever say anything?" This was my first encounter with something known among grammarians as "the pathetic fallacy."
>
> A certain precision, you see, was what the professor was after and I was lucky to be made to toe the line early. Also, it was not a permissive era. Blackburn graded his themes with rigid unsentimentality. That theme of mine, I recall, received a D-minus, and through discreet inquiry I discovered that it was the lowest grade in the class (I think the highest was a C). Chastened, I began to regard Professor Blackburn with apprehension and awe, and both of these feelings were heightened by his redoubtable appearance and demeanor. A large, bulky, rather rumpled man (at least in dress), he tended to slump at his desk and to sag while walking; all this gave the impression of a man harboring great unhappiness, if not despair. Nor did he smile effortlessly. He was ill at ease with strangers, including students, and this is why my first impression of Blackburn was one of remoteness and bearish gloom. Only a remarkably gentle South Carolina voice softened my initial feeling that he was filled with bone-hard melancholy and quiet desperation. For several weeks it seemed to me impossible that one could ever draw close—or be drawn close—to such a despondent, distant man.
>
> But before too long my work got much better, and as it did I found myself able to strike through the Blackburnian mask. Possibly because I was so eager to meet his demanding standards, I sweated

like a coolie over my essays, themes and fledgling short stories until my splintered syntax and humpbacked prose achieved a measure of clarity and grace. Blackburn in turn warmed to my efforts—beginning to sprinkle the pages with such invigorating phrases as "Nice!" and "Fine touch!"—and before the term was half through I had begun to acquire a clutch of Bs and As. More importantly, I began to know Blackburn, the great-hearted, humane, tragicomical sufferer who dwelt behind the hulking and lugubrious façade. . . .

Blackburn readily admitted that there was a great deal of logic in the accusation, so often leveled at "creative writing" courses, that no one actually could be taught to write English narrative prose. Why, then, did he persist? I think it must have been because, deep within him, despite all his doubts (and no man had so many self-doubts) he realized what an extraordinarily fine teacher he was. He must have known that he possessed that subtle, ineffable, magnetically appealing quality—a kind of invisible rapture—which caused students to respond with like rapture to the fresh and wondrous new world he was trying to reveal to them. Later, when I got to know him well, he accused himself of sloth, but in reality he was the most profoundly conscientious of teachers; his comments on students' themes and stories were often remarkable extended essays in themselves. This matter of caring, and caring deeply, was of course one of the secrets of his excellence. But the caring took other forms: it extended to his very presence in the classroom—his remarkable course in Elizabethan poetry and prose, for instance, when, reading aloud from Spenser's *Epithalamion* with its ravishing praise, or the sonorous meditation on death of Sir Thomas Browne, his voice would become so infused with feeling that we would sit transfixed, and not a breath could be heard in the room. It would be too facile a description to call him a spellbinder, though he had in him much of the actor manqué; this very rare ability to make his students feel, to fall in love with a poem or poet, came from his own real depth of feeling and, perhaps, from his own unrequited love, for I am sure he was an unfulfilled writer or poet too. Whatever—from what mysterious wellspring there derived Blackburn's powerful and uncanny gift to mediate between a work of art and the young people who stood ready to receive it—he was unquestionably a glorious teacher. Populate a whole country and its institutions of learning with but a handful of Blackburns, and you will certainly have great institutions of learning, and perhaps a great country.[132]

William Blackburn's Literary Composition class. For reasons of personal modesty and academic hostility to courses in imaginative writing, Father called his famous creative writing course "Literary Composition." During pauses in its two-hour sessions, he served tea to students to create an atmosphere of informality. In this photo published in the Durham Morning Herald *(23 February 1947), one can see atop the bookcase the samovar that had been presented to his parents upon their arrival in Iran in 1896.* (Reprinted, by permission, from Charles Cooper/Durham Herald-Sun.)

Mac Hyman (1923-63) was a native of Cordele, a small, sleepy town in south Georgia where his father operated an auto parts store; his mother was a former actress who was given a screen test for the role of Scarlett in *Gone With the Wind*. A B-29 navigator for three years during the Second World War, he took pictures of Hiroshima immediately after the atomic bombing. Enrolling at Duke University in 1946, he too found in Father's writing classes stern guidance. When he got Ds and Fs, Hyman used to grin at his teacher and joke, "You don't know how much I hate you!" He dedicated his best-selling novel, *No Time for Sergeants*, to this man he once "hated."[133]

Hyman was restless as an isolated artist who had found only in those writing classes the sense of an audience responding seriously to his work. When Hyman died of a sudden heart attack, his friend, poet and critic Guy Davenport, summed up the tragedy of Hyman's life succinctly in his *New York Times* review of *Love, Boy*, Hyman's letters collected and edited by Father: "Genius chooses its vessel with abandon, and in Mac Hyman it chose a quiet boy from Cordele, Ga., who nourished its gifts painstakingly and honestly, but paid for it with nerves, constant anxieties and the armor he constructed of whimsy and insouciance to protect himself from an all but defenseless sensitivity."[134] His unimpressed, Twain-like gaze at the world found its way into the letters; for example, "He might be sane as hell, but he's not too bright," or, "I've found myself twice now in the ridiculous position of arguing against women's suffrage," or, "I don't care to read anything else that is called complex but is really confused."

While *No Time for Sergeants* was successfully running on Broadway as a farce starring Andy Griffith, Mac shared my New York apartment with me for a period in 1956. I was teaching weekdays at a private school and struggling with my own writing on weekends, whereas Mac, working in the apartment, produced twenty typescript pages a day on a new novel. It gave him no satisfaction. "I just can't get the names right," he fretted one evening after reading aloud to me the day's brilliant output. "If the name of a character comes to me immediately, without my thinking about it, I get half the character." On another evening he had a different complaint: "Everybody wants me to write comedy, but all I can feel is tragedy." We went together to my informal writing class, a group led by John Farrar, the publisher, and Mac joined the proceedings enthusiastically.[135] As Davenport observes, "One suspects that what he was looking for was society's equivalent of that calm classroom at Duke, with its community of strivers, its wise master and its atmosphere of unabashed idealism."

Reynolds Price came from Wake County, and attended high school in Raleigh (as did, later, his student and Father's, Anne Tyler, who like Styron would become a Pulitzer Prize-winning novelist). He was an undergraduate at Duke from 1951 to 1955 and with Father's encouragement competed for and won a Rhodes Scholarship to Oxford. He returned to teach at Duke in 1958. Reynolds has frequently spoken and written about Father, as in the following piece:

We have been very closely involved with him because that was part of his genius as a teacher—his ability to be a friend in the best sense of the word. He is such a tremendously generous, kind man. If he believed in you —that you were a gifted writer—he would go to almost any lengths to do whatever he could for you.

He did what few teachers did ten or twenty years ago or do now. He took students seriously as human beings. He did not treat them as though they were just kids to be dealt with for 50 minutes. He dealt with them as though they were important people whom he respected because they had something that he honored and that was creative ability, however elementary it might be at that point.

He gave you something that was harder to get than technical advice and that was tremendous confidence in you and a very sane enthusiasm. He was measured in his praise and ungushing about it, but you knew you could believe him.

And he didn't have any secret methods. People always say, "How really did he do it?" He didn't know how he did it, like so many great teachers—so many great anything—it was a form of magic. I've known some very great teachers at Duke, Harvard and Oxford, but I have never known another teacher like him in my life.[136]

Fred Chappell came to Duke in the late 1950s from the North Carolina mountain town of Canton. Father took him under his wing and encouraged a career that has yielded prizes for both fiction and poetry (T.S. Eliot Prize, Bollingen Prize). He has taught creative writing for many years at the University of North Carolina at Greensboro.

Father discussed his relationship with Chappell in an article published in 1972:

> Fred had been writing epic poems and long stories since he was 14, perhaps. He came to Duke much against his will, sent there by his parents. He came into my class the last semester of his senior year and read a manuscript called "January." I called him aside and said, "Fred, there's certainly nothing I can teach you. There is something I can give you, though, and that is time. Don't come to class. Just cut for the semester and see what happens." So he came up with the first three chapters of his first novel, *It Is Time, Lord*.

Father introduced Chappell to Peter Taylor, dramatist, novelist and short story writer, who sent the first chapter of Chappell's novel to *The Sewanee Review*, in which it was published. Chappell stayed on at Duke another year to work on his master's degree.

> At the end of his first year of graduate studies, he asked, "Are you going to be around this semester?" I said, "Yes." He said, "Would you mind if I brought you 10,000 words of my novel every Friday afternoon around 4:00?" I said, "No, I wouldn't mind in the least," and so there it was for seven weeks running. He completed his novel, and by August he had sent it to Hiram Haydn, editor of Atheneum, who agreed to publish it.[137]

The following piece by Fred Chappell was written shortly after Father's death:

> He wasn't always right, but he was more valuable than if he had been. It takes a long time for a teacher to realize that his task is only partly that of the critic. He must uphold substantive critical values, right enough, but he is never to rank or grade literary production. Some teachers never learn this fact, but Dr. Blackburn probably knew it by temperament.
>
> This is to say, he erred on the side of the angels. His mistakes were those of precipitate enthusiasm and generous sympathy—not forced or dishonest. When he liked something you had written you felt momentarily equal to Sidney or Drayton. . . .Well, to Arthur Hugh Clough, anyway. And though you knew at the time that the exhilaration was fleeting and would have to be tempered by knowledge of his generosity, the excitement was no less heady.
>
> He never taught writing merely as writing. He never said, "*Playboy* will buy this story," or, "I can almost see this in *Sewanee Review*." He taught writing as literature, as part of a civilized discourse that always had been and always would be going on. When you wrote a story, no matter how naive or clumsy, he made you feel that you had contributed to that great conversation.
>
> He impressed you with the idea of writing as a moral act. When a story was phoney or cute or pretentious or callow, you felt that you had done a wrong thing, like telling an inadvertent lie. Not something to ponder remorsefully, but something to correct; an error curable by earnest labor.

That's how it was: he taught pride and humility all at once. I know of no other teacher who can do it.[138]

‡ ‡ ‡

On February 3, 1963, Father, together with Styron, Hyman, Price, and Chappell, was featured on a program called "Meet the Professor." Part of a series sponsored by the American Association for Higher Education, the program was broadcast to millions of people over ABC radio and television.

Mac Hyman wrote a letter to his friend, novelist and story writer Max Steele, describing his version of the rehearsal for that network show:

> Speaking of B. . . . I am. . . just. . . getting back from New York where I had been in order to appear on a TV show called "Meet the Professor" with Blackburn (he was the prof. being honored) with Styron, Reynolds Price, and another fellow from Duke by the name of Fred Chappell who has a book coming out soon. It was kind of fun in a way; they paid the expenses so we stayed at the Plaza and lived elegantly. It was to be one of the cultural things, a kind of impromptu discussion that Blackburn kept trying to plan in detail. "I'll say this to you and then you say that." We went through two hours of that kind of rehearsal the day before and it got worse and worse and Blackburn got more and more nervous. . . . .Everybody would chitchat and nobody would take his planning seriously. Then the TV men would try to explain how they wanted it, and this would embarrass him. They wanted to show him as the good professor with us saying nice things about him. They wanted to show we were all friends. Blackburn would say he didn't see any sense in saying things like that. "The mere fact that we are all sitting here," he would say, "shows that we are getting along. I don't see any point in mentioning things like that." Instead, he wanted to discuss high school teachers who influenced us as writers and the theory that most writers had had lonely childhoods between the ages of thirteen and sixteen during which period they did a lot of reading. I told him that I personally didn't care to sit on TV with a bunch of people watching and discuss my lonely childhood. All the others agreed with this, and

Blackburn pouted. Reynolds wanted to discuss the time that he (Blackburn) threw a chair at one of his students. The TV people didn't like this line, and finally Blackburn came up with the notion that we discuss the way writers become aware of things. He mentioned Styron's great feeling for water and things like that. I said I thought that would be embarrassing too. If Willie wanted to discuss how he became aware of water, it would be all right, but I didn't want to discuss things like that. Blackburn began to get right miserable. And the more miserable he got, the happier everybody was.

Did you see it by any chance? It was on last Sunday. I haven't seen it myself. Actually it went off all right. We went down the next day and they taped about forty-five minutes of profound discussion with the idea of trimming it down later, and I believe it worked all right. Blackburn and Styron carried the ball most of the way, and we chit-chatted all right. We got off on one or two silly subjects. One of them was how young writers are influenced by other writers and whether or not it was a good idea to read (this was after the subject began running away with us) good writers or not, and we went on about this until we reached the dead-end of the whole question which unfortunately ended with me so that I came out with the bright remark: "Well, if you are not going to read good writers, who are you going to read?" which I thought was bright at the time, but suddenly succeeded, I thought, in making all of us—me especially—look kind of silly. Anyhow, we dropped that then and went on to some more impromptu profundity.[139]

James L. W. West III and August J. Nigro have edited the transcript of "Meet the Professor" and published it as "William Blackburn and His Pupils: A Conversation" in *The Mississippi Quarterly*.[140] The writers, they point out, were not aware of a technique used in the production of the program: several times the soundtrack cut away from the conversation so that, as each writer spoke and the cameras focused on him, Blackburn's voice could be heard telling about each of them. Even on this occasion, which was supposed to honor him, he managed to turn attention away from himself and onto his students. Their conversation provides us with an extraordinary peek into educational decorum in process.

In the following excerpts from the transcript the participants discuss compositions they wrote as undergraduates in Father's classes:

Left to right, William Blackburn, Fred Chappell, William Styron, Reynolds Price, and Mac Hyman on the stage of the 1963 national television show, "Meet the Professor." Two years later an editorial in the London Times Literary Supplement *singled Blackburn out as the teacher of writers most gifted with the critical acumen and the charisma feasible for the discipline.* (Photograph courtesy of Duke University Archives.)

BLACKBURN: Fred, you wrote a sketch, perhaps your first one, which I am running in *Under Twenty-five*, about a little boy and girl, brother and sister, walking through a very cold wintry evening. I believe your novel grew out of that first sketch, in a way. I'm not asking you how it did, of course, but is that a fact?

CHAPPELL: Well, it did. It was a very short sketch. It was only 900 words, I think—one page. I wrote it as a one-page sketch and I started thinking about it. The thing gathered more and more energy until it wasn't something made up after a while. It became something I remembered really happening. After a while it gathered to this sketch. And there just happened to be enough energy to make a novel out of it.

BLACKBURN: Mac, could you remember your first paper?

HYMAN: Oh yeah. It was strictly Hemingway stuff. At that time, I was reading Hemingway. And so I handed it in and I kept waiting for you to read the thing. Nothing was right except Hemingway to me at the time. So I kept waiting it out. I'd been looking for somebody to help me write, and I thought to myself, "Well, if he doesn't like this, I'm just going to quit the class tomorrow and go to another place!"

BLACKBURN: Either/or ethic.

CHAPPELL: An ultimatum!

BLACKBURN: I was wondering if this business of steeping your-self in a contemporary writer, or any writer, is one way of making great progress as a young writer. The old saying is that you always crawl up on somebody's back anyhow in this life. Do you feel that reading Hemingway, steeping yourself in Hemingway, did you good?

HYMAN: Well, I don't know. I think it took me about a year or two to unlearn a lot of things I had learned—that I thought I had learned. Sooner or later, you are going to have to throw the rules out. But I do think it helps you, it gives you something to be going on—a point of view, at least, that maybe is not your own, and you are trying to find your own.

STYRON: I wonder if a very young person has really absorbed enough experience to encompass the idea of a novel. It's a tentative beginning in a short story; it's probably the logical extension of the essay or the composition. The novel is a rather formidable undertak-ing for somebody who's still trying his wings, so to speak.

PRICE: The short story also makes a young writer aware, makes him attentive to the whole texture of a given experience, so that he has to notice it in great detail.

CHAPPELL: The thing you don't get from short stories is bal-ancing the masses of material.

STYRON: Also, a novel does involve a tremendous adventure and a multiplicity of characters. I still feel, at least if my own experience is any guide, that when you are of college age, you probably haven't really had enough experience to encompass all of these characters that you eventually project into a novel.

PRICE: Well, you've probably had it, but you haven't got the understanding to deal with it.

CHAPPELL: Maybe I just can't write English well enough. That's a great deal of the problem. How much experience do you have to have to write a novel?

STYRON: I don't know. That's one of the thorniest questions. I think it was Hemingway who said something to the effect that all the experience needed to write a novel a man had accumulated before he was 25 years old. That's quite arbitrary and you can take it for what it's worth. But I think there's something to it. But I do think that one has to wait until a period, let us say, being arbitrary, after 25, before you can make use of that experience in the novel form.

HYMAN: That's probably because Hemingway wrote his first book after he was 25.

PRICE: Well, you don't have to have any experience at all. Emily Brontë just sat there in the vicarage.

STYRON: Oh no. She had plenty of experience.

PRICE: Of course, it was interior.

STYRON: You're right.

PRICE: She was a genius. If you are going to write *Wuthering Heights*, you don't have to get out and go be a hobo and/or anything. You don't have to be a gypsy to know what it's like to be Heathcliff. You just have to be Emily Brontë.

STYRON: But at the same time you have to have lived. How many novels do we have from people who are 18 years old, 20 years old?

PRICE: Precious few, right?

STYRON: None. The idea of experience is certainly apposite and completely important to the idea of a novel. I do think there is something to what Hemingway says in that after this age—let us say it's 25—you have absorbed so much that from then on, you could sit in a room somewhere.

HYMAN: One thing he means, too, is the fact that after you have begun writing, you might become more conscious of the experience as experience. Therefore, it is not as strong inside. It is not something that you automatically just pick up. It's something you observe, when looking at it.

CHAPPELL: It doesn't have the same effect as experience. You can't go and look for certain types of experience and have them, and come home and write them up.

PRICE: That's very sad, because too many people do that!

BLACKBURN: I'm always asking this question, or rather, quoting Jane Austen to the effect that she wished she had read more and written less in her younger years. I'm wondering if this is not another way of saying what you gentlemen have said: that one can hardly hope to write anything worth reading until one is 25 or so.

CHAPPELL: Well, you've read a great deal more too by that time. It's not that you've got more experience. Have you ever heard a student say he is afraid to read a certain author because it might influence him too much?

BLACKBURN: Oh yes, of course.

PRICE: It's a real fear at times.

STYRON: Yes, but I don't think it makes much difference at an early age. It's healthy to imitate because you immerse yourself—immerse yourself deeply. We all can recall the moments when we were smitten by, let us say, Conrad, and these great orotund marvelous syllables kept haunting us. And so we wrote like Conrad for a while or we wrote, on the other hand, like Hemingway—this marvelously sparse lean prose. There's hardly anybody who hasn't, at one time, been influenced by it. But I think these are important transitional stages that young people should go through. If they've got it, and if

200

they are going to be writers, they'll eventually shake loose of these influences. They are bound to in the scheme of things.

HYMAN: Yeah, if they are not going to read the good ones, what are they going to read?

BLACKBURN: Well, I'm all for it.

CHAPPELL: I read "Batman" comics myself.

STYRON: A good example would be a friend of mine, James Jones, who was smitten, by his own account, with Thomas Wolfe. That's the reason he chose Scribner's as a publisher, and Maxwell Perkins, the late Maxwell Perkins, for an editor. But look what happened. He wrote a marvelous book, *From Here to Eternity*, which was, so far as anyone can tell, totally free of the Wolfeian influence. The real writer is going to shake loose, on his own, from these early influences.

PRICE: The whole business of influence is a very interesting question, because it is the invariable thing that any reviewer says about a book. It's the first thing he can think of. "This book sounds like Faulkner. This book sounds like Conrad. Ergo, Mr. Blotz has been influenced by Conrad."

BLACKBURN: One of the worst things you can say is that it came out of a writing course, isn't that right?

STYRON: The combination of the two—the "This man has obviously read all of his Faulkner in college"—is the ultimate insult.

PRICE: Speaking quite personally, no one ever guessed what my influences were, because they weren't the ones that sounded obvious. The obvious thing is to say that I sound like Faulkner. I think that's because Faulkner is from Mississippi and I'm from North Carolina. But I was influenced by Tolstoy because he just seemed so great that he gave me great courage and a desire to emulate anyone who calmly knew what it was like to be everyone who'd ever lived. And I think continually of Leo Tolstoy and read *Anna Karenina* about once a year.

BLACKBURN: You want someone who's going to stretch your imagination.

PRICE: It's very liberating because you realize you can never be that good. And yet it looks so easy when you read it. You feel like you could do it, if you really just tried another day.

CHAPPELL: You feel that, but you know you can't.

BLACKBURN: I'm wondering about the rough-and-ready school, the hobo school, the hobo preparation for the writer. Don't go to college at all. Just experience life. I'm wondering if you gentlemen have any feeling about that—looking back?

HYMAN: Tell you one thing, I think there is a danger in school. It's this business of analyzing a story to such an extent that if a young student gets in, starts with symbols and one thing after the other, then he kind of gets the cart before the horse. He starts out trying to write through symbols and it's not a story. A story's got to work on the surface or it doesn't work. That is one danger of too much studying and analyzing of stories.

BLACKBURN: Yes. You want to get inside the writer, but not be aware of his "parts" so much as the whole feeling of the man.

STYRON: On the other hand, what you term the "rough-and-ready school" often betrays a total lack of reading, total lack of attention to prose. There's a nice compromise that most good writers eventually hit. Certainly it's true that some of our great predecessors, in fact most of them, didn't go to college. Faulkner had a year at Ole Miss. Hemingway, so far as I know, had no college.

HYMAN: Yeah, but he had a terrific education, even leaving out college. You couldn't go to college and get Gertrude Stein.

STYRON: Yes, he was lucky. So was Faulkner, for that matter, because Faulkner had Sherwood Anderson as a teacher. But the important thing here is this early exposure to the great—to your Tolstoy and to your Conrad. The college itself can be outside the walls, like Hemingway.

CHAPPELL: How much of the immediately contemporary writer do you think a young writer should read—someone he knows, or someone next door, or someone whose book was published last week? Do you think he should spend a lot of time reading people that just came out last week or should he read the earlier stuff?

STYRON: I don't think it's important to read the latest bestseller because I think the works of value eventually find their own level. Good books are often damned out of hand, bad books praised out of hand. Five years pass and then all of a sudden you understand which is the good and which is the bad.

HYMAN: Somerset Maugham said one time he waited a year before he read any books. That way, they were sifted out. Said it was amazing how many books he didn't have to read!

CHAPPELL: Very discouraging to a guy who just started to write—when Maugham said that!

BLACKBURN: Malcolm Cowley was saying in a piece about a year ago that everyone who writes has been through a period, a rather lonely youth, and has been a great reader, and has been encouraged by some particular person—it may be an uncle, an aunt, a teacher, a fellow writer, or what not. I was just wondering if that sounds true to you.

STYRON: Certainly it's true in my case. In spite of whatever reservations I might have already made about college, it's quite apparent to me that when I was fortunate enough to be sent to Duke in the Marine Corps and ended up in your class, it was the propitious moment for me. I found the person who, symbolic or otherwise, gave me that particular encouragement.

BLACKBURN: Well, that's very handsome of you and I appreciate it. I wasn't trying to make you say that, of course.

STYRON: I think most all of us here would subscribe to that.

TWELVE

The Long Habit of Living

I saw Father for the last time in the fall of 1972. He was by then, at the age of seventy-three, a legend in certain quarters. Throughout a long career as The Professor, most of it at Duke University, he had been sensitive, conscientious, and respectful in all things pertaining to the art of leading students to discover their own powers. An annual literary festival bearing his name had been permanently established at Duke. Former students, some already famous, some about to be, had cornered him on national TV and paid homage to their frowning master before he could duck back into his characteristic diffidence. In 1965 an editorial in the London *Times Literary Supplement* had singled him out as the teacher of writers gifted more than anyone else with the critical acumen and charisma feasible for the discipline of creative writing.[141]

Renown, however, had done little to alleviate his lifelong burden of self-doubt. While others cheered, we in the family anxiously awaited the day when his teeth-clenching efforts to accept himself as worthy of esteem would be relaxed. Sometimes enervated by moods which

we would nowadays attribute to depression, he was nevertheless pro-
fessionally composed, courtly in manner, humorous in inclination, and
great-hearted in sentiment. Yet for most of his life and away from the
public eye, he had pulled himself up by his love-of-life bootstraps to
fight endlessly plucky rounds in what seemed to him an endless series
of losing battles. On the wall of his office at Duke he had tacked up a
cartoon which depicted an X-eyed fighter prone on the canvas while
his manager exhorts him, "Up, Rodney! Up like a sport!" This was
Father's emblem all right.

When I saw him for the last time, he had been remarried for six
years, an achievement much to the delight of his children and to the
mortification of those who had chalked up his quest for the perfect
mate to a madness akin to that which unseated the reason of Don
Quixote. He had, after all, remained single for fifteen years and ought
not at the age of sixty-seven be sallying forth in search of whatever
peerless Dulcinea del Toboso the enchanted realm of Durham had to
offer. He had managed a courtship and re-entry into matrimony that
scandalized no one except his mother. She was in Wisconsin, far away
in a nursing home for giantesses.

Let us once again place this romance of chivalry in perspective. In
boyhood Father had been raised by the iron will of his mother in expectation of becoming a Puritan minister in the harvest field of lost
souls. Should he discover for himself the importance of liberty and
learn to breathe the atmosphere of boundless intelligence, the Lord's
hand would surely, he had been admonished, be extended in chastise-
ment. By the time he entered college he had liberated himself from
the predestined ministry, having no vocation for it, but a latent dread
of divine wrath continued to plague his mind. Then having been a
Rhodes Scholar at single-sex Oxford and knowing little about women
save their apparent obsession with having babies, he sought refuge in
Pygmalionism and desired to love a statue.[142] While still scoffing at
women, he established criteria, namely, the statue must not only provide him with hot meals, clean laundry, and a limited passel of prog-
eny, she must also be intelligent, literary, and free of the poor house.
In 1926 he met the new Eliza—Mother—and married her. Although

Three Blackburn generations: Father with me and grandsons Philip William and David Alexander, August 1964, Philadelphia. Having completed a doctorate degree at Cambridge and a year of teaching literature and creative writing at the University of Pennsylvania, I am suddenly a professor meeting The Professor. (Photograph by Jane Blackburn.)

she lacked a college degree, a fact that would fester like a boil in his heart for years, she in most respects incarnated his hopes for a combination of Jane Austen and Cinderella. When the marriage ended in divorce in 1951, Father's mother once more swooped down upon his conscience. Believing in the absolute veracity of every statement in the Bible, she warned him about the sinfulness of a second marriage, thus renewing in him the conflict between will and terror. He, with a knight's armor protecting sensitivity, clutched his private parts at cocktail parties and protested in a squeaky voice that he had been castrated. But he intended to commit "sin," so there! Then Roma Goodwin, a widow from Montreal and mother of the young provost of Duke, swam into his ken and whipped the offending theology into a wholesome subordination. She was daughter of the governor of Prince Edward Island, a province noted for its clans of dour no-nonsense Scots; she was a lawyer with a quality of mercy; her late husband had been a banker; she was bright, witty, still very attractive in her early sixties. He married Roma on July 12, 1966.

I admired my new stepmother. I would champion her integrity, as will appear. But as a mature person I had come to recognize in my mother a commitment to her beloved that could be enshrined. Her love for my father—a womanly, purely human experience of love for a person, involving the courage to suffer for it—lasted from the moment they met in 1926 to the day she died in 1994 at the age of ninety-six, twenty-two years after his death. Would it seem profane, here, to recall the twelfth-century romance of Abélard and Héloise? That middle-aged Parisian professor, we recall, married the girl Héloise, gave her a child, was castrated by her uncle, entered the monastery of Saint Denis as a monk; he sent his wife, in obedience to his wish, to the convent of Argenteuil as a nun. For ten years after their separation, he never wrote her, though he was famed for eloquence, a single line. Then she wrote him. He was still her god:

> When little more than a girl I took the hard vows of a nun, not from piety but at your command. If I merit nothing from thee, how vain I deem my labor! I can expect no reward from God, as I have done nothing from love of Him. . . . God knows, at your command I would have followed or preceded you to fiery places. For my heart is not with me, but with thee.[143]

Father and Roma purchased a two-story brick house on Pinecrest Road in Durham. Instead of avoiding intimacy with his new wife, as he had done in his first marriage, by working all day in his campus office and grabbing lunch at a beanery, he now studied at home, ate nutritious meals, and took restful naps. Instead of traveling abroad alone, he had taken Roma with him for a month in Florence, his favorite city in the world. I joined them there and for three days watched two equal and tender partners strolling hand in hand from the Carmine to the Campanile. He had stopped smoking cigarettes. In Durham he swam laps at the YMCA, and at Roma's summer cottage in Vermont he took regular dips in a frigid lake, this a man who for most of his life could not have been dragged into violent exertion by a team of wild horses goaded by the Surgeon General. His 215 pounds were now proportionately distributed over his big frame.

Even his handwriting improved. As one of his century's last practitioners of epistolary art, he wrote Chesterfield-quality letters by dipping a nib pen in ink and scratching sentences on bond paper in fluid, unruled lines. When he felt happy he sent everyone thick envelopes stuffed with pages inscribed with bold strokes. When, however, his daemons got the better of him, his trembling hands produced words so cramped and wriggly that one wondered if the author were not, after all, King Lear, a bare, unaccommodated soul lost on a blasted heath. During the years of his marriage to Roma, when I received from him a letter, I no longer needed to decipher his calligraphy.

At the age of twenty-seven, while teaching at the American School in London, I met and married an English woman, Jane Allison, a psychiatric social worker from a family of doctors.[144] For a while we shuttled back and forth across the Atlantic, here at a graduate school or job for me in Virginia, there at Cambridge University, 1959-60, 1961-63. We had two sons, David and Philip, and in 1963 the four of us went to live in Philadelphia where I had landed employment as an instructor of English at the University of Pennsylvania. I taught creative writing and a freshman Honors class. Then the first of a series of crises erupted, a personal crisis: who was I to be teaching writers, I asked myself, when I had never put myself to the test of writing a novel? I loved my students—Candace Bergen would soon be starring in movies and Steve Berg would soon be founding *The American Poetry Review*—but my bliss since the age of about six had been writing, not teaching. I had little to show for my compulsion beyond a few published poems and stories and an unpublished doctoral dissertation. In

1964 at the age of thirty-five, I was jolted out of complacency by the death of my first cousin, Emily Knapp Pitkin, only thirty-six. Attending her memorial service in an old church in Harvard Square and listening to the eulogy delivered by Professor Leo Marx of M.I.T., I learned that Emily had deliberately taxed her poorly functioning heart in order to bring her child full-term. "She was," Marx said, quoting his mentor and Emily's godfather, Professor F.O. Matthiessen of Harvard, "'a Jamesian heroine'." Life, itself, the most precious gift, had been sacrificed that another person might live. At that moment I made a vow to myself, that for the rest of my life I would strive to give birth to art.

My wife's health was poor. Because Jane wished to be cared for by her uncle, Mr. Philip Allison, Nuffield Professor of Surgery at Oxford, I resigned my position at Penn, and we returned to England in 1965. By 1968 I had completed the draft of a long novel. Encouraged by my friend, novelist and poet (later Oxford Professor of Poetry) John Wain, and by Father, who found my novel "strong," I secured the services of a New York literary agent, James Oliver Brown, who anticipated a success. Meantime, I was struggling to make ends meet. Although I had patched together part-time jobs at R.A.F. bases in the University of Maryland's European Division, at Oxford Polytechnic, and at St. Clare's Hall, Oxford, for a total of 90 to 100 hours per week of preparation and contact time, proceeds were slim for a family renting a 200-year-old Cotswold stone farmhouse in Berkshire even for just $30 a week. Several years of this strenuously fruitless existence passed. Then Jim Brown, baffled by editors who were turning down my novel—corporations were taking control of publishing houses and introducing the "bottom line" mindset—cut me loose. When I proposed to move the family back to the States, Jane gave me an ultimatum: go alone. We separated. While I continued to support her and to send our sons to excellent schools, I rented a cheap bed-sitter in Oxford for myself and my banished Sheltie. This was the situation that Father would be encountering during his visit in the fall of 1972.

In the process of meeting The Professor, I had long ago recognized that a code of honor lay at the very basis of his personal attitude toward life. Truly, honor meant something essential to him. There had been

The Professor reading an exam book. (Photograph by John Menapace in *Duke Alumni Register*, 54:6, November 1968. Courtesy of Duke University Archives.)

that occasion when the dean of Duke University had demanded from him proof that Yale had actually awarded to him the Doctor of Philosophy Degree, a slanderous complaint, to the effect that Father lacked the degree, having been lodged by a jealous colleague with the administration. Father produced the proof. Afterwards he said to me in a vehemently triumphant tone of voice, "I defended my honor!"—not "I showed that rascal and saved my job" but "I defended my honor!" It was a very personal thing. Although he could relish a Falstaff's cynical rejection of honor—"Who hath it? He that died a-Wednesday" (*King Henry IV*, Part I, V.1.136)—he maintained a disciplined personal standard for living his life. In this respect as in certain others he reflected his Southern ancestry and upbringing. Ben Robertson, who, we recall, wrote a book that Father wished he had written, expresses the matter succinctly:

> As Southerners, it is essential to my kinfolks that they live by an ethical code, that they live their lives with dignity to themselves, that they live them with honor. A Southerner who loses his honor loses all, and he had rather die than live in disgrace. . . . It is not defeat that we fear, it is the loss of our intimate honor.[145]

This ideal of honor fostered in Father's spirit a deep vision of the necessity of upholding good conduct and good government. At its most profound level it was a vision of our national life.

This was my father, The Professor, who was coming to England. As long as his code of honor—my own code, one learned from him—remained satisfied, my defeat in marriage would not trouble him unduly.

With the prospect of a job at the University of Colorado at Colorado Springs opening up for me, I had already received from him not only encouragement but also heady praise. He knew I was now a sort of Rip Van Winkle, having slept in the alien corn so long that the native land in which I would soon reawaken loomed in my imagination as an improbable place, as precarious and unreliable as a colony on Mars. What I didn't know was this: he was dying.

‡ ‡ ‡

He looked depressed. Perhaps he was suffering from jet lag. When we were seated in my Ford Escort and driving from Heathrow airport toward Oxford, I finally asked, "You all right, Dad?"

"I'm sunk," he said. "I may have to get a divorce."

I was stunned. "Oh?"

"She's thinking about another man."

"Roma?" I geared down for a round-about, dodged an oncoming lorry, geared up. "What makes you think she would leave you for another man? She's the last person —"

"— I know," he interrupted with a snap. He had his protuberant jaw, the so-called "Hapsburg" jaw of a Renaissance man, set firmly.

"I'm sure you're mistaken," I said after a long pause. "Do you want to talk about it?"

Presently he told the story. Roma had been reading a book about Flaubert and had expressed admiration for the French critic.

"Anyone we know? Where does he live?"

He fell silent and gazed out the window at England's green and pleasant land. Suddenly he sighed, chuckled in his throat, and said, "Jane Austen wished she'd written less at sixteen and read more." With this non sequitur his Othello moment seemed to vanish.

Years before, when Mother was deconstructing marital problems, she had recalled similar moments with Father. He could imagine unkind glances from her where they did not exist. He could accuse her of incredible disloyalties, even for having thoughts he suspected her of having, and then he would punish her with cold silence. He projected upon her, she believed, the image of a psychotic invalid.[146]

"I don't think I can endure the stress of another divorce," Father said in a resigned tone. He half smiled at me. Perhaps he understood what Jane and I and the children were going through. Probably he realized he didn't have a thread of Desdemona's handkerchief as evidence of disloyalty. I quoted to him one of his favorite sayings: "A gentleman is too indolent to harbor malice."

Again he chuckled in his throat. His moods could be as capricious and fleeting as English weather, foggy one moment, sunny the next. They were something to watch for, that was all.

Now, it happened that I'd been reading a few new books about the suburban malaise in America in order to cushion myself against culture shock upon return. One of these books, *Open Marriage*, had recommended that married couples swap partners in order to be liberated from jealousy, guilt, and remorse. Because it was quite possibly the silliest book I had ever read, I thought it might serve as an over-the-counter drug for Father's depression. One glimpse of the sexual revolution at its most absurd might dispel doubt about his marriage to a loving and absolutely honorable lady. "Have you read *Open Marriage*, Dad?" I plunged. He replied that he hadn't heard of this bestseller. "Have a look," I suggested.

We drove on in silence. Because the purpose of his visit, I believed, was to inspect family conditions, he was going to be pleasantly surprised that everyone was, in English parlance, "coping." The boys had not missed a beat at their schools and stood a good chance of eventual admission to universities. Jane, always a good mother, was looking after the home and receiving therapy. She had graciously invited Father to stay at the farm that he might have a long visit with his grandchildren. As for myself, according to a stress test in the *Reader's Digest*, I needed a score of 1,200 in order to go mad. So far, I had managed only a measly 800.

Upon arrival at the farm the family sat down to tea. Father's mood brightened. His "imagination of disaster," that Huckleberry Finn aspect of his personality, had eased itself away.[147] Unfortunately, just as I was preparing to leave for my bed-sitter and a hungry dog, he remembered the book I had facetiously recommended. "*Open Marriage*," he said. "I'd like to read it tonight."

I looked at Jane in hopes she had tossed the book in the garbage during the ritual purge of my belongings. She went and fetched it. A conviction of a sort of medical malpractice grazed my conscience.

Next morning when I came to pick Father up for a drive to Oxford, he looked at me accusingly. "I read that book," he sighed.

"Oh?" I feigned indifference but waited for an explosion. "Open adultery? I don't think that's for Blackburns."

A smile tightened the corners of his mouth. His eyes had in them a touch of whimsy. "Don't take the gloomy view," he said.

That was vintage Father. He was coping, too.

We spent that day and others strolling about a city he had loved in his youth. We stopped at Hertford, his college in Rhodes Scholar years, for a chat with an ancient Jeeves at the Porter's Lodge, who remembered him. They talked about freezing winters in the 1920s;

Father recalled having sat on the radiator in his digs when he was preparing for examinations. At a department store he purchased a Liberty scarf for Roma. At Blackwell's he purchased for himself a LP recording of songs composed in the seventeenth century by Henry Purcell. Back at the farmhouse he placed this treasure on my Bang & Olafson phonograph turntable with the studious devotion of a priest celebrating a sacrament.

My alarm about his health was rekindled when he revealed he had had a cancer removed by a surgeon in Montreal. Titans, I thought, never die, though Polyphemos had an eye problem, Prometheus a liver complaint. Is Dad not immortal? Could the world lose him? Although he told me the biopsy had been negative, I secretly telephoned Professor Allison—Uncle Philip—at the Radcliffe Infirmary. He told me that a spreading cancer could cause muddled thinking.

One noon we drove to Botley, near Oxford on the Upper Thames River, for lunch at "The Perch," a thatched-roof pub reputed to be a setting for Chaucer's *Miller's Tale*. After a game of shove ha'penny, we dined heartily on pig-in-a-poke and fries and settled down to drinking pints of bitter ale, an amber liquid packing a friendly wallop.

"I've read your novel and told you it is strong," he said. "Don't lose faith in it. I've not lost mine." These were the kindest and highest words of praise and encouragement for my writing I had ever received from Father. He went on to speak of sundry other matters: the promise he perceived in his grandchildren, his expectation of a flourishing career for me in Colorado. Suddenly he clenched his fist, made a chopping motion of it in the air, thrust out his "Hapsburg" jaw—for the first time I saw the scar from his surgical incision—and declared with the intensity of an Old Testament prophet: "I'm finally beginning to understand the English sentence!"

I had no idea what had prompted this outburst. The inference I made from it left me gazing at him in disbelief. If he, The Professor, were now just beginning to understand the English sentence—not the poem, story, novel, not the paragraph, just the sentence—the rest of us must have been speaking prose all our lives, like Molière's bourgeois gentleman, without understanding it. Did it require a lifetime to

catch a glimpse of glory behind a grammatical arrangement of words?
Did this devotee of the Word, this veteran of the Bonehead English
wars, mean that the subject and object of a sentence, their interaction
fueled by a verb, constituted spiritual geometry? Perhaps Father was
intimating at Sophoclean depth that nothing is more wonderful than
Man, and that the most wonderful of Man's achievements is his capture of winged words.[148]

Father without explaining the basis for his minimalist confidence
finished his pint of ale and asked for another.

"Strong for mid-day," I cautioned.

Over spectacles lowered to his nose he peered at me mockingly
in his professorial manner. "Sweeten the cup," he ordered.

A girl in a mini-skirt brought us more pints of ale. Her adventur-
ous pelmet attracted our attention. Although hardened to the fashion
by nymphs at the Polytechnic, I had never ceased to feel ridiculous as
I lectured them on "silence, exile, and cunning" and other profundi-
ties.[149] I wondered what Father's reaction to the mini-skirt would be.

Lifting his glass and closing his eyes, Father recited with a dramatic sigh,

> That is no country for old men. The young
> In one another's arms. . . . .[150]

and I chimed in with,

> The Lord has pitched his mansion in
> The place of excrement. . . . .[151]

He opened his eyes and in another voice recited:

> Oh, I have been to Ludlow fair,
> Left my necktie God knows where,
> And down in lovely muck I've lain
> Happy till I woke again. . . . [152]

We finished our pints, left the pub, went and stood in a
meadow beside the Thames. He put an arm around my shoulders. We

watched sunlight dancing on the river and contemplated the distant spires of Oxford. He gestured toward them and recited:

> Into my heart an air that kills
>   From yon far country blows:
> What are those blue remembered hills,
>   What spires, what farms are those?
>
> That is the land of lost content,
>   I see it shining plain,
> The happy highways where I went
>   And cannot come again.[153]

He was in a mood of belatedness.

"I loved your mother for the first ten years of our marriage," he said as if in reply to a nagging doubt I had never expressed.

"I know," I said. I was glad to say this sincerely. Although an iodine-painted wishbone had not granted me my wish for his total happiness, I knew he had found a measure of it. "Don't take the gloomy view, Dad."

He swept an arm toward the river. "'Sweete Themmes! runne softlie, till I end my Song'."[154] A mood of exaltation had been aroused in the heart of his being.

‡   ‡   ‡

His own Song began to fade before dawn. As I was brewing coffee in my mini-kitchen, there came a knock on my door. I opened it to find my landlady standing in the rain, an anxious look on her face. She was a tiny Jewish lady who had shown compassion for an alien American and his dog when they needed shelter after their declaration of independence. Except when her telephone upstairs, the only one in the house, rang for me, which was seldom, she never disturbed my privacy. I invited her to enter.

"That won't be necessary, doctor, thank you very much," she said. "I like rain. We never have an ample sufficiency. . .Your wife says you are to come at once. Your father has suffered the loss of sight in one eye. . . I'm dreadfully sorry."

Half an hour later I found waiting for me at the farmhouse an American professor of medicine whom Jane had had the presence of mind to summon from his residence on nearby Boar's Hill. He had already examined Father and given him a black patch to wear over his blind eye. "Professor Blackburn," he said, leading me away from the house, "has an incurable cancer. He cannot be expected to live more than a few weeks, a few months at most. I have informed him that he has suffered only a mild stroke and may expect the recovery of his eyesight, but that he must return immediately to Durham." The doctor's voice was a vehement whisper. "For god's sake, do not tell him the truth!"

I drove Father to Heathrow next morning. The black patch gave him the menacing and curiously invincible look of a retired commander of freedom fighters. He had somehow contrived to tie his polka-dot bow tie. His gray felt hat was as handsome as its twin had been on Humphrey Bogart in *Casablanca*. He spoke of himself as someone inconvenienced by the need for a prescription for new reading glasses. He looked forward to presenting Roma with the Liberty scarf. I parked the car and went with him to the gate where his flight was being boarded. I brushed my lips across the sandpaper bristles of his cheek. We did not say goodbyes. As he was disappearing in the crowd, he gave me a backward glance and nodded his head. It was a blessing.

In those days some of us living on a shoestring budget could ill afford the expense of transoceanic telephone calls or cables. I relied for news of Father upon letters from Aunt Mallie, who had come down from Washington to be at his bedside once he was admitted to Duke Hospital, and from Mary April, who had flown in to Durham from Palo Alto.[155] He went completely blind in both eyes. He lost his rapturous voice. He disappeared into a black hole of depression. Reynolds Price brought a phonograph to his hospital room and filled it with Mozart. The music gave him peace. One day in December my landlady knocked on my door and I went to the telephone and Mary April told me that Father was dead. I, like some of his students, was reminded of a passage in *King Lear*:

William Blackburn's gravestone in the Presbyterian churchyard, Marion Street, Columbia, South Carolina. Father's ashes were buried next to the gravestones of his Waring kin. The gravestone is inscribed, simply, "William Maxwell Blackburn, 1899-1972."(Photograph by Inés Dölz Blackburn.)

O! let him pass; He hates him
That would upon the rack of this tough world
Stretch him out longer.[156]

‡ ‡ ‡

The memorial service is held in the afternoon of December 17, 1972, in Duke Chapel. The sun outside is bright. The stained-glass windows, like those in the cathedrals of Chartres and of Notre Dame de Paris which had inspired them, shimmer in its blaze. Soaring through vaulted arches, reverberating amidst sibilant murmurs of the gathering of a thousand people, tones of the great organ give me the feeling of falling forever in space, powerless to know the unknowable. Father had once described this Gothic chapel as "a study, in terms of stone, of how the spirit of man may escape the fetters of the earth."[157] I am

The Chapel tower. When William Blackburn joined the Duke faculty in 1926, President William Preston Few took him aside and said, "Come for a ride with me. Let me show you where we're going to build the 'Oxford of the South.'" Blackburn watched Few's dreams take tangible form: forest cleared, thousands of workers brought to Durham, carload after carload of materials delivered, and finally the skeleton structures gave way to magnificent greenish gray Hillsborough stone buildings. The most imposing of the buildings is the Gothic chapel, its tower seen here from the south end of the main quadrangle. A memorial service for Blackburn was held in the Chapel on December 17, 1972. (Photograph from William Blackburn, *The Architecture of Duke University, 1939.* Courtesy of Duke University Archives.)

thinking: he never wished to escape the earth. Wonder was always in him, here and now.

The eulogy is brief. James Applewhite mounts to the elevated pulpit and reads Donne's "Hymn to God My God, In My Sicknesse." Fred Chappell reads Henry Vaughan's "They are all gone into the world of light." Reynolds Price reads one of Milton's poems. The selections are apposite to the feeling of inwardness—of vital and passionate living—Father had always communicated.

In a hush William Styron mounts to the pulpit and begins to read from Sir Thomas Browne's *Hydriotaphia, Urne-Buriall, or, a Brief Discourse of the Sepulchrall Urnes Lately Found in Norfolk*. One sentence is, "'The long habit of living indisposeth us for dying'." After reading this sentence from the seventeenth century, Bill Styron pauses to explain that Father considered it to be one of the greatest understatements in the English language.

My *Reader's Digest* Stress Test score is well over the terminal 1,200 mark. I am still okay, released by the irrepressible lurch of tears. There is work to be done, a family tradition to be honored. I am beginning to understand an English sentence.

William Blackburn, Riding Westward

James Applewhite

Here in this mild, Septembral December, you have died.
Leaves from the black oaks litter our campus walks,
Where students move, or stand and talk, not knowing
Your wisdom's stature, illiterate in the book of your face.

So often we walked along the old stone wall at night,
Looked up at your window, where lamplight cleft your brow,
And knew you were suffering for us the thornier passages,
Transfixed by Lear, or staring ahead to the heart
Of Conrad's Africa. Sometimes we ventured inside,
To be welcomed by an excellent whiskey, Mozart's Requiem.
This clarity of music and ice revealed once in air
A poem as you read it: as Vaughan created "The World,"
Eternity's ring shining "calm as it was bright."

On a wall was the picture of you riding on a donkey,
Caught in mid-pilgrimage, to a holy land I do not remember.
But your missionary parents had birthed you in Persia,
And after we'd learned that we saw you as explorer;
From hometowns scattered on an American map marked

Terra incognita for the heart, you led treks
Into our inward countries, and still seem discovering before,
Through straits to "the Pacific Sea," or the "Eastern riches."
Left on these New World shores—so thoroughly possessed,
So waiting to be known—on all sides round we see
Great trees felled and lying, their bodies disjointed,
Or standing in all weather, broken, invaded by decay.

The worn landscape of your features, the shadows
Days had cast under eyes, were part of the night
That steadily encroaches on the eastward globe, as it rotates
In sunlight. Out of your age shone a gleam of youth,
Which seems with cedars' searing to sing in the forest
In wolf's ears of green flame.

                              Still, you are dead.
Your system is subject to entropy. Cells' change
Reduced your monarchical features to a kingship of chaos.
"With faltering speech, and visage incomposed,"
You said good night, between pangs of the withering hunger
Which filled your dying dreams of apples and cheeses.

In spite of the revolt of your closest ally, your body,
You died with the nobility you'd taught, and teaching, learned.
And now you roam my brain, King Lear after death.
The broken girl in your arms is only your spirit,
A poor fool hanged by Cordelia, by the straits of fever.

We visit your old office in grief.
Outside, trees lift winterward branches toward
A sky in chaos. The patterning which spins the stars
Exists outside this weather we live under.

We see only branches against those clouds' inclemency.[158]

A Memorial Letter

by Max Steele

William Blackburn taught a writing class at the University of North Carolina at Chapel Hill from 1970 to 1972. The letter below—from Max Steele to Wallace Kaufman, his colleague at U.N.C.—was read at the memorial service for Blackburn on December 17, 1972. William deBuys of Santa Fe, New Mexico, received his B.A. with highest honors in American Studies and honors in Creative Writing from U.N.C. His second book River of Traps, *one of three finalists for the 1991 Pulitzer Prize, combines memoir, biography, and photography.*

December 16,1972

Dear Wally:

Since you were his student at Duke and his colleague at Chapel Hill, I think it should naturally be you who read about his teaching on our campus. We can in no way claim him; but we can hope that the two years from 1970 to 1972 were a happy footnote to the history of his great teaching career at Duke.

To talk of William Blackburn's teaching at Duke is to talk generally in names of his students: Applewhite, Chappell, Davenport, Felker, Mac Hyman, Price, Tyler and Styron. To talk of his teaching at Carolina we must talk in terms of that one talented student who received his full devoted attention: William deBuys.

When Blackburn began here in Sept. 1970 I noted in a journal: "At lunch he seems disappointed. We've given him our best students but I'm afraid, though he doesn't say, he finds them difficult and sees no talent. . ."

But a late October entry says: "Blackburn at his jovial best at lunch. He mentions a manuscript by a young man named deBuys which is *extraordinary*. He can make that word roll so marvelously I can see how students have worked their hearts out to hear it."

A later entry says: "Blackburn has left deBuys' story on my desk. It is called 'Watching the Edge' and I'm inclined to agree with Daphne Athas that the writing is good but that the story is cold."

Over lunches that fall he mentioned the story and the superb rewrites deBuys was doing, how much more human the story was becoming, and began making plans for deBuys to take Honors in Writing with him in the spring and to work mainly on a novel. A January journal entry says: "Blackburn has found his student and on Thursdays when I pass his office I see them poring over pages, word by word, or Blackburn sitting back, that fine chin stuck straight out as if his collar were cutting, his eyes apparently closed, listening. He wants us to help deBuys obtain an extension of his Morehead Fellowship for a full semester of nothing but writing."

But in March there is a different sort of journal entry: "At lunch today Blackburn is perplexed. He sighs and often says, rhetorically, 'Well, Professor?' Finally he comes out with it. deBuys has handed him 40 pages, the first chapter, and Blackburn says. 'I'm sure it's brilliant. . .' (No one can make brilliant sound so brilliant and I'd rather have that one word from him than a gold medal from the State.) '. . . . but I haven't the *foggiest* notion what it's about.' He is to meet deBuys Tuesday to go over the pages."

The following Tuesday there was a note on my desk written late in the afternoon in that familiar handwriting: a scholarly print spaced out wide by a trembling hand: "deBuys tells me the 40 pages are from the viewpoint of a *dog*. The dog is apparently looking at a modern painting!"

When I saw him again the following week for lunch Blackburn seemed exhausted. Finally he said: "God knows he may be right. Who am I to say? But I just don't believe you can ask a reader to read 40 pages and not tell him he's in the mind of a *dog*." The entry continues: "Most of lunch he is silent but on the way back across campus, wielding his umbrella with the conservative authority of an Englishman, he stops suddenly. His head goes back and his down-slanting eyes shut and his face crumples like a baby's about to cry before that great laugh rolls out and he says in what Reynolds calls the archbishop voice: "Dammit, it's not even a very perceptive dog . . . . I mean, weeelll. . . ."

A week or so later there was a note from Blackburn saying deBuys was considering changing his viewpoint. The note ends: "I hope I have done the right thing."

The rest of the story is shorter and told in Blackburn's letter forwarded to the Morehead Foundation dated September 21, 1971:

I am pleased to write you about Mr. Wm. deBuys.

He has just rewritten his short story for the fifth or sixth time—"Watching the Edge"—and I have urged him to send it off . . . before his perfectionism gets the better of his good sense and he throws it in the wastepaper basket. In form and style he has indeed perfected it. It is the story of an old man, who clings to the slice of land he owns, who must of necessity, be moved into a rest home. It is told with great feeling for the human condition but also without a soft spot in it.

My judgment of the first version of his novel-in-progress was "brilliant but odd." His second first chapter was almost entirely different—less odd and mannered, more human and readable . . . Given his sensibility, his intuitive knowledge of human nature, and his command of language, I have high hopes for his novel.

High hopes but no promises. From a humanistic point of view it really doesn't matter whether he turns out, as the saying is, a publishable novel at all: he will have learned something about himself in the process of writing it—and that knowledge, I take it, is part, if not the end itself, of a liberal arts education.

All I am sure of at this point is that Mr. deBuys is among the best students who have come my way in a long career of teaching.

DeBuys's story was printed; his fellowship was extended; he worked exclusively with Blackburn for a year and is now in New Mexico completing the novel.

That is all of Blackburn's teaching story at Carolina. In July of this year he wrote from Magog, Canada: "Dear Max, I'm resigning my job at Chapel Hill as of August 31." The letter ends "I am just out of the hospital." In a note written Sept. 19th he returned the keys to the elevator and to his office. There were telephone calls but essentially that was all.

As his colleague, I do think it is of touching significance, Wally, that the semester ended Friday, December 8th and that he died Saturday, December 9th. Again, whether through long habit or through a lifetime sense of responsibility to students, he had made it through another semester to a final examination period.

All week I have been thinking of the short poem Helen Keller left on the desk of Ann Sullivan Macy, that woman who had led her out of darkness:

"Teacher?"
And yet again, "Teacher?"
And that is all.
And it will be my answer
When Death calls.

Always,

Max

A Feminist Perspective

During the years immediately before and just after the divorce of William and Elizabeth Blackburn in 1951, my mother sought reasons for the breakdown of the marriage by reading extensively in psychological studies then available. By far the most impressive of these studies, to her way of thinking, was Karen Horney's *Neurosis and Human Growth* (1950), in her copy of which she made marginal notes when passages struck her as applicable to "Bill & Tris."[159]

According to Horney, women incorporate their social devaluation as well as oppose it and internalize the values that presume female inferiority. This conflict produces neurosis, a term of derision in popular usage but not to Horney, who argued that the neurotic is a victim whose suffering is not an individual failure but the rational human response to a culture that is sick. Especially during the 1920s romantic love and marriage emphasized a woman's dependency on a man, but a "new" woman began to appear who was free to take on responsibility and to pursue self-improvement.

Two of the cultural prototypes described by Horney are the "proud perfectionist" and the "morbid dependent." Passages describing these types were underlined by Mother. In quoting them one needs to be on guard because Horney's generalizations are sometimes derived from somewhat extreme examples of "neurotics." Horney on the whole believed that people have the capacity to grow with others and in accordance with what she called "the real self."

The proud perfectionist:

> He should be the utmost of honesty, generosity, considerateness, justice, dignity, courage, unselfishness. He should be the perfect lover, husband, teacher. He should be able to endure everything, should like everybody, should love his parents, his wife, his country; or, he should not be attached to anything or anybody, nothing should matter to him, he should never feel hurt, and he should always be serene and unruffled. He should always enjoy life; or, he should be above pleasure and enjoyment. He should be spontaneous; he should always be in control of his feelings.

> The more he feels himself to be the measure of all things, the more he insists—not upon general perfection but upon his particular norms being measured up to. The failure of others to do so arouses his contempt or anger. Still more irrational is the fact that his own irritation with himself for not being, at any moment and under all conditions, what he should be may be turned outward. Thus, for instance, when he is not the perfect lover. . . he may turn angrily against those he failed and build up a case against them.

Mother underlined the following passage twice in red pencil:

> He is a past master in frustrating others—frustrating their small and big hopes, their needs for attention, reassurance, time, company, enjoyment.

> The need for triumph and the need to deny positive feelings,

both stemming from an unfortunate childhood situation, are thus, from the beginning, intimately interrelated. And they remain so because they reinforce each other. The hardening of feelings, originally a necessity for survival, allows for an unhampered growth of the drive for a triumphant mastery of life. But eventually this drive, with the insatiable pride that accompanies it, becomes a monster, more and more swallowing all feelings.

The morbid dependent:

The partner becomes the sole center of her existence. Everything revolves around him. Her mood depends upon whether his attitude toward her is more positive or negative. She does not dare make any plans lest she might miss a call or an evening with him. Her thoughts are centered on understanding or helping him. Her endeavors are directed toward measuring up to what she feels he expects. She has but one fear—that of antagonizing and losing him.

———————

The trouble may set in, full fledged, right at the beginning. But sometimes things look fairly auspicious for a while. In certain neurotic ways the two seem to fit together. He needs to be master; she needs to surrender. . . But sooner or later clashes are bound to occur between the two temperaments. . . which in all essentials are diametrically opposed. The main clashes occur on the issue of feelings, of "love." She insists upon love, affection, closeness. He is desperately afraid of positive feelings. Their display seems indecent to him.

———————

Her need for total surrender also makes it necessary to idealize the partner. Because she can find her unity only with somebody to whom she has delegated her pride, he should be the proud one and she the subdued.

Psychoanalysis does not have the last word about anybody, especially someone as complex as William Blackburn—a genius. Mother, who loved Father as Héloise loved Abélard, found little solace in reading Horney. The "analysis" nevertheless opens to inspection a shadow side of his personality.

The Conrad Letters

Father's teaching of Joseph Conrad's *Heart of Darkness* was a powerful experience for many of his students, who felt that they were taking a journey into themselves. What they didn't know was that their professor felt a special bond to Conrad: they were both in a sense "aliens," both terrified of debt, both at times powerless to produce even while their imaginations remained extremely active. Father especially admired Conrad's triumph over periods of depression and demoralization.

Father's ten-year search for Conrad letters was a personal as well as a scholarly triumph, culminating in 1958 with the publication of his edition of *Joseph Conrad: Letters to William Blackwood and David S. Meldrum*.

The following are excerpts from a staff article published in January 1959 in the *Duke Alumni Register*:

> Even if the career of an author is well documented, research often sheds new light on his work. Take the life of Joseph Conrad, for example. The outlines of the career of this Polish-English author are

well accounted for in available published documents. Yet certain letters between him and one of his publishers, found and edited by a Duke English professor, place a new emphasis on a particular segment of time in Conrad's dramatic and complex career—the years between 1897 and 1903, when he was producing some of his most enduring work.

These letters have been brought to light by Professor William M. Blackburn and their discovery recaptures a lost chapter in Conrad's writing career. They comprise correspondence between Conrad and his publisher, William Blackwood, head of the noted Edinburgh, Scotland, publishing firm of William Blackwood and Sons, and correspondence between Conrad and David S. Meldrum, who was literary advisor in the London office of the firm. It is, in fact, a three-way correspondence—Conrad to Blackwood, Blackwood to Conrad, and Meldrum to Blackwood—thus the letters give an insight not only into the personality and the problems of Conrad but also into the relationship between author and publisher at the turn of the century. Two portraits, other than that of Conrad, emerge from the letters, that of Blackwood, a shrewd but kindly editor, and that of Meldrum, one of the earliest of Conrad enthusiasts. . . . Of significance is the fact that the letters unearthed by Mr. Blackburn give the background of Conrad's writing *Lord Jim* and the volume of stories which includes "Heart of Darkness" and "Youth."

The interest of Mr. Blackburn in the letters of Conrad started about 10 years ago when Margery Gray Wynne, now in charge of the Rare Book Room, Yale University Library, informed him this library had 100 unpublished letters of Conrad's. With this beginning, Mr. Blackburn searched everywhere for letters, finally collecting copies of about 300 of them. When all these letters were put together, however, the collection seemed very miscellaneous indeed. It was not until he discovered Conrad's letters to Blackwood, a first batch (1897-1901) in the National Library of Scotland, then another batch (1900-1903) in the letter books of the firm in Edinburgh, that he began to feel that he had a collection unified enough to warrant publication. His discovery at Kirkcaldy, Scotland, in the summer of 1956 of 73 Conrad letters addressed to David Meldrum made a complete, coherent volume possible. . . .

"The survival," Mr. Blackburn points out in the preface, "is owing first of all to the strong historical sense of the firm, as well as to the happy accident of geography, namely that the House of William

Blackwood and Sons is to be found at 45 George St., Edinburgh. The files of many London publishers, including those in Blackwood's London office, went up in flames when Paternoster Row was leveled in the great fire raid of December 29-30, 1940. Other London publishers of Conrad, not situated on Paternoster Row, have felt obliged to get rid of their old correspondence for lack of storage space. But in Edinburgh the vast correspondence addressed to the firm since its inception in 1804 or to the editor of Blackwood's *Edinburgh Magazine* (Maga) since its beginning in 1817 has escaped the ravages of time and circumstance."

It wasn't an easy task to assemble the letters between Conrad, Blackwood and Meldrum. Many obstacles faced Mr. Blackburn and a less determined person might have given up the project. To cite one example, Wing Commander Douglas Blackwood, present head of the firm, was reluctant to let him copy the letters. "Once he decided to let me use them," Mr. Blackburn said, "he showed me every courtesy and kindness. I believe I was the first to ask to use the letters in the Blackwood letterbooks."

Mr. Blackburn found that Meldrum wrote from the London office to Edinburgh nearly every day during his tenure as literary advisor. In these letters he frequently told Blackwood of his having heard from Conrad. This fact led Mr. Blackburn to believe that letters from Conrad to Meldrum were in existence and the only problem was finding them.

"Accordingly," Mr. Blackburn related, "I searched out Meldrum's will in Edinburgh and found that his daughter Elizabeth was his literary executor. The next problem was finding out where Miss Meldrum lived. I wrote to the Town Clerk of Kirkcaldy, Fifeshire, Meldrum's birthplace, and asked if any of his kin still lived there. He replied that a Miss Meldrum lived at 5 Rosebery Terrace but did not identify her as Meldrum's daughter."

Mr. Blackburn wrote Miss Meldrum and explained his discoveries about Conrad in the Meldrum-Blackwood correspondence. He added that he would telephone her the following morning, as his ship was sailing to the United States within a few days.

When Mr. Blackburn telephoned, Miss Meldrum identified herself as Meldrum's daughter, said she had some letters addressed by Conrad to her father, but that they were personal letters and she did not imagine Mr. Blackburn could use them.

"I asked her not to decide the matter over the telephone," Mr.

Blackburn recalled. "Finally Miss Meldrum invited me to her home for tea, but once there I found her reluctant to let me use the letters—or even see them!"

After a pleasant tea and much talk of Conrad and of the friendship between him and Meldrum, Mr. Blackburn asked whether he might leave the Conrad-Blackwood letters with Miss Meldrum, suggesting that she please read them of the week end.

"On leaving the letters," Mr. Blackburn said, "I remarked that if she did not see how the letters to her father were in fact part of the Conrad-Blackwood correspondence, enriching it and completing it, then I would not press my request. When I returned a few days later I was delighted to have her entrust me with 73 new letters of Conrad's." These letters, one of the finest collections of Conrad letters in America, were bought by the Duke University Library.[160]

This account of Father's search for letters should dispel his early, self-deprecating image of a scholar's life as dull. It reads, in fact, like a short story by Henry James, or like the synopsis for a BBC production of "Masterpiece Theatre"—minus a murder mystery.

But the story is not complete. Father had tactfully omitted the real reason behind Miss Meldrum's reluctance to show him Conrad's letters to her father. As Father told the story to me, Conrad had alluded in his letters to the fact that Henry James and John Galsworthy had generously given him money to tide him over desperate times. Miss Meldrum, perhaps following instructions from her father but in any case acting upon a code whereby the gentlemen's gifts were to remain a secret, hesitated. After reading the Conrad-Blackwood correspondence, however, she discovered, as Father knew she would, that the secret was already known, whereupon she changed her mind.

The William Blackburn Literary Festival

During his career at Duke University, WMB often worked closely with *The Archive*, the undergraduate literary magazine that began publication in 1887. This collaboration evolved into The Literary Arts Celebration in 1959. It was renamed the Archive Festival in 1962, and again renamed the William Blackburn Literary Festival in 1969, as it is called to the present day. The following list of guest authors has been compiled by Benjamin Morris, Editor, *The Archive*, 2003-04. Currently unavailable from Duke records are dates and names omitted here.

1959: Randall Jarrell, William Styron, Burke Davis, Frances Gray Patton
1960: Richard Wilbur, Mac Hyman, Ovid W. Pierce, Lodwick Hartley, Helen Bevington
1961: Richard Eberhart, Hiram Haydn, Jessie Rehder, Reynolds Price
1962: Peter Taylor, Robert Watson, John Allen, Donald Sanford

1963: Eudora Welty, Reynolds Price, X.J. Kennedy

1964: Joan Williams, Robert Watson, Doris Betts, Fred Chappell

1965: George Garrett

1966: Romulus Linney

1967: Joseph Heller, Stephen Spender

1968: Robert Lowell, John Knowles

1969: Louis Simpson, W.D. Snodgrass

1970: Louis Simpson, W.D. Snodgrass, Tennessee Williams, Fred Chappell, James Applewhite

1971: Gregory Corso, Robert Creeley, William Styron, Willie Morris, Saul Bellow

1972: Richard Howard, John Barth, Anais Nin

1973: James Wright

1974: Margaret Atwood, Robert Penn Warren

1975: Willie Morris

1976: Stanley Kunitz

1978: Andrew Lytle, James Applewhite, Reynolds Price, Allan Gurganus, Elizabeth Bishop, Wallace Fowlie

1979: Howard Nemerov, Emmet Gowin, Ann Deagon, Allan Gurganus, Reynolds Price, James Applewhite, W.S. Merwin

1980: Allen Ginsberg, Reynolds Price, John Balaban, Richard Price, Bruce Davidson, Cliff Haac, John Menapace

1981: Fred Chappell, Reynolds Price, Maxine Kumin, James Applewhite, James Dickey

1982: Carolyn Forché, Galway Kinnell, Reynolds Price, James Applewhite, Toni Morrison

1983: Maya Angelou, Mark Strand, John Frederick Nims, James Applewhite, Reynolds Price

1984: James Laughlin, Joe Ashby Porter, Howard Moss, Willie Morris, Fred Chappell

1985: Bernard Malamud, John Irving, George Plimpton, Jonathan Williams, James Applewhite

1986: Joe Ashby Porter, Reynolds Price, Philip Levine, James Baldwin

1990: Toni Morrison

1992: Dave Smith, Clyde Edgerton, Lee Smith, Bobbie Ann Mason
Affiliated Conference: "Southern Writing and the Crisis of
Memory": Reynolds Price, Dan T. Carter, James Applewhite, Hal
Crowther, Anne Firor Scott, Julius S. Scott III
Affiliated Conference: "Language and Memory": Ron Butters, Jaki
Shelton Green, Karla Holloway, Derek Walcott
1993: Carlos Fuentes
1994: Leslie Marmon Silko
1995: Judith Ortiz Cofer
1996: Robert Coover, John Ashbery, Joyce Carol Oates
1997: Li-Young Lee, Ariel Dorfman, Frank Lentricchia, Eve Sedgwick,
Deborah Pope, Joe Ashby Porter, James Applewhite
1998: Marge Piercy, Michael Ondaatje, Ariel Dorfman, Lucille Clifton,
Philip Shabazz, James Seay, Alan Shapiro
Tribute to William Blackburn (reading): Elizabeth Cox, Deborah
Pope, Melissa Malouf, Reynolds Price, James Applewhite
1999: Lucille Clifton, Joyce Carol Oates, Marilyn Chin, Sharon Olds,
Elizabeth Spencer, Elizabeth Cox, Melissa Malouf, Joe Ashby Por-
ter, Reynolds Price, Jonathan Cullen, Frank Lentricchia, Susannah
Waters, Khaled Mattawa
2000: Barry Lopez, Amy Hempel, Andrea Selch, Joe Ashby Porter,
Maxine Kumin, Fred Chappell, James Applewhite
2001: Ron Hansen, Joe Ashby Porter, Reynolds Price, tribute to
Gwendolyn Brooks (with the Blue Roach)
2002: Michael Malone, Joe Donahue, Elizabeth Cox, W.S. Merwin,
Don DeLillo
Panel Discussion on Literary Translation: W.S. Merwin, Reynolds
Price, Carol Flath, Peter Burian, Erdag Goknar
2003: Robert Morgan, Michael Cunningham, Betty Adcock, Richard
Ford
2004: James Applewhite, Orson Scott Card, Joyce Carol Oates, Alice
Walker

Notes

Abbreviations Used

ALB	Alexander Lambert Blackburn
ECB	Elizabeth Cheney Blackburn
WMB	William Maxwell Blackburn

Epigraph

Joseph Campbell, *The Mythic Dimension: Selected Essays, 1959-1987* (San Francisco: Harper San Francisco, 1997), 185.

1. Legacy

1. Letter from ECB to ALB, 24 March 1950.
2. See Leo Marx, *The Machine in the Garden: Technology and the Pastoral Ideal in America* (New York: Oxford University Press, Galaxy Books, 1967), 3.
3. Robert Cushman, quoted in Larzer Ziff, *Puritanism in America: New Culture in a New World* (New York: Viking Press, 1973), 41.

2. Sketches of Father

4. On the side of Malvina Sarah Black Gist Waring, WMB's maternal grandmother, there is apparently a line of descent from John Howland that, according to the late George S. Blackburn, can be traced through "The Book of Hinman." Robert M. Hill has traced the line of descent from George Washington's grandfather, as follows: Joseph Ball (1649-1711) first married Elizabeth Romney; from their daughter Ann, the line goes through George Conway, Edwin Conway, Sarah Ewell, and John Blair Black, father of Malvina. Joseph Ball's second wife was Mary Montague (Johnson); they were Washington's grandparents.

5. WMB was eldest of the four children. George Stebbins B. (1901-1988) graduated from Yale in 1926 and devoted his career to teaching French in small private schools. Malvina ("Mallie") B. (1905-1995) began a career as a nurse; she married Archibald Robertson of Louisville, Kentucky, in 1934, and after their divorce worked as a secretary in government offices in Washington, D.C., until retirement. Clark Waring B. (1908-2003), after graduating from Yale, earned an M.A. in social work from the School of Applied Social Sciences, Case Western Reserve University in Cleveland. He directed Family Service agencies in Plainfield, New Jersey, Hartford, Connecticut, and Minneapolis, Minnesota; from 1952 to 1974 he was general director of the Family Service Association of America, now known as the Alliance for Children and Families. Clark directed a federation of over 330 family counseling agencies in the United States and Canada, with headquarters in New York. For further details see Daisy Hernandez, "Clark Waring Blackburn, Who Promoted Family Counseling, Dies at 94," *New York Times*, 26 January 2003.

6. For a university to associate itself with what has come to be called "creative writing" was something of a novelty in the 1930s and 1940s; for a university press to publish creative work by students and faculty was virtually unheard of. Duke University Press published three volumes of such work, all edited by WMB, *One and Twenty: Duke Narrative and Verse, 1924-1945* (1945), *Under Twenty-five: Duke Narrative and Verse, 1945-1962* (1963), and *A Duke Miscellany: Narrative and Verse of the Sixties* (1970).

7. The subject of WMB's 1943 doctoral dissertation at Yale was a painstakingly annotated edition of Matthew Arnold's *Literature and Dogma*. A few chapters were thereafter published in *Modern Philology* XLIII (1945): 130-39; *Philological Quarterly* XXV (1946): 70-78; and *Modern Language Quarterly* IX (1948): 199-207. WMB's pioneering scholarship was recognized in 1968 with the appearance of R.H. Super's edition of *Dissent and Dogma*, vol. VI of *The Complete Prose Works of Matthew Arnold* (Ann Arbor: University of Michigan Press).

8. WMB edited *Joseph Conrad: Letters to William Blackwood and David S. Meldrum* (Durham: Duke University Press, 1958). For an account of his discovery of the letters, see Appendix B.

9. WMB edited *Love, Boy: The Letters of Mac Hyman* (Baton Rouge: Louisiana State University Press, 1969).

10. See Larzer Ziff, *Puritanism in America*, 5, 14, 121, 199.

11. "[A]s respectfully as he could, without parade or remonstrance, he took a human being's privilege to fashion his inner life for himself": Edmund Gosse, *Father and*

Son (London: Penguin Books, 1949), 250. Sir Edmund's central thesis is that Puritan theology is an unwholesome influence on human life.

12. "William Maxwell Blackburn," in *Dictionary of American Biography*, vol. I (New York: Charles Scribner's Sons, 1927), 317-18.

13. Conversation of ALB with Clark W. Blackburn in Littleton, Colorado, 28 March 2002.

14. When Sherman's army burned the city of Columbia one night in February 1865, the house at 1428 Laurel Street was set on fire three times by burning torches being thrown on the shingled roof. Each time the house was saved with little damage. Four years later, Clark Waring and his wife, Malvina, moved into the house; their five children were born there, and the house eventually became the property of Elizabeth Waring McMaster. It was torn down in the early 1980s to create an asphalt parking lot.

15. See A.V. Williams Jackson, *Persia Past and Present: A Book of Travel and Research* (New York: Macmillan Company, 1906) 88-90, 102-3. Jackson was in Urumiah when Father was four years old.

16. Amy Blackburn's letters home, some apparently published in Columbia newspapers, were collected, typed, and mimeographed by Mallie B. Robertson. They describe the journey from the Black Sea to Urumiah, the welcome there on 23 September 1896, and customs she observed during the next six weeks. When Amy was ninety-three years old, she revealed in conversation with ALB the stories of her breast-feeding, of her enthusiasm for Mount Ararat, and of transportation by ox-cart. George S. Blackburn also in conversation with ALB remembered the ox-cart. It seems likely that it was employed in 1904 during the Blackburns' return journey from Urumiah.

17. WMB quoted in Marcia Norcross, "William Blackburn," *The Archive (Literary Quarterly of the Students of Duke University)* 62:2 (January 1949): 20. On the murder of Benjamin Woods Labaree, see "Benjamin Labaree," *Who Was Who in America*, vol. I.

18. Ben Robertson, *Red Hills and Cotton: An Upcountry Memory* (Columbia: University of South Carolina Press, 1960), 7, 10-11, 32-33, 34, 126-27. I have selected passages that by inference may shed light upon WMB's personality.

19. WMB, "Sketches for a Memoir," *Duke Alumni Register* 58 (1973): 18-21. In presenting this memoir for publication, Reynolds Price also states a belief that it was written in 1948. The date is significant because WMB at that time was experiencing an emotional crisis and may have been seeking to reestablish his identity by means of memory.

3. Tris

20. Donald Ogden Stewart, Class of 1916, Yale, and a member of the Skull & Bones Society (with fellow writers H. Phelps Putnam and Archibald MacLeish as well as with Farwell Knapp), met ECB when he was living in her mother's New York apartment in 1921. His career was about to be launched through introductions to Edmund Wilson and F. Scott Fitzgerald. By 1924 in Paris he became part of a literary group that included Ernest Hemingway. In his autobiography, Stewart refers to a "new girl"—ECB:

I had a new girl. Or, at least, I undeservedly had a wonderful girl who loved me, and with whom I "necked" shamelessly in the best *This Side of Paradise* tradition. The fact that she really loved me quite desperately was hard on her, but very good for my own *amour propre* which had never experienced anything like this before. Or, let us say, the 1920s were enthusiastically letting down the bars everywhere, and by playing the role of a Fitzgerald character I found the girls were willing to listen to my suggestion of a romp in a taxi without becoming insulted—or (which was my worst fear) laughing. But the romp never crossed the borderlines, perhaps because of my old-fashioned Yale ideals, but more because of my fear of rejection. I had, however, discovered a wonderful hotel on Broadway where you told a Negro elevator boy that you had come to call on Mrs. Haviland, and up you went. (*By a Stroke of Luck! An Autobiography*, with a note by Katharine Hepburn, New York: Paddington Press Ltd., 1975, 102-3.)

ECB noted in the margin of her copy of this book, next to the cavalier revelation about "Mrs. Haviland," "I knew nothing of this. It would have cured my admiration for him instantly." Ella Winter, widow of Lincoln Steffens (d. 1936) and Stewart's last wife, paints an engaging portrait of him in *And Not to Yield: An Autobiography* (New York: Harcourt, Brace & World, Inc., 1963).

21. ECB in conversation with ALB revealed the anecdote about *The Varieties of Religious Experience*. She never read it.

22. ECB's sister Helen ("Hen") inspired jealousy in ECB. Her cousin Harriet Cowles was daughter of Will Cowles, a West Coast publisher, and made her home in a Spanish-style mansion atop Eucalyptus Hill in Santa Barbara, California.

23. This is probably "Sock and Buskin," a junior-senior dramatic club that became a regular feature of Manchester High School. Its first vice president and Mother's lifelong friend was F. Cowles Strickland, who later directed plays in New York, Washington, and St. Louis, and was a pioneer in summer theater work. In 1956 when he was head of the Speech and Drama Department of Stanford University, he published a 300-page book, *The Technique of Acting*. "Stricky" encouraged Mother in her theatrical talents and was an invaluable friend during her lonely years at the school.

24. "The Lamp Beside the Golden Door" (completed in 2002), typescript, 157-59. In its unpublished form it has been awarded the 2003 International PeaceWriting Prize.

25. Letter of WMB to ECB, 29 February 1928, is affectionate even though in the passage quoted here his stereotyping of the relationship—dull scholar meets Lost Generation flapper—suggests genuine vacillation of feelings.

26. *Tomorrow Magazine* purchased but for unexplained reasons never published ECB's tightly written short story about a grand old lady's attempt to cover up the dark side of her deceased husband's character. The story may have been inspired by some incident in the life of ECB's Cheney grandmother. WMB may have been discomfited by psychologizing about a shadow personality.

27. "Paid this day for lumber," quoted in Alice Farley Williams, *Silk & Guns: The Life of a Connecticut Yankee, Frank Cheney, 1817-1904* (Manchester, Conn.: The Manchester

Historical Society, 1996), 5, from an account book dated 1784. The house may have been begun at an earlier date or completed, as I suggest, a year later. Cheney Hall, not to be confused with the Homestead, was built by Cheney Brothers as a community center and theater in 1867.

28. For a general history, see Mathias Spiess and Percy W. Bidwell, *History of Manchester, Connecticut* (S. Manchester, Conn.: Centennial Committee of the Town of Manchester, 1924). Source material about the Cheney family is compiled from the following: Ednah Dow Cheney, *Memoir of Seth W. Cheney, Artist* (Boston: Lee & Shepard, 1881) and *Memoir of John Cheney, Engraver* (Boston: Lee & Shepard, 1889); Helen Cheney Bayne, "Some Memories of 'The K.Ds,' an Old Fashioned Family" (typescript, 140 pp., 1914); Elizabeth Dow Leonard, *A Few Reminiscences of My Exeter Life*, edited by Edward C. Echols (Exeter, N.H.: The 2x4 Press, 1972); Margreta Swenson Cheney, *If All the Great Men: The Cheneys of Manchester*, 57 pp., 1975; Antoinette Cheney Crocker, *Parents and Children: A Family Vignette* (Concord, Mass.: 1984); Alice Farley Williams, *Silk & Guns*. ECB's marginalia in her copy of *If All the Great Men* are invaluable amendments and additions.

29. The main sources are F.O. Matthiessen, *Russell Cheney (1881-1945): A Record of His Work* (New York: Oxford University Press, 1947) and Louis Hyde, ed., *Rat & the Devil: Journal Letters of F. O. Matthiessen and Russell Cheney* (Hamden, Conn.: Archon Books, 1978). A useful article is Ina Sizer Cassidy, "Russell Cheney," *New Mexico Magazine*, March 1935, 26, 39.

30. Hugh Aiken Bayne's unpublished memoirs exist in three bound typescript volumes, i.e., copies were made for each of his children. Sentimental and pretentious, the memoirs are nevertheless a valuable record of a colorful life. During his lifetime many people found him charming and defended his exhibitionism as that of a genial and generous soul. ECB, ALB, and Farwell Knapp were among those aware of his flaws.

31. After graduating from Yale in 1916, Farwell Knapp went to Harvard Law School, a fact which scandalized family devotees of Yale, and practiced law in Hartford. His marriage to "Hen," ECB's sister, was a happy one, but he died young, leaving Hen to raise two daughters, Emily (Mrs. Donald Pitkin) and Betsy (Mrs. Peter Packard).

32. Excerpts from "Putnam Battle Cry" and from "Words of an Old Woman" are from *The Collected Poems of H. Phelps Putnam*, edited by Charles R. Walker with a foreword by Edmund Wilson (New York: Farrar, Straus & Giroux, 1971). This edition contains a reprint of F.O. Matthiessen's critical essay, "To the Memory of Phelps Putnam." On his early reputation see Paul Rosenfeld, "An Affirmative Romantic: Phelps Putnam," *Bookman* (March 1932): 607-13, from which I partially quote ("Putnam's verse has the force of purity, a trumpet-like forthrightness, an iron clangour"). ECB, in a letter to James P. Gelatt, 9 September 1975, wrote: "'Phelpie' was indeed my friend and we shared a home in Colorado Springs the winter of 1918 along with my mother, my uncle Russell Cheney, the artist, and my cousin Alfred Cowles Jr." Because Uncle Russell was being treated for tuberculosis at the Cragmor Sanitarium in Colorado Springs, Putnam came there and sought care for the asthma that was afflicting him and that would eventually destroy his creative energy.

33. ECB's marginal notes in her copy of Karen Horney, *Neurosis and Human Growth*

(New York: W.W. Norton & Company, 1950), 194, indicate her belief that Stewart and Bayne represented a "type." See Appendix A.

34. A carbon copy of this letter from H.Phelps Putnam to Helen Bayne, 8 November 1921, was discovered by ALB in 2002 folded inside ECB's copy of Stewart's novel, *Mr and Mrs Haddock Abroad.*

35. I am indebted to Betsy Packard for these details of upper-class behavior.

36. The story of "The Wee-Wee's" (also known as "The Annies") was hand-written by ECB inside her copy of Margreta Swenson Cheney's *If All the Great Men.* The story of ECB's wedding is told by her in a letter to the Manchester Historical Society, September 1973.

4. Crying Hither

37. See William Kenneth Boyd, *The Story of Durham: City of the New South* (Durham: Duke University Press, 1927).

38. Edmund Wilson's disdain for Greece and the description of the Bull Durham tobacco factory are noted by Helen Bevington, *Along Came the Witch: A Journal in the 1960s* (New York and London: Harcourt Brace Jovanovich, 1976), 171, 192.

39. Doris Betts, *Souls Raised from the Dead* (New York: Alfred A. Knopf, 1994).

40. William Kenneth Boyd, *The Story of Durham*, 60, 159.

41. See Hugh Talmadge Lefler and Albert Ray Newsome, *North Carolina: The History of a Southern State*, rev. ed. (Chapel Hill: University of North Carolina Press, 1963), 567.

42. WMB assumed responsibility for his siblings, in effect taking on his father's role. He and ECB helped Clark to complete his education—a loan promptly repaid—and he and Clark gave financial assistance to Mallie throughout her life.

43. See WMB, "An Awareness of the Arts: An Essay in Retrospect," *Duke Alumni Register* 49:4 (April 1963): 5-9. In this essay he expresses his conviction that the arts are necessary for an understanding of "the human predicament." He is scathing in his attitude toward Puritanism: "Indifference to the arts finds its ultimate historical source in the Protestant ethos, namely, the conviction that art, if not downright immoral, is at best a decoration to life and therefore a luxury for which a pioneering society can discover neither inclination nor time."

44. A Durham fictionalized as "Poe's Hill" appears, "located" west of Durham, in *The Cold War of Kitty Pentecost* (Chicago: Swallow Press, 1979) and in "The Lamp Beside the Golden Door." A fictionalized Duke appears in these novels as "South Atlantic University." Such links notwithstanding, the novels are not romans à clef.

45. ALB, *The Cold War of Kitty Pentecost*, 51, 100-102, 213, 215. Completed in first draft in 1968, revised in 1975, it was published by agreement between a fiction collective, Writers West Books, and Swallow Press in 1979. It was subsequently sold and distributed by Swallow Press/Ohio University Press.

46. While ECB was in New York awaiting birth of their first child, WMB wrote her every day from Durham. The letters of October 2, 3, 4, 5, and 7 in 1927 were treasured by ECB; if there were others, she didn't keep them. A portion of the letters is published in ALB, *Creative Spirit* (Berkeley: Creative Arts Book Company, 2001), 40-44.

47. Now torn down, 303 Swift Avenue stood on the north side of an unpaved road connecting Duke's East and West Campus sites.

48. Clarence Gohdes, *Pioneers in English at Trinity and Duke*, a 51-page booklet published in 1988, gives a detailed history of the English Department and its faculty, but the socializing of these professors and their wives is what I observed. The "circle" for home parties included Newman Ivey and Marie White, Lewis and Frances Gray Patton, Clarence and Celestine Gohdes, Merle and Helen Bevington, and Ashbel Brice, and from outside the department Loring and Suzanne Walton, Karl and Ann Zener, Douglas and Frances Hill, Fred and Mollie Bernheim, and Mildred Hendrix. Other close friends such as Banks and Louisa Rhine were not party-goers. WMB also gave parties for his students and for junior faculty, as well as for visiting writers (Elizabeth Bowen, Malcolm Cowley, et al). Altogether, WMB gathered about him a brilliant circle, something of a rarity because its members did not behave as an academic or political clique nor as a salon of movers and shakers.

49. ECB's handwritten "book" about and for ALB exists in a single copy. Intended as an intimate record, it can be taken as a reliable index of her struggle for self-esteem.

50. I learned this bit of folklore from Juliana Busbee of Jugtown, North Carolina.

51. Letter from ECB to ALB, 21 March 1950: "Your Grandmother and Great-Grandmother both kept copies of Marcus Aurelius on their bedside tables and read him as the Blackburns and Warings read their Bibles." ECB was at this time discovering just how stoical she herself had become.

52. The professor's ideas found their way into print. See George E. Dimock, Jr., "The Name of Odysseus," in *Homer: A Collection of Critical Essays*, edited by George Steiner and Robert Fagles (Englewood Cliffs, N.J.: Prentice-Hall, 1962), 106-21.

53. *King Lear*, 4. 6. 180.

54. See Tony Tanner, *The Reign of Wonder: Naivety and Reality in American Literature* (Cambridge: Cambridge University Press, 1965).

55. "Ecclesiastes is the fine hammered steel of woe," from Herman Melville, *Moby-Dick, or, The Whale*, edited by Luther S. Mansfield and Howard P. Vincent (New York: Hendricks House, 1952), 422.

56. Richard Harris published two lengthy and carefully researched articles about the history of Medicare in *The New Yorker* 42:19 (2 July 1966) and 42:20 (9 July 1966). I quote from the first article, p. 30.

57. "To what base uses we may return, Horatio! Why may not imagination trace the noble dust of Alexander, till a' find it stopping a bung-hole?" (*Hamlet*, 5. 1. 197-99).

58. Outraged by Bayne's behavior, Farwell Knapp bluntly told his father-in-law that he was offering a bribe to satisfy his own vanity.

59. Matthew Arnold, "Dover Beach," ll. 14, 17-18, 33-34.

60. "Hell is empty, And all the devils are here": *The Tempest*, 1, 2, 213-14.

5. Chaotic Splendor

61. Patricia Hampl, *Spillville* (Minneapolis: Milkweed Editions, 1987), 31. Hampl develops a theme of "falling on the breast of existence, knowing it will bear you up"

(p. 32) while discussing the 1893 visit of Antonín Dvorák to the Czech community of Spillville, Iowa.

62. Robinson Jeffers, "Credo," ll. 16-18.
63. See William Kenneth Boyd, *The Story of Durham*, 5-7. The Occaneechi belonged to the Siouan family and came to be known as the Dakotas (or Lakotas). The Eno Indians, in custom and religion like the Pueblos of the Southwest, established a village on the Eno River, Adshusheer, probably located six miles west of Durham. I give a general account without distinction between Occaneechi and Eno.
64. *The Cold War of Kitty Pentecost*, 3-4.
65. Flannery O'Connor, quoted in Stanley Edgar Hyman, *Flannery O'Connor* (Minneapolis: University of Minnesota Press, 1966), 44.
66. William Faulkner, *Absalom, Absalom!* (New York: Vintage Books, 1972), 122.
67. Dylan Thomas, quoted in Andrew Sinclair, *Dylan Thomas: No Man More Magical* (New York: Holt, Rinehart & Winston, 1975), 227-29.
68. Letter of ALB to Mary April Blackburn, 2 May 1935.
69. Translated from the French by ALB, Gustave Flaubert, *Correspondence* (Paris: Louis Conard, 1926-33), III, 61.
70. Letter of ECB to Cheney relative, "Auntie Neppie," 9 July 1935.
71. Michel de Montaigne, *The Complete Essays*, translated and edited by M.A. Screech (New York: Penguin Books USA, 1991), 8.
72. Letter of ECB to Helen Cheney Bayne, 10 January 1934.

6. Whiskey-Wow-Wow!

73. William Bradford, *Of Plymouth Plantation 1620-1647* (New York: Alfred A. Knopf, 1952), 59.
74. In any edition of *Moby-Dick* this sentence appears in the first paragraph of the first chapter.
75. The story of the hurricane is partly based upon ECB's letter to Amy Blackburn, 11 September 1935, published in *Creative Spirit*, 44-48.
76. See Hugh Talmadge Lefler and Albert Ray Newsome, *North Carolina: The History of a Southern State*, 3-11.
77. See Lee Miller, *Roanoke: Solving the Mystery of the Lost Colony* (New York: Penguin Books, 2002). Miller makes a convincing argument for the survival and enslavement of the colonists.
78. *Slow Train to Yesteryear* and *That Old-Time Religion* were Archibald Robertson's most popular books.

7. Home

79. See Betsy Holloway, *A Proud History: Durham, North Carolina: The Story of George Watts School* (Orlando, Fla.: Persimmon Press, 1998), 23-26. For further details about George Watts School, I have consulted pp. xiv, 5, 10, 13, 17, 27, 28, 42, 44-50, 51-55, 90.
80. Montaigne, *The Complete Essays*, 122.

81. *The Cold War of Kitty Pentecost*, 209.

82. Following service in Vietnam, Yusef Komunyakaa enrolled in the College of Letters, Arts & Sciences of the University of Colorado, Colorado Springs, in 1973 only a new, small institution with about 1,200 students. Then recently hired to develop courses in creative writing, I read Yusef's poems (perhaps a hundred of them, a few already published) and invited him to join my writing class. It was clear from the start that I had little to teach him, so extraordinary was his gift, but for the next two years I did what I could to encourage him to pursue postgraduate studies in writing. It was no coincidence that I founded *Writers' Forum* in March 1974: Yusef had given me permission to publish dozens of his poems, and I had little doubt that they would earn him recognition from John Williams and John Edgar Wideman, who had been invited to judge the contents of the first volume. Yusef went to Colorado State University to study for his M.A. degree under the tutelage of the poet Bill Tremblay; in Fort Collins he was discovered by Gwendolyn Brooks, who told me, "Yusef is the finest young Black poet in America."

83. I remember being shown by a sixth-grader his collection of "funny-paper" favorites such as Maggie and Jiggs "performing" sexually.

84. Frances Gray Patton's first "Miss Dove" short story was published in *The New Yorker* in 1947.

85. *The Cold War of Kitty Pentecost*, 25-26.

86. Keats, "On First Looking into Chapman's Homer," ll. 9-10.

87. Outward shows of affection and the use of terms of endearment were usually missing from William Blackburn's family in spite of Mother's protests.

8. Away School

88. William James chided his brother Henry for living in England because he suffered from "the skinniness and aridity of America," phrase quoted in R.W.B. Lewis, *The Jameses: A Family Narrative* (New York: Farrar, Straus & Giroux, 1991), 367. Having lived in England, 1956-57, 1959-60, 1961-63, and 1965-73, I must say I never considered my residence as an exile. Moreover, having lived in the West since 1973, I do not share the Eastern view of it as a cultural backwater. Like WMB, however, I deplore American anti-intellectualism and indifference to the arts.

89. ALB, *The Myth of the Picaro: Continuity and Transformation of the Picaresque Novel, 1554-1954* (Chapel Hill: The University of North Carolina Press, 1979).

90. Inés Dölz was born in Santiago, Chile, 18 December 1935, and graduated with B.A. and M.A. degrees from the Universidad de Chile before coming to the United States in 1961 to Saint Mary's College, University of Notre Dame, South Bend, Indiana, where she was invited to teach Spanish language and literature. She subsequently completed her Ph.D. degree in Latin American literature at the University of Colorado at Boulder and is the author of numerous books and articles in that field. When she joined the faculty of the University of Colorado at Colorado Springs in 1975, we met and married.

91. Pierre Teilhard de Chardin, *The Future of Man*, translated from the French by Norman Denny (New York: Harper & Row, 1969), 124.

92. Richard Hofstadter, *Anti-intellectualism in American Life* (New York: Vintage Books, 1963), 341-42.

93. Washington Irving, "The Legend of Sleepy Hollow," in *Washington Irving: Selected Prose*, edited by Stanley T. Williams (New York: Holt, Rinehart & Winston, 1966), 165.

94. *Romeo and Juliet*, I. 5. 44-46.

95. Robert Frost, "The Road Not Taken," ll. 14-15.

96. Joseph Campbell, *An Open Life* (Burdett, N.Y.: Larson Publications, 1988), 24.

97. Richard Hofstadter, *Anti-intellectualism in American Life*, 356.

98. ALB, *Suddenly a Mortal Splendor* (Dallas: Baskerville, 1995), 145-47.

9. Things Fall Apart

99. See Delavan L. Pierson, *The Sunday School Times*, 1 December 1945, pp. 955-56, obituary of George C. Stebbins. I am also indebted to Dr. Philip Blackburn for information about Stebbins's career and musical composition. The long and much publicized association of Stebbins with evangelists Moody and Sankey gave him exalted status in the eyes of WMB's parents.

100. See Lionel Trilling, *Matthew Arnold* (New York: Columbia University Press, 1949), 266.

101. From Matthew Arnold's *Culture and Anarchy*, quoted in ibid, 268.

102. Yale Professor Chauncey Brewster Tinker, an influence on WMB at graduate school, was the author of *The Poetry of Matthew Arnold* (New York: Oxford University Press, 1940).

103. Matthew Arnold, *Culture and Anarchy*, ed. J. Dover Wilson (Cambridge: Cambridge University Press, 1960), 70.

104. Arnold, "Dover Beach," ll. 35-37.

105. William Butler Yeats, "The Second Coming," ll. 3-4.

106. A.E. Housman, "When I Was One-and-Twenty," line 1.

107. WMB, "Flight to Firenze," *The American Oxonian* (April 1946), 90, 93, 95, 96. WMB's feeling for the city of Florence was enhanced through a friendship with the Marquesa della Robbia whom he met when he was employed by University Command. She belonged to the family famed since the Renaissance for its artists and sculptors.

108. Paul Boyer, *By the Bomb's Early Light: American Thought and Culture at the Dawn of the Atomic Age* (New York: Pantheon Books, 1985), xv, xvi.

109. Many of my Yale classmates who had not previously served in the armed forces were either conscripted soon after graduation or were commissioned or joined the C.I.A. I volunteered as a private in the Regular Army in July 1951. Following basic training at Camp Gordon, Georgia, in the Signal Corps, instead of being sent to the combat zone in Korea, I was "frozen" as a weapons instructor and thus came to be ordered to Nevada as an observer of an atomic test. In 1952, I spent six months in New Jersey at Signal Corps O.C.S., was briefly assigned to supply school at Fort Holabird, Maryland, and later served in Fort Bragg, North Carolina, as a psychological warfare officer until the end of the Korean War, whereupon I was honorably discharged. Operation Desert Rock was the first atomic

test in which large numbers of soldiers (mostly officers) were involved. We observed the test from a distance of six miles. No "dirty" bomb was used—as contrasted with subsequent tests in Nevada.

110. *The Cold War of Kitty Pentecost*, 177-78.

111. These names have been fictionalized to serve dramatic purpose. "Mountain Man" represented a way of life that I would increasingly find appealing. On my second western trip, the summer of 1950, I stayed as a guest at his home in Seattle. I was in Nevada for Operation Desert Rock late in October 1951, and in the summer of 1956 toured the entire West by automobile; in 1964 I briefly explored coastal California. When I moved to Colorado in 1973, I felt sufficiently informed about and attuned to the West to establish *Writers' Forum* as an outlet for contemporary western literature.

112. The West "has a shine on it; despite its mistakes, it isn't tired": Wallace Stegner, *The Sound of Mountain Water* (Garden City, N.J.: Doubleday & Company, 1969), 37.

113. WMB left home on 11 January 1948. I was not informed.

114. WMB's project, a textbook on the English poets, was rejected suddenly by Houghton Mifflin.

115. WMB's words are quoted exactly from memory.

116. Letter of ALB to ECB, 12 April 1948. On the psychiatrist Dr. Agnes Greig, see Note 146.

10. The Education

117. Feodor Dostoevsky, *Crime and Punishment*, translated by Jessie Coulson (New York and London: W. W. Norton & Company, 1989), 390 (Part 6, Chapter 2). One of WMB's axioms was that writers have to suffer in order to have something to say. He did not, of course, have the crime and penitence of Raskolnikov in mind. I was torn—at college and for many years thereafter—between the material benefits of education and the spiritual benefits of the experience that leads to effective writing.

118. ECB to ALB, 8 June 1948, and 19 January 1949.

119. Letters of ALB to ECB, 19 June 1949, and 26 June 1949.

120. Willa Cather, *My Ántonia* (Boston: Houghton Mifflin, 1918), 7-8.

121. Wordsworth, *Book IV, The Prelude, or Growth of a Poet's Mind* (text of 1805), ll. 150-52. An English teacher at Phillips Academy, when I was seventeen, had assigned us pupils to buy and to read *The Prelude* in its entirety.

122. See W.Y. Evans-Wentz, *Cuchama and Sacred Mountains*, edited by Frank Waters and Charles L. Adams (Athens: Swallow Press/ Ohio University Press, 1982).

123. David Bohm, *Wholeness and the Implicate Order* (London and Boston: Routledge & Kegan Paul, 1981), 2.

124. Preparing for Comprehensive Exams in English at Yale, I steeped myself in New Criticism by means of a thorough study of Cleanth Brooks, *The Well-Wrought Urn: Studies in the Structure of Poetry* (1947).

125. "Among contemporary poets, European or American, Jeffers is unique in that he has been the only one to project and sustain a truly cosmic vision of man, induct

a whole cosmology, as Homer and Dante and Milton did before him." —William Everson, *Robinson Jeffers: Fragments of an Older Fury* (Oyez, 1968), 3.

126. In 1951 Professor Van Baumer summarized the modern age exclusively in terms of "anxiety" and "un-reason." Almost twenty-five years later he recognized that not all twentieth-century philosophers of history are pessimistic. He included a selection from Teilhard de Chardin's *The Phenomenon of Man* in the third revised edition of his *Main Currents of Western Thought* (New York: Alfred A. Knopf, 1974).

127. See *Creative Spirit*, 204-6.

11. Meet the Professor

128. Gilbert Highet, *The Art of Teaching* (London: Methuen, 1963), 203.

129. Ibid, 27.

130. Quoted in Marguerite Hays, "William Blackburn: Teacher of Writers," *Furman Magazine* 19 (Spring 1972): 28.

131. William Styron, quoted in James L. W. West III, *William Styron: A Life* (New York: Random House, 1988), 96. The chapter is entitled, "Duke and William Blackburn," 93-108.

132. William Styron, *This Quiet Dust and Other Writings* (New York: Random House, 1982), 253-54, 256.

133. Mac Hyman achieved fame and financial success with the publication in 1954 of his phenomenal bestseller, *No Time for Sergeants*. It is happily worth noting that his daughter, Gwyn Hyman Rubio, is author of *Icy Sparks* (1998), a best-selling novel selected by Oprah's Book Club.

134. Guy Davenport, review of *Love, Boy* in the *New York Times Book Review* (4 January 1970), 8.

135. During the winter and spring of 1956 John and Margaret Farrar led a group of aspiring writers at weekly meetings in New York. I had been introduced to the Farrars by the family of Hervey Allen whose book, *Anthony Adverse*, had been published by the firm of Farrar & Rinehart.

136. Reynolds Price, quoted in Marguerite Hays, "William Blackburn: Teacher of Writers," 28-29.

137. WMB, quoted in ibid, 24. On Chappell's recollection of the relationship, see Georgann Eubanks, "Fred Chappell: The Bard of Canton," *Duke Magazine* (November-December 1972): 10.

138. Fred Chappell, quoted in Hays, 29.

139. Letter of Mac Hyman to Max Steele, 7 February 1963, in WMB, *Love, Boy*, 223-24.

140. James L. W. West III and August J. Nigro, "William Blackburn and His Pupils: A Conversation," *Mississippi Quarterly* 31:4 (Fall 1978): 605-14.

12. The Long Habit of Living

141. "Writing Schools," *Times Literary Supplement*, 8 April 1965, 275.

142. WMB's letters to ECB in 1927 when she was in New York awaiting birth of their first child refer with good-humored self-mockery to a bachelor's pose, namely, a

fear that women are "obsessed" with having babies. His years at traditionally male Oxford may have sharpened the attitude, one associated with Shaw's characterization of Professor Higgins in *Pygmalion*.

143. Letter of Héloise to Abélard, cited in Joseph Campbell, *The Masks of God: Creative Mythology* (London: Secker & Warburg, 1968), 59.

144. ALB married Jane Ruth Allison of Filey, Yorkshire, England, in 1957. There are two sons of this marriage. David Alexander Blackburn, born 5 February 1959, in Charlottesville, Virginia, graduated from Warwick University and the University of California, San Diego; a composer and sound engineer, he lives in Fallbrook, California. Philip William Rhodes Blackburn, born 15 October 1962, won a choral exhibition to Clare College, Cambridge University, and after graduation there attended the University of Iowa (Ph.D. in Music). He is Senior Program Director of the American Composers Forum in St. Paul, Minnesota, and publisher of Innova Records. His biography of American composer Harry Partch received the ASCAP Deems Taylor Award in a ceremony at the Lincoln Center in New York on December 3, 1998.

145. Ben Robertson, *Red Hills and Cotton*, 11.

146. ECB believed that Dr. Agnes Greig, a Washington psychiatrist, had violated professional ethics and advised her clients, WMB and his sister Mallie, to divorce their spouses. In letters to Greig, 24 April 1948, and May 1948, ECB defends herself against presumed allegations, claiming WMB "hated me so at times, was so convinced that I was the cause of his nervousness, so afraid of inherited insanity," adding, "love and faith in Bill and pity for him have held me steady." In the same vein ECB wrote to WMB 6 April 1948: "You are a very precious, lovable, wonderful, talented, congenial and (potentially) understanding and affectionate friend. . . . You are your own enemy, not me. If you want to destroy your life, I can't stop you. Meantime, I am not the psychotic invalid Mallie and Dr. Greig invent, for their own sick purposes." Dr. Greig denied any wrongdoing but, significantly, refused to meet ECB.

147. In his introduction to Mark Twain, *Adventures of Huckleberry Finn* (Boston: Houghton Mifflin, 1958), xix, Henry Nash Smith gives a pithy description of Huck's character: "Wise beyond his years in the mischances of life, he has the imagination of disaster." WMB's childhood insecurity—experience of poverty, of uprooting from place to place, of a father's confusion in financial matters—suggests the comparison.

148. Often called Sophocles's "Hymn to Man," lines 331-370 of *Antigone* celebrate among other human achievements an expropriation from the gods of the power of language. The lines are not without irony but still convey a feeling of wonder.

149. In any edition of James Joyce's *A Portrait of the Artist as a Young Man* these words appear near the end of the novel. ALB was a part-time lecturer on American and modern literature for the "Publishers Course" at Oxford Polytechnic, 1969-73, and often encountered students whose interests lay in business, not in arts and artists.

150. Yeats, "Sailing to Byzantium," ll. 1-2.

151. Yeats, "Crazy Jane Talks with the Bishop," ll. 15-16.

152. A.E. Housman, the 67nd poem of *A Shropshire Lad* ("Terence, this is stupid stuff"), ll. 29-30, 35-36. WMB with a sigh of mock resignation often quoted aloud these lines as he remembered them (he misquoted l. 30, substituting "lost" for "left").

153. Housman, the 40th poem of *A Shropshire Lad*.

154. Spenser, "Prothalamion," the refrain.

155. Mary April Blackburn attended the University of North Carolina at Greensboro and Duke University before she married Robert M. Hill in 1947. The couple soon moved to Palo Alto, California, where she established a reputation as an artist under the name April Hill. The Hills moved in 2003 to Medford, Oregon.

156. *King Lear*, 5. 3. 312-14.

157. WMB, *The Architecture of Duke University* (Durham: Duke University Press, 1939), 25. The book reveals WMB's astonishing knowledge of the art and history of architecture.

158. James Applewhite, "William Blackburn, Riding Westward," *Sewanee Review* 82:1 (Winter 1974), also appears in his book, *Statues in the Grass* (Athens: University of Georgia Press, 1975).

Appendix A

159. See Karen Horney, *Neurosis and Human Growth*, 65, 78, 81, 198-99, 203, 247, 248, 254. ECB purchased this book in June 1952 and wrote marginal notes in it. The feminism in Horney's psychology is emphasized in Marcia Westkott, *The Feminist Legacy of Karen Horney* (New Haven and London: Yale University Press, 1986).

Appendix B

160. "A Lost Chapter Recovered," *Duke Alumni Register* (January 1959), 16-19.

(*Photograph by Pat Pollard.*)

Alexander Blackburn, novelist, essayist, editor, and educator was born in Durham, North Carolina, in 1929, and educated at Phillips Academy, Yale University (B.S.), The University of North Carolina (M.A.), and Cambridge University (Ph.D.). He and his Chilean-born wife, Inés Dölz-Blackburn, make their home in Colorado Springs, Colorado, with occasional residence in Taos, New Mexico.